BOURDIEU AND LITERATURE

John R.W. Speller is Head of Foreign Languages and teaches the sociology of organisations at the International Faculty of Engineering, Łódź University of Technology in Poland. He is also co-editor (with Jeremy Ahearne) of *Pierre Bourdieu and the Literary Field* (2012).

Bourdieu and Literature

John R.W. Speller

http://www.openbookpublishers.com

© 2011 John R.W. Speller

Version 1.1. Creative Commons licence changed and minor edits made, July 2013.

This book is licensed under a Creative Commons Attribution 3.0 Unported license (CC-BY 3.0). This license allows you to share, copy, distribute and transmit the work; to adapt the work and to make commercial use of the work providing attribution is made to the author (but not in any way that suggests that he endorse you or your use of the work). Attribution should include the following information:

> John R.W. Speller, *Bourdieu and Literature* (Cambridge: Open Book Publishers, 2011), and the appropriate DOI.

Further copyright and licensing details are available at http://www.openbookpublishers.com/isbn/9781906924423

As with all Open Book Publishers titles, digital material and resources associated with this volume are available from our website:

> http://www.openbookpublishers.com/isbn/9781906924423

ISBN Hardback: 978-1-906924-43-0
ISBN Paperback: 978-1-906924-42-3
ISBN Digital (PDF): 978-1-906924-44-7
ISBN Digital ebook (epub version): 978-1-78374-005-5
ISBN Digital ebook(mobi version): 978-1-78374-006-2

DOI: 10.11647/OBP.0027

Cover image © Craig Richardson (all rights reserved).

All paper used by Open Book Publishers is SFI (Sustainable Forestry Initiative), PEFC (Programme for the Endorsement of Forest Certification Schemes) and Forest Stewardship Council (FSC) certified.

Printed in the United Kingdom and United States by
Lightning Source for Open Book Publishers

Contents

Abbreviations	11
Introduction	13
1. Positions	17
The field of reception	19
The field of production	23
Lévi-Strauss and structuralism	26
The death of intellectuals	29
Post-structuralism	31
Appendix: the composition of *Les Règles de l'art*	34
2. Methods	39
Epistemological preliminaries	40
The author's point of view	45
The field of power	46
The literary field	50
Habitus and trajectory	59
The space of possibilities	64
World literary space	71
Appendix: reflexivity and reading	75
3. Autonomy	79
The evolution of the literary field	80
Art and money	85
Zola and the Dreyfus affair	89
Reversals	92
Autonomy and value	96
4. Science and Literature	103
L'Éducation sentimentale	103
'Le démontage impie de la fiction'	109
Cross-overs	115
Fiction and realism	123

5. Literature and Cultural Politics — 131
   The production of the dominant ideology — 131
   'La Pensée Tietmeyer' — 135
   On aesthetics and ideology — 138
   A politics of form — 143
   For a collective intellectual — 146

6. Literature and Cultural Policy — 153
   Reproduction and distinction — 153
   Proposals for the future of education — 163
   Between the state and the free market — 175
   For a corporatism of the universal — 181

Conclusion — 185

References — 191
   A. Works by Pierre Bourdieu — 191
   B. Secondary sources — 194
   C. Collectively or anonymously authored works — 200

Index — 201

Acknowledgements

I would like to thank Open Book Publishers for their help with editing and revising this book. I am grateful to Jeremy Ahearne, who has been my mentor on Bourdieu from the beginning. I am also grateful to Jeremy Lane for reading and commenting on draft versions. Finally, I would like to dedicate this book to my wife, Magda, who has borne its writing with patience and good humour.

Abbreviations

AA   L'Amour de l'art: les musées d'art européens et leur public (The Love of Art, European Art Museums and their Public)
CD   Choses dites (In Other Words)
CF1 Contre-feux 1 (Firing Back: Against the Tyranny of the Market)
CF2 Contre-feux 2 (Firing Back: Against the Tyranny of the Market 2)
CP   Propos sur le champ politique
D   La Distinction: critique sociale du jugement (Distinction: A Social Critique of the Judgement of Taste)
DM   La Domination masculine (Masculine Domination)
E   Esquisse pour une auto-analyse (Sketch for a Self-Analysis)
ETP Esquisse d'une théorie de la pratique (Outline of a Theory of Practice)
FCP The Field of Cultural Production: Essays on Art and Literature
H   Les Héritiers: les étudiants et la culture (The Inheritors: French Students and their Relation to Culture)
HA   Homo academicus (Homo Academicus)
I   Interventions 1961-2001: science sociale et action politique (Political Interventions: Social Science and Political Action)
ID   La Production de l'idéologie dominante
IRS An Invitation to Reflexive Sociology
LE   Libre-échange (Free Exchange)
LL   Leçon sur la leçon
LPS Langage et pouvoir symbolique (Language and Symbolic Power)
MM   La Misère du monde (The Weight of the World)
MP   Méditations pascaliennes (Pascalian Meditations)
MS   Le Métier de sociologue: préalables épistémologiques (The Craft of Sociology: Epistemological Preliminaries)
NE   La Noblesse d'État: grandes écoles et esprit de corps (The State Nobility: Elite Schools in the Field of Power)

QS *Questions de sociologie* (*Sociology in Question*)
R   *La Reproduction: éléments pour une théorie du système d'enseignement* (*Reproduction in Education, Society, and Culture*)
RA *Les Règles de l'art: genèse et structure du champ littéraire* (*The Rules of Art: Genesis and Structure of the Literary Field*)
RP *Raisons pratiques: sur la théorie de l'action* (*Practical reason: On the Theory of Action*)
SP *Le Sens pratique* (*The Logic of Practice*)
SSR *Science de la science et réflexivité* (*Science of Science and Reflexivity*)
T   *Sur la télévision: suivi de l'emprise du journalisme* (*On Television*)

References to the French editions of Bourdieu's published works will be given in the text, using the abbreviations listed above. Translations are supplied in the footnotes, using shortened forms of the English titles. In view of the range of literature referred to in the text, it has not proved possible in every case to trace English translations of works originating in other languages. The author's own translations are given on such occasions, indicated by the initials J.S. Full details of translated works are given in the bibliography at the end of the book.

Introduction

At the time of his death in 2002, Bourdieu was a contender for the position of France's foremost intellectual, and one of the most influential sociologists in the world. A Chair in sociology at the Collège de France from 1981, he wrote on a wide range of topics from Kabyle society to French cultural taste, and from housing policy to fine art. Translated into some forty languages, his works have become standard points of reference in the fields of anthropology, linguistics, art history, cultural studies, politics, sociology, and beyond. Yet Bourdieu's work on literature has so far received relatively little attention, especially in the Anglophone world. If few literature students in French universities have read even a single page of Bourdieu, this is even more likely to be true of their counterparts across the Channel and the Atlantic.[1]

Certainly, Bourdieu's sociology of culture can appear bleak and pessimistic – to the extent that some critics have even interpreted it as an 'attack' on cultural creators, intellectuals, and critics, and on the very institutions of art and literature. To these critics, Bourdieu's sociology would seem to reduce all high art and literature merely to so much 'cultural capital', denying it any role other than that of reproducing and naturalising class distinction. Individual literary works would appear merely as the euphemised expressions of struggles for power and prestige within a narrowly defined literary field. Writers, and the battery of critics, scholars, and publishers supporting them, would ignore or deny the commercial and symbolic interests which drive them, so involved are they in the literary game, and so accepting are they of its unspoken rules and premises (what Bourdieu calls the field's *illusio*). Not only is this sociology 'reductionist', the critics argue, but the sociologist, who steps in as a self-styled 'de-mystifier', commits the double (and sometimes simultaneous) *faux pas* of stating the obvious and the taboo.

---

[1] See Jean-Pierre Martin, 'Avant-Propos. Bourdieu le Désenchanteur', in Jean-Pierre Martin, ed. *Bourdieu et la Littérature* (Nantes: Cécile Defaut, 2010), 7-21 (p. 7).

DOI: 10.11647/OBP.0027.01

This study sets out to go beyond these superficial arguments, which have been debated often enough (not least by Bourdieu). First, it examines Bourdieu's methodology for analysing literary works, and demonstrates that it offers genuine insights for those involved in literary study. Second, it will show that although Bourdieu was keenly aware of the role that consecrated literature could play in reproducing class distinctions, his sociology also accorded literature a privileged status in struggles for political and aesthetic autonomy. This study seeks therefore to examine precisely how Bourdieu understood the relationship between literature and politics, and how he reconciled his emphasis on literature's distinctive function with a continued belief in its emancipatory potential. Thirdly and finally, this study will show how Bourdieu's belief in literature as a force for emancipation was reflected in the series of concrete proposals he made for the reform of literary education, at both school and university level.

The opening chapter provides a first notion of the spaces of positions and position-takings in which Bourdieu's theories of the literary field were developed, expressed, and received. This chapter positions Bourdieu in relation to the major figures in the French intellectual field in the 1960s, Jean-Paul Sartre and Claude Lévi-Strauss, and to the later schools of structuralism and post-structuralism, including post-modernism and deconstruction. The chapter introduces the *problématique* regarding Bourdieu's work on literature from the point of view of the Anglophone field of reception, explaining its relatively belated reception in Britain and America. This exposition then serves as a starting point for the chapters that follow.

Chapter 2 provides a generative blueprint for conducting a 'Bourdieusian' analysis of a literary work, author, and field. It compares Bourdieu's approach with more established literary theories, including Russian Formalism, literary structuralism, and literary Marxism. It assesses Bourdieu's claim to have forged a link between internal reading and external analysis (of biographical, social, economic, and other determinations). It addresses previous and possible criticisms of Bourdieu's method, and discusses recent attempts to apply Bourdieu's framework to other national traditions and to extend it to the transnational level of 'world literary space'.

The third chapter traces Bourdieu's historical account of the genesis of the French literary field and its development over time, using the concepts presented in Chapter 2. This chapter shows how literature developed with other fields (the scientific field, the economic field, the political field), as

part of a single process of evolution, autonomisation and
Focusing on the critical period of the nineteenth century,
creation of a restricted and relatively autonomous field of prod
writers including Théophile Gautier, Charles Baudelaire and G
Flaubert. It also discusses Bourdieu's account of the invention of the figure of the engaged intellectual by Émile Zola, which brought the French literary field to a level of autonomy from economic and political power it has not exceeded since. The chapter concludes by outlining Bourdieu's claim that the literary and cultural fields have now entered a phase of 'involution' in the face of commercial and political pressures, bringing with them new forms of censorship and patronage.

Chapter 4 examines Bourdieu's claim to have produced a 'science of works', and the opposition he sets up between a 'scientific' sociology and 'literature'. It places Bourdieu's theory of sociological knowledge in the context of Gaston Bachelard's philosophy of science, from which he develops his epistemology. It then reads Bourdieu's analysis of Gustave Flaubert's *L'Éducation sentimentale* as an exploration of the difference between a 'scientific' and a 'literary' representation of social reality. The chapter shows how Bourdieu drew inspiration from literary writers in his own sociological writing; and how literary writers, most notably Annie Ernaux, have in turn been influenced by Bourdieu. Bourdieu's position with regard to the relations between literature, science, and reality is finally contrasted with those of contemporary post-structuralist and post-modernist theories of 'textuality'.

Chapter 5 explains Bourdieu's interest in literature in terms of its ability to convey critical messages to very wide audiences. It begins by showing how Bourdieu himself made use of literary devices and techniques in his political writings, starting with his 1976 article on 'La Production de l'idéologie dominante'. It then looks at examples of engaged art and literature that served as models for Bourdieu, including works by Günter Grass and Karl Krauss. The chapter, finally, follows Bourdieu's efforts to establish intellectual groupings that could combine the skills and resources of writers, artists, and researchers, including with plans for the International Parliament of Writers and *Liber,* a European book review, and explores the reasons for which these projects ultimately failed.

The last chapter explores the cultural policy implications of Bourdieu's work on literature. Focusing on two reports commissioned by the French government in the 1980s, it shows how Bourdieu envisioned a literature that would fit into a more integrated education system, and would equip students to live in a multi-cultural world and a modern democracy. It also follows his arguments in favour of state protection and subsidies for literature and the arts, and consequently against the 'neo-liberal' policy agenda of the 1990s, including the 2000 GATS negotiations. Finally, the chapter shows how Bourdieu urged cultural producers and agencies of diffusion (publishers, libraries, teachers, researchers) to work together to defend and disseminate intellectual and therefore literary culture, by forming what he calls a 'corporation of the universal'.

In short, against the limited reading of Bourdieu's work on literature as a form of sociological reductionism, the key arguments this study presents are (1) that Bourdieu's sociology offers a new and penetrating method of reading literature, (2) that such readings retain a keen sense of the specificity of literature and its political potential, (3) that Bourdieu saw literature as a useful store of ideational and expressive resources, which could also be of use to sociologists, and (4) moreover, all this feeds into the various proposals Bourdieu made regarding literary education over the course of his career. Far from an 'attack' on literary culture, then, Bourdieu's sociology of literature represents a theoretically sophisticated and wide ranging exposé of the literary game, which, while at times disenchanting, offers a fresh perspective on some of the most enduring problems in literary criticism, and on some of the most urgent issues facing literature today.

1. Positions

Are Bourdieu's analyses of literature any more than a diversion from his more 'serious' sociological research? Unlike his other major studies of social fields, which were written in collaboration with teams of researchers and co-authors, Bourdieu's work on literature seems to have been a largely solitary affair, suggesting that it was something of a sideline to which he returned when he needed a rest from his 'hard' scientific labours. Again, while literature provides an important source of anecdote, illustration, and insight across much of the rest of Bourdieu's work, it appears most often in the form of epigraphs, footnotes, and annexes, contributing to the impression that literature was somehow marginal, or even ornamental, in his work. Perhaps unsurprisingly, in the vast meta-discourse of Anglophone introductions and general studies on Bourdieu, his work on literature has itself been sidelined, rarely receiving even an entire chapter's attention.[1] And while we have had books on *Culture and Power: The Sociology of Pierre Bourdieu* (1997), *Bourdieu and Education: Acts of Practical Theory* (1998), *Bourdieu and Culture* (1999), *Bourdieu and the Journalistic Field* (2004), *Art Rules: Pierre Bourdieu and the Visual Arts* (2006), *Bourdieu's Politics: Problems and Possibilities* (2006), *Pierre Bourdieu and Literacy Education* (2008), and most recently *Bourdieu in Algeria* (2009), there had yet to be written a single-authored work on Bourdieu and Literature.[2]

---

[1] See e.g. David Swartz, *Culture and Power: The Sociology of Pierre Bourdieu* (London: University of Chicago Press, 1997); Jeremy Lane, *Pierre Bourdieu: A Critical Introduction* (London: Pluto, 2000); Bridget Fowler, *Pierre Bourdieu and Cultural Theory: Critical Investigations* (London: Sage, 1997); Michael Grenfell, *Pierre Bourdieu: Agent Provocateur* (London: Continuum, 2004); Deborah Reed-Danahay, *Locating Bourdieu* (Bloomington, ID: Indiana University Press, 2005).

[2] Michael Grenfell and David James, with Philip Hodkinson, Diane Reay and Derek Robbins, *Bourdieu and Education: Acts of Practical Theory* (London: Falmer Press, 1998); Derek Robbins, *Bourdieu and Culture* (London: Sage, 2000); Rodney D. Benson and Erik Neveu, *Bourdieu and the Journalistic Field* (Cambridge: Polity Press, 2005); Michael Grenfell and Cheryl Hardy, *Art Rules: Pierre Bourdieu and the Visual Arts* (London: Berg, 2007); Jeremy Lane, *Bourdieu's Politics: Problems and*

Other facts, however, suggest that literature occupied a far more important position in Bourdieu's own mind and work than has so far been widely acknowledged. Literature was an early and recurrent theme in Bourdieu's publications. He first brought literary themes into his argument in 'Champ intellectuel et projet créateur' (1966),[3] and elaborated his vision of the literary field in 'Le Marché des biens symboliques' (1971).[4] Subsequently, a substantial fraction of his work centred on cultural production, and included a specific focus on literature. Many of these writings were collected, revised, and re-published in 1992 as *Les Règles de l'art*. Literature also played an important role in the development of Bourdieu's theory. His key concept of *field* was first developed through his studies of literature,[5] which determined its initial properties, and oriented its future applications. Finally, Bourdieu frequently expressed a strong sense of personal identification with his literary and artistic heroes, an identification he reiterates on the final page of his final book, *Esquisse pour une auto-analyse* (2004).

There may be other reasons, then, why Bourdieu's work on literature has not received the same levels of attention as, say, his ethnographic research on Algerian peasant households, in *Esquisse d'une théorie de la pratique* (1972) and *Le Sens pratique* (1980); his study of patterns in European gallery and museum attendance, in *L'Amour de l'art: les musées et leur public* (1966); his research into French education, in *Les Héritiers* (1964), *La Reproduction* (1977), *Homo academicus* (1988), and *La Noblesse d'État* (1989); or his survey-analysis of French cultural tastes, in *La Distinction* (1979), all of which have become classic points of reference in their respective fields. This chapter sets out to outline the principal criticisms and complaints that have been levelled at Bourdieu's work on literature by scholars in the Anglophone field of reception. It then provides a first notion of the French intellectual space in which Bourdieu's theory of the literary field was first developed and

---

Possibilities (London: Routledge, 2006); James Albright and Allan Luke, eds. *Pierre Bourdieu and Literacy Education* (New York: Routledge, 2008); Jane E. Goodman and Paul A. Silverstein, eds. *Bourdieu in Algeria: Colonial Politics, Ethnographic Practices, Theoretical Developments* (Lincoln, NE and London: University of Nebraska Press, 2009).
3 Pierre Bourdieu, 'Champ intellectuel et projet créateur', *Les Temps Modernes*, 246 (1966), 865-906.
4 Pierre Bourdieu, 'Le Marché des biens symboliques', *L'Année Sociologique*, 22 (1971), 49-126.
5 In Bourdieu, 'Champ intellectuel et projet créateur'.

1. Positions   19

received. This route is taken partly to test Bourdieu's theory (which will be discussed in more detail in the next chapter) that in order to form a closer understanding of cultural works, including of his own texts, it is advisable to subject them to what he terms a *double historicisation*:

> Il s'agit pour cela de reconstituer à la fois l'espace des positions possibles (appréhendé à travers les dispositions associées à une certaine position) par rapport auquel s'est élaboré le donné historique (texte, document, image, etc.) à interpréter, et l'espace des possibles par rapport auquel on l'interprète. Ignorer cette double détermination, c'est se condamner à une 'compréhension' anachronique et ethnocentrique qui a toutes les chances d'être fictive et qui, dans le meilleur des cas, reste inconsciente de ses propres principes (*RA*, 505).[6]

By going through this process, Bourdieu contends, we can control our preconceived ideas regarding the work, and gain a greater comprehension of the author's understanding of his creative project. Only then can we begin to make an unbiased or 'objective' judgment of the work, and perhaps even find points of correspondence and constructive engagement between the author's position and our own. Let us begin, then, by meeting Bourdieu on his own terms, and applying to his own work on literature the same method he uses to study great literary authors including Flaubert and Baudelaire; that is, by constructing the spaces of 'positions' and 'position-takings' in the 'fields' of production and reception.

The field of reception

Bourdieu anticipated that his work on literature would not be welcomed by scholars in literary studies. Indeed, he seems to have relished the thought of 'scandalising' his readers with what he describes grandiosely in the opening pages of *Les Règles* as 'la dernière et peut-être la pire des blessures infligées, selon Freud, au narcissisme, après celles que marquent les noms de Copernic, Darwin et Freud lui-même' (*RA*, 12).[7] Arguably

---

6 'This requires the reconstruction both of the space of possibles (apprehended through the dispositions associated with a certain position) in relation to which the historical given (text, document, image etc.) to be interpreted is elaborated, and of the space of possibles in relation to which one interprets it. To ignore this double determination is to be condemned to an anachronistic and ethnocentric "understanding" which is likely to be fictive and which, in the best of cases, remains unaware of its own principles' (*Rules*, 309).
7 'the last and perhaps the worst of those wounds inflicted, according to Freud,

this claim to scandalise is more likely to provoke the 'resistances' of his readers than anything in Bourdieu's actual sociology. Bourdieu's case, in these opening pages, is that the sociologist dispels the belief in 'creators' as unique and gifted individuals by analysing the manifold social and historical determinations that made them and their works what they are. This has however long been the aim of literary histories and biographies. If Bourdieu's theory differs, it is in the methods he deploys to perform the literary scholar's traditional tasks more effectively.

A more common accusation is that sociology 'reduces' aesthetic works and experiences, most dramatically to numerical statistics, but also to their social uses. This preconception, Bourdieu warned, had been given new life by 'deconstructionist' and 'post-modernist' critics in the 1980s, who looked to expose the ways in which other people, experiences, or texts, could not be contained in a single 'totalising' description or theory. Bourdieu's strong claim to 'science', especially, appears to expose him to such a critique, as it suggests he was aiming to discover some 'fundamental' or 'objective' (in the positivist sense) truth or reality. Several English-language critiques of Bourdieu's work on literature have taken this line of attack, perceiving an 'essentialism' at the heart of Bourdieu's sociology.[8] This impression cannot be blamed entirely on critics who, influenced by the dominant academic trends of the time, saw in Bourdieu's work what they expected to find. Bourdieu is prone to making rather sweeping and finalising remarks – which he explains by his desire to 'twist the stick in the other direction', and emphasise what his intellectual opponents left unsaid or denied (*RA*, 304). Yet as I will attempt to show throughout this study, it is more meaningful and productive to take these isolated and sometimes contradictory position-takings as elements in a more complex system under continual development than to dismiss the whole edifice on the basis of partial or incomplete readings (one might only wish that Bourdieu had paid some of his own opponents the same courtesy).

Another consistent concern regards Bourdieu's writing style. As Bourdieu himself writes in the preface of the English translation of *Distinction*, his 'long, complex sentences may offend', particularly those with literary sensibilities.[9] Added to this is an initially intimidating

---

upon narcissism, after those going under the names of Copernicus, Darwin and Freud himself' (*Rules*, xvii).

8 For example, see Stephen Thompson, 'The Instance of the Veil: Bourdieu's Flaubert and the Textuality of Social Science' in *Comparative Literature*, 55:4 (2003), 275-92.

9 Pierre Bourdieu, *Distinction, A Social Critique of the Judgment of Taste*, trans. Richard

system of concepts and technical terminology, which at best enables him to communicate complex and nuanced points, and at worst makes simple points unnecessarily opaque. These obstacles are compounded in *Les Règles de l'art*, the book in which Bourdieu's work on literature is concentrated, and which is arguably his worst (at least, it has been the least well received, and perhaps the least well read). A patchwork of ideas and essays spanning decades, it suffers from inner inconsistencies and poor organisation.[10] As a result, the cogency of Bourdieu's argumentation, and the coherence of his methodology, can become lost, particularly to readers in the field of literary studies, who are unfamiliar with his wider work.

In the view of Toril Moi, 'the difficulty that Bourdieu represents for literary critics has to do with the fact that he inherits a philosophical tradition that remains poorly understood in U.S. literary criticism'.[11] On Moi's reading, Bourdieu takes his place among the group of twentieth-century thinkers including Freud, Heidegger, Sartre, Beauvoir, Merleau-Ponty, J.L. Austin, and Wittgenstein. This is true, although one might think there is nothing particularly unfamiliar about the names Moi has chosen. More to the point would have been to cite, from the sociological and anthropological tradition, Max Weber, Émile Durkheim, Norbert Elias, Claude Lévi-Strauss, and Marcel Mauss; and from the philosophy of science, Gaston Bachelard, Ernst Cassirer, Georges Canguilhem and Alexandre Koyré, as well as a number of contemporaries, sociologists, and historians less famous than these.[12] That said, there is also a surprising number of parallels and crossovers between Bourdieu's sociology and established literary theories, and even with literature itself – so many, in fact, that he tried for a long time to bury or repress his proximity to literary writers and critics, because he was working in a scientific milieu.

According to John Guillory, 'what seems to have troubled Bourdieu's U.S. readers most is the implication that social change cannot be the conscious and intended effect of individual or collective action'. This is particularly true, Guillory argues, in the humanities, where it has become increasingly

---

Nice (London: Routledge, 1989), p. xiii.
10 As one reviewer put it: 'It is as if Bourdieu cleaned out his desk and put a staple through everything that involved literature'. Wendy Griswold, 'Review of The Rules of Art, Genesis and Structure of the Literary Field', *The American Journal of Sociology*, 104 (1998), 972-75 (p. 974).
11 Toril Moi, 'The Challenge of the Particular Case', *Modern Language Quarterly*, 58 (1997), 497-508 (p. 498).
12 For a more exhaustive list of Bourdieu's sources, see Bernard Lahire, 'Présentation: pour une sociologie à l'état vif', in *Le Travail sociologique de Pierre Bourdieu*, ed. Bernard Lahire (Paris: La Découvert, 1999), pp. 5-20 (p. 11).

important for critics and scholars to justify their academic practice in terms of promoting positive social change. 'Literary and cultural critics', Guillory writes, 'would like to believe that vanguard theoretical discourses can lead to transformative struggles, by which the various forms of domination can be brought to an end'.[13] Yet Bourdieu held just such beliefs in the emancipatory power of sociological knowledge, as David Swartz has shown. Swartz cites Bourdieu making such hopeful claims as 'genuine scientific research embodies a threat for the "social order" and inevitably produces a political effect'; or, 'the sociologist unveils and therefore intervenes in the force relations between groups and classes and he can even contribute to the modification of those relations'.[14] As we will see, Bourdieu cherished similar hopes for literature, which he believed can challenge and overturn our most deep-seated prejudices and preconceptions, and give voice and visibility to dominated social groups. To this end, Bourdieu urged greater collaboration between writers, artists, and researchers, whom he encouraged to join their skills and resources to promote progressive causes.

Then again, Bourdieu's theories and models do appear to present a society in which there is little room for resistance or change. His is a world of 'reproduction', where 'determinations' and 'mechanisms' seem to trap individuals into perpetuating the *status quo*. This picture is as much at odds with the literary celebration of creativity and liberty, as it is with the popular self-image of cultural producers and consumers as non-conformists, and even revolutionaries. Even more unsettling are his suggestions that, by pursuing their 'disinterested' ends, lovers of art and literature are still engaged in games of social distinction and 'symbolic capital' accumulation. Cultural tastes and competences are really only transformed (or 'sublimated') expressions of class divisions, which they help to consolidate. Yet, Bourdieu's defence of cultural fields, especially in the later part of his career, will complicate this reading. And when it came to preparing two reports on the future of education at the request of the French government, he turned to emphasise the positive role of cultural education, including as an instrument of social cohesion and as an initiation in critical thinking. As we will argue in Chapter 4, these two positions are not simply contradictory. Indeed, an awareness of how

---

13 John Guillory, 'Bourdieu's Refusal', in Nicholas Brown and Imre Szeman, eds. *Bourdieu: Fieldwork in Culture* (Lanham, MD: Rowman & Littlefield Publishers, 1999), pp. 19-43 (pp. 20-21).
14 David Swartz, *Culture and Power: The Sociology of Pierre Bourdieu* (Chicago and London: University of Chicago Press, 1997), p. 260.

'cultural capital' is distributed and accumulated could assist teachers and policy-makers in extending access to culture to economically and culturally deprived groups.

A final complaint to be examined here is that Bourdieu's work is 'too French': too involved in a specifically French intellectual problematic, and too focused on the particular case of France. This criticism has also been aimed at Bourdieu's work on literature, which, with its focus on Flaubert and the French nineteenth-century literary field, has raised questions both about the generalisability of Bourdieu's theory, and its restriction to the national level. In the next chapter, we will discuss recent efforts to extend Bourdieu's theory of literary fields to the transnational level, and to different national traditions. In the next section, we will provide an overview of the French intellectual field in which Bourdieu's work on literature was written and his broader intellectual project elaborated: which, as Bourdieu himself insisted, is necessary to understand an author's intention (which need not always be explicit or even conscious), and the significance of that author's work in its original context.[15]

The field of production

Why was the author of *La Reproduction* and *La Distinction* drawn to literary topics? Literature holds a particularly important place in French culture, in comparison with other European states and America.[16] Many literary trends have originated in France, and French literature has long been regarded as one of the world's finest. Paris represents, for many, the capital of the 'World Republic of Letters': a hub for writers of all nationalities, and one of the most prestigious sources of literary consecration. Writers are commemorated in the Pantheon in Paris, have given their names to street signs and metro stations, and their faces used to appear on French coins and banknotes. Politicians pay homage to literary writers in public ceremonies, with literary references in their speeches, or by simply

---

15 See Pierre Bourdieu, 'Passport to Duke', in Brown and Szeman, eds. *Bourdieu: Fieldwork in Culture*, pp. 241-46 (first publ. in *International Journal of Contemporary Sociology*, 33 (1996), 145-50); and Pierre Bourdieu, 'Concluding Remarks: For a Sociogenetic Understanding of Intellectual Works', in Craig Calhoun, Edward LiPuma, and Moishe Postone, eds. *Bourdieu: Critical Perspectives* (Cambridge: Polity Press, 1993), pp. 263-75.

16 In this section, I draw in particular on Priscilla Parkhurst Ferguson, *Literary France, The Making of a Culture* (Berkeley, CA: University of California Press, 1987), especially pp. 25-29.

expressing their appreciation for the Classics. Several career politicians have even become published authors themselves. There is also a tradition of French writers taking political duties, from Chateaubriand, who worked as foreign secretary during the Restoration, to Victor Hugo, who was a deputy and sat in the *Chambre des pairs*, and André Malraux, who served as the first minister of culture in the Fifth Republic. Finally, literature receives extensive media coverage in France, with dedicated television programmes and designated review sections in national newspapers. All these are signs of literature's prestigious place in French society, or, in the terms Bourdieu uses, of its 'cultural capital'.

During Bourdieu's formative years, the dominant figure on the French intellectual scene was not, however, a 'pure' literary writer, but 'l'intellectuel total' Jean-Paul Sartre. For the students of Bourdieu's generation, Sartre represented a sort of ideal of intellectual accomplishment, as well as the main opposition to overcome. In a prolific career, Sartre combined the roles of philosopher, writer, and *engagé* intellectual, writing plays, novels, literary criticism, and philosophical treatises, founding his own literary and political review, as well as making frequent interventions in the political arena.[17] As a consequence, literary studies became almost an obligatory point of passage for any aspiring French intellectual who wished to follow in his footsteps, or to challenge him on his own ground.

It is little surprise, then, to find that as a youth Bourdieu identified naïvely with Balzac (*E*, 87), and that for a long time he appeared set on a career as a philosopher, perhaps even the next Sartre, passing, like Sartre before him, the *agrégation* in philosophy at the prestigious École Normale Supérieure (ENS), in the same year as Jacques Derrida. Yet for reasons he links to his relatively underprivileged social background, Bourdieu always held an ambivalent attitude towards both literature and philosophy. Bourdieu's trajectory to the apex of French academia was far from typical.[18] Born in a village in the Béarn region of southern France, where his father had been a postal worker and his grandfather a sharecropper, Bourdieu was the first in his family to finish high school, and was marked out at the ENS by his thick regional accent amongst his predominantly Parisian colleagues. No doubt, Bourdieu's social background contributes to explain his bitter critique of

---

17 See Anna Boschetti, *Sartre et 'Les Temps Modernes': une entreprise intellectuelle* (Paris: Éditions de Minuit, 1985).
18 See Scott McLemee, '"Not a Fish in Water": Close Colleague of Bourdieu Reflects on His Influence', *The Chronicle of Higher Education*, 25 January 2002.

the 'ideology of gifts', and his thinly-veiled *ressentiment*[19] of conspicuous displays of verbal fluency and cultural prowess. It also explains why he always figured himself as an outsider in the academic community, and sought always to ground his work in ordinary reality. Bourdieu came to see his conversion first to ethnography in the late 1950s and then to sociology, with their measurements, interviews, and observations, as in part a reaction to the bookish culture of the closed, self-referential French academic universe of the 1960s and 1970s which was still dominated by literature and philosophy, and as an attempt to break away from its 'aestheticising' and 'de-realizing' tendencies (*E*, 59).

'Infinitely close, and infinitely distant', is how Bourdieu describes his feelings about Sartre, in an article first published in 1993.[20] Bourdieu's conversion to the social sciences, which the author of *L'Être et le néant* held in low esteem; his strong commitment to science, against Sartre's attempt to be all people and all things; his critique of the ideology of the 'uncreated creator', to which Sartre's existentialism had given new life; and his scepticism of intellectuals who sought too keenly the celebrity status Sartre had acquired, can all be understood as a reaction against everything that the Sartrean enterprise represented in his eyes. Yet in order to challenge Sartre, Bourdieu knew that he must also engage with him, and it was above all in his work on literature that this contact and combat took place. Bourdieu's first article on literature, 'Champ intellectuel et projet créateur', was published in Sartre's journal *Les Temps Modernes*, and appears to pay tribute to Sartre's theory of the 'projet originel', but then attempts to find a new way forward. Likewise, Bourdieu's enduring focus on Flaubert should be understood in the light (or shadow) of Sartre's final work: his monumental, interminable, and increasingly amphetamine-fuelled biography of the same author, *L'Idiot de la famille*.[21]

It is in *Les Règles*, however, that Sartre's presence can be felt most clearly. The section entitled 'Questions de méthode' deliberately echoes the first part of *Critique de la raison dialectique*,[22] in which the existentialist philosopher outlines the method of enquiry he uses in *L'Idiot de la famille*. This section also

---

19 When we condemn in others what we wish for ourselves.
20 Pierre Bourdieu, 'My Feelings about Sartre', *French Cultural Studies*, 4 (1993), 209-11 (p. 210).
21 Jean Paul Sartre, *L'Idiot de la famille: Gustave Flaubert de 1821 à 1857*, 3 vols (Paris: Gallimard, 1971-1972).
22 Jean-Paul Sartre, *Critique de la raison dialectique*, 2 vols, vol. 1 (Paris: Gallimard, 1960).

contains a re-worked version of Bourdieu's analysis of the Sartrean project, upon which Anna Boschetti's full-length study *Sartre et 'Les Temps Modernes': une entreprise intellectuelle* is based (*RA*, 291-350).[23] Bourdieu's analysis in the prologue and first part of *Les Règles* of Flaubert's paradoxical social position and the determinations which weighed upon it is intended explicitly to counter what Bourdieu interprets as Sartre's vision of Flaubert as an 'uncreated creator', who had chosen freely his own destiny (*RA*, 310). And in the post-script, 'Pour un Corporatisme de l'Universel' (*RA*, 545-58), Bourdieu proposes a course of political action by intellectuals, which promises to overcome the limitations of the Sartrean model of charismatic intervention on every contemporary issue. Published at the peak of Bourdieu's career, and at the commencement of his more prominent political activism, the appearance of *Les Règles* (which inevitably drew comparisons with Sartre) can be understood as an attempt to affirm at once his proximity and distance from France's last great public intellectual, and as a bid for his crown.

Lévi-Strauss and structuralism

Sartre was not the only major player on the French intellectual scene who had a formative influence on Bourdieu. As Bourdieu recalls in the preface to *Le Sens pratique*, the anthropologist Claude Lévi-Strauss exerted a tremendous influence over his contemporaries, by offering 'à toute une génération une nouvelle manière de concevoir l'activité intellectuelle qui s'opposait de façon tout à fait dialectique à la figure de l'intellectuel "total"' (*SP*, 7-8).[24] Lévi-Strauss gave legitimacy to the social sciences, at a time when they were structurally subordinate in relation to literature and philosophy, but also in relation to the natural sciences (*E*, 29). Situated in the Faculty of Letters, the social sciences were defined doubly negatively, as neither literary nor scientific, and as applied and empirical rather than pure and theoretical (*HA*, 160). Indeed, Bourdieu goes so far as to describe sociology in the early 1960s as a 'discipline pariah' (*E*, 52), looked down upon as a refuge for failed philosophers, and considered close, because of its object, to journalism (*CD*, 15; *E*, 28). Bourdieu admits that the new prestige Lévi-Strauss brought to ethnology helped him subjectively to make the transition

---

23 Pierre Bourdieu, 'Sartre', *London Review of Books*, 22 (1980), 11-12.
24 'a whole generation was led to adopt a new way of conceiving intellectual activity that was opposed in a thoroughly dialectical fashion to the figure of the politically committed "total" intellectual represented by Jean-Paul Sartre' (*Logic*, 1-2).

from philosophy, then at its apogee, to ethnography, where his first works were those of a self-confessed 'structuraliste heureux' (*SP*, 22).²⁵

Yet even Lévi-Strauss, who played detached scientist to Sartre's *engagé* humanist, was still altogether too 'literary' for Bourdieu. In Bourdieu's view, Lévi-Strauss had never fully 'rompu avec la tradition du voyage littéraire et le culte artistique de l'exotisme' (*E*, 61),²⁶ focusing, in his famous work *Tristes Tropiques*,²⁷ on far-away lands, rather than studying more pressing and immediate realities. Lévi-Strauss had also set the trend for 'literary structuralism', by switching seamlessly, in an influential essay with Roman Jakobson,²⁸ from the analysis of myths and kinship structures to the study of literature. Lévi-Strauss's transposition of structuralist principles from the linguistic structuralism of Ferdinand de Saussure to the study of social constellations implied they could be turned towards the study of any other social reality, such as rites, myths, matrimonial strategies, or works of art and literature, which could all be studied as 'languages'. Bourdieu came to see 'la propension à étendre presque sans limites la posture du lector, qui a caractérisé certaines formes du structuralisme ethnologique et sémiologique' (*RA*, 498-99)²⁹ as the faulty principle behind systematic errors in empirical research, including that of Lévi-Strauss. Firstly, because it introduced a 'theoretical bias' that ignored how the theory was played out in practice. Secondly, because it by-passed the dimension of symbolic power, which over-determines any literal signification. Thirdly, because it fixed the sense of words and documents, of which the meaning is often contested in reality (*SP*, 56-70; *CD*, 132-43).

Sartre and Lévi-Strauss represented to Bourdieu two sides of a false alternative. The originality of structuralism, Bourdieu argued in his early article 'Structuralism and Theory of Sociological Knowledge', was paradoxically to have 'contributed to wiping out the fictitious originality assigned to anthropological knowledge by the spontaneous theory of such a knowledge' by applying the 'relational' or 'structuralist' principles that were

---

25 'a blissful structuralist' (*Logic*, 9).
26 'broken with the tradition of the literary journey and the artist's cult of exoticism' (*Sketch*, 43).
27 Claude Lévi-Strauss, *Tristes Tropiques* (Paris: Plon, 1955).
28 Raymond Jakobson and Claude Lévi-Strauss, '"Les Chats" de Charles Baudelaire', *L'Homme*, 2 (1962), 5-21.
29 'the propensity to extend almost limitlessly the posture of lector, which has characterized certain forms of ethnological and semiological structuralism' (*Rules*, 393).

used already to discover natural or physical laws to the study of human relations and practices.[30] Yet by focusing on structures, structuralism had lost sight of the element of individual agency upon which existentialism placed its emphasis. Existentialism insists on the role of the freely choosing subject, who determines his or her own destiny. Bourdieu's theory of the 'dialectical relation' between habitus and field, according to which our 'subjective' ability to interpret and respond to the world is limited by our 'objective' conditions of existence (i.e., our position in the social structure or field, and the access to economic and cultural resources it provides) was formulated to overcome this opposition, and the agency/structure problem.[31]

In the early part of his career, Bourdieu was careful to distance himself from structuralism, especially from its literary 'formes mondaines' (*CD*, 16).[32] His only contribution to the structuralist debate, aside from certain critical analyses destined for specialist revues, was the aforementioned 'Champ intellectuel et projet créateur' (*E*, 101). Yet by combining the notion of field, with its structuralist overtones, with that of a 'projet créateur', with its echoes of Sartre's 'projet originel' and its emphasis on agency, the article was quite clearly a riposte to both opposing camps. At the same time, he delayed or downplayed the publication of his articles treating literary themes. He postponed the publication of his major article on the 'Le Champ littéraire' (written and presented back in 1983) until 1991. He waited until 1994 before publishing a similar article in *Raisons pratiques*, which he had delivered at a conference back in 1986. And several of the texts Bourdieu later republished in *Les Règles* with only minor revisions, 'The Field of Cultural Production, or: The Economic World Reversed' (1983), 'The Genesis of the Concepts of Habitus and Field' (1985), 'The Historical Genesis of a Pure Aesthetic' (1987), and 'Flaubert's Point of View' (1988), were first published in British reviews.[33]

Indeed, in an interview published in 1996, Bourdieu admits he had hidden (*enfoui*) his proximity to writers and literary critics, because he was working in a 'scientific' milieu. Now, he says, 'je suis arrivé à un point où

---

30 Pierre Bourdieu, 'Structuralism and Theory of Sociological Knowledge', *Social Research*, 35 (1968), 681-706.
31 See Swartz, *Culture and Power*, pp. 8-9.
32 'merely fashionable forms' (*Other Words*, 6).
33 Pierre Bourdieu, 'The Field of Cultural Production, or: The Economic World Reversed', *Poetics*, 12 (1983), 311-56; 'The Genesis of the Concepts of Habitus and Field', *Sociocriticism*, 2 (1985), 11-24; 'The Historical Genesis of a Pure Aesthetic', *The Journal of Aesthetics and Art Criticism*, 46 (1987), 201-10; 'Flaubert's Point of View', *Critical Inquiry*, 14 (1988), 539-62; Le Champ littéraire', *Actes de la recherche en sciences sociales*, 89 (1991), 3-46.

je suis reconnu et où je peux me permettre, sans me suicider, d'aborder les problèmes que j'avais jusque là étouffés. Bien sûr, des gens diront maintenant: voyez! Bourdieu — nous l'avons toujours dit — ce n'est pas un vrai savant'.[34] Bourdieu was concerned to avoid being seen as too 'literary', not just in order to distinguish his position from those of existentialism and literary structuralism, but also in case his studies on education and culture were not treated with the 'seriousness' they in his view required and deserved, as 'objective' works of 'science'.

The death of intellectuals

By the early 1990s, Bourdieu was both in a position and pressed by changes in the social status and conditions of intellectual culture to publish his work on literature and art more prominently. Traditional 'humanist' intellectuals, he warned, were losing their prestigious place in French society, and were increasingly cut off from the public sphere. The shift to new media, radio, and television favoured the least 'autonomous' producers, who were willing to play along with the market-driven needs of journalists and television producers. Such 'journalist-intellectuals' and 'journalist-writers', to use Bourdieu's polemical terms, were monopolising public access at the expense of writers, intellectuals, and others with greater specific competence in their fields. Meanwhile, more traditional avenues to the public sphere were being closed down, as the concentration of the publishing and bookselling industries reduced the numbers of outlets for specialised and experimental works. Even in their traditional bastion, the education system, the humanities were losing their dominant position to the natural sciences, and other more obviously 'useful' (i.e., immediately marketable) disciplines, such as management and engineering. In the midst of all this, intellectuals had interiorised a sense of their own irrelevance, as shown by the strangely self-defeating discourse on 'the death of intellectuals', and by rampant anti-intellectualism even in their own ranks.[35]

---

34 Isabelle Graw, trans. Véronique Gola, 'Que Suis-Je? Une Entrevue avec Pierre Bourdieu' (first publ. as 'Ein Interview mit Pierre Bourdieu von Isabelle Graw', *The Thing*, 1996), http://www.homme-moderne.org/societe/socio/bourdieu/entrevue/quesui.html consulted on 27/08/11. 'I have come to the point where I am recognised and where I can allow myself, without committing suicide, to address problems which I had until now stifled. Of course, there are people who will now say: "Look at Bourdieu! We knew it, he's not a real scholar"' (trans. J.S.).

35 It is difficult not to see the themes of deconstruction, silence, death, *désoeuvrement*, and so on, which recurred in this period, as a sort of sublimated expression of the

Swiftly, Bourdieu repackaged his work on literature and art as offering 'une vision plus vraie (...) des conquêtes les plus hautes de l'entreprise humaine' (RA, 16),[36] which could provide the basis for an informed defence of the menaced 'virtues' and 'values' of cultural producers who struggle to make 'the universal' progress (RA, 545-58). Concessions were made to the 'heroism' of Flaubert and Baudelaire, whose transgressions of the norms imposed by the Church, market, and State, were offered as examples to be emulated (RA, 85-191). And Bourdieu appended an explicitly 'normative' post-script, entitled 'Pour un corporatisme de l'universel', in which he calls on intellectuals from across the faculties, and from across Europe and beyond, to join forces to protect the social and economic conditions of their 'autonomy': to analyse and resist the new forms of patronage and censorship imposed by commerce and the State; to restore the integrity of specific instances of consecration from political and economic influence; to protect independent publishers and bookshops from commercial takeovers and competition; and to struggle against 'les prophètes du malheur', 'philosophes journalistes', and 'doxosophes', who were usurping and eroding confidence in intellectual authority (RA, 557).

Yet despite these revisions, additions, and a normative post-script, the bulk of *Les Règles* remains predominantly critical, with few ideas for positive action, nor even explanations why 'autonomous' literature should be thought to be worth defending. Bourdieu's discourse on 'the universal' can seem confusing, especially as much of his earlier work (for instance, in *L'Amour de l'art* and *La Distinction*) was meant to explode the myth of 'universal' cultural values. As the main proposal Bourdieu derives from these 'realistic' analyses, his project for an 'international of intellectuals' seems rather unrealistic, and proved to be so in practice. Several critics have argued that *Les Règles* does not really repair the damage done by Bourdieu's own critiques of 'legitimate' culture and institutions (museums, schools, the *Grandes Écoles*), which could themselves have contributed to the pervasive climate of anti-intellectualism.[37]

---

deteriorating social condition of intellectuals (and one that only added, no doubt, to their sense of despondency and demobilisation).

36 'a vision more true and, ultimately, more reassuring, because less superhuman, of the highest achievements of the human enterprise' (*Rules*, xx).

37 Indeed, according to Fredric Jameson, Bourdieu provides 'the most complex rationale for anti-intellectualism available today'. Frederic Jameson, 'How Not To Historicize Theory', *Critical Inquiry*, 34 (2008), 564-82.

Post-structuralism

By the time of the publication of *Les Règles*, both existentialist and structuralist moments had passed, and a new intellectual movement was establishing itself. Bourdieu was just as critical of the various forms of 'post-structuralism' that were gaining recognition in France, via a detour by America. Bourdieu saw their successes in literature and philosophy departments as a defensive reaction against the rise of the natural sciences, and to the perceived threat from the social sciences, which had both social and epistemological consequences. Derrida and Foucault's theories, Bourdieu protests, had 'given new life, throughout the world but especially in the United States, to the old philosophical critique of the social sciences, and fuelled, under the cover of "deconstruction" and the critique of "texts", a thinly-veiled form of irrationalist nihilism'.[38] By opening scientific texts, which were meant to be tested by empirical observation, to the infinite play of signifiers, their results could be absorbed and belittled. By deconstructing the objects of sociological analysis (especially when it came to works of art or literature), any attempt to analyse their structure and meaning could be dismissed as 'reductive' (*MP*, 155). By treating science as one discourse among many, its truth-claims could be placed on the same level as religion, literature, or ideology. The result was a loss of trust in scientific progress, and the rise of an 'anything goes' mentality (*SSR*, 59).

The most extreme position in this cluster of theories, however, was the semi-mystical strain of deconstruction, that can be recognised by frequent references to Derrida, Levinas, Heidegger, Hölderlin, Mallarmé, and Sade, and by mournful meditations on death, transcendence, and the irreducibility of persons and things to any abstract conceptualisation. Modernist literature holds a privileged place in this literary-philosophy, as a discourse that exploits the inherent polysemy of language, and frustrates any effort to impose a unitary meaning. For Blanchot, one of the principal theorists in this loose movement, the truth of literature, and perhaps the truth of truth, is its *ambiguity*, which outstrips any single reading, particularly in terms of historical context or authorial intent.[39] All these theories were extremely popular (especially in literature departments in the 1980s and 1990s) not least because they enabled literary scholars and philosophers to reassert themselves in the face of the

---

[38] Loïc Wacquant, 'Towards a Reflexive Sociology: A Workshop with Pierre Bourdieu', *Sociological Theory*, 7 (1989), 26-63 (p. 49).
[39] Here I am following Simon Critchley, *Very Little... Almost Nothing* (London: Routledge, 1997), pp. 31-76.

rising natural and social sciences, as guardians of a 'deeper truth' (even if this was reduced to inter-textuality, relativism, or ambiguity).

The publication of *Les Règles* offered Bourdieu the opportunity to deliver a riposte on behalf of sociology, to position himself on the side of the scientific community, and to mark his distance from 'post-structuralists' and 'post-modernists' with whom he was sometimes confused.[40] In the avant-propos, Bourdieu launches into a lively tirade against (mostly unnamed) philosophers and literary scholars, whom he accuses of having resigned from the attempt to relate cultural works and producers to their social contexts, and for lapsing instead into repetitive affirmations of literature's 'ineffable' and 'transcendent' character. Against what he decries as this too ready capitulation to 'la défaite du savoir' (*RA*, 10),[41] Bourdieu cites Goethe and Kant, so inscribing himself in an Enlightenment tradition that had gone recently out of fashion:

> A tous ces défenseurs de l'inconnaissable, acharnés à dresser les remparts imprenables de la liberté humaine contre les empiétements de la science, j'opposerai ce mot, très kantien, de Goethe, que tous les spécialistes des sciences naturelles et des sciences sociales pourraient faire leur: 'Notre opinion est qu'il sied à l'homme de supposer qu'il y a quelque chose d'inconnaissable, mais qu'il ne doit pas mettre de limite à sa recherche'. Et je crois que Kant exprime bien la représentation que les savants se font de leur entreprise lorsqu'il pose que la réconciliation du connaître et de l'être est use sorte de *focus imaginarius*, de point de fuite imaginaire, sur lequel la science doit se régler sans jamais pouvoir prétendre s'y établir (*RA*, 12-3).[42]

As we will discuss in more detail in Chapter 4, Bourdieu saw the task of sociology (like that of any science) as being *to build a model*, which, while it may never match the complexity of the thing it describes, can always be made more accurate.

Bourdieu's critique of post-modernism seems to position him on the side of Jürgen Habermas and the Frankfurt School,[43] with whom and which he is sometimes associated. In fact, the relationship between

---

40 See Pierre Bourdieu, 'Passport to Duke', pp. 241-42.
41 'the defeat of knowledge' (*Rules*, xvi).
42 'Against all those defenders of the unknowable, bent on manning the impregnable ramparts of human liberty against the encroachments of science, I would oppose this very Kantian thought of Goethe's, which all natural scientists and social scientists could claim as their own: "Our opinion is that it well becomes man to assume that there is something unknowable, but that he does not have to set any limit to his enquiry"' (*Rules*, xvii).
43 See Jürgen Habermas, 'Modernity Versus Postmodernity', *New German Critique*, 22 (1981), 3-14.

1. Positions   33

Bourdieu's critique of postmodernism and Habermas's is more complex than it appears, and is explicitly spelled out by Bourdieu in *Méditations pascaliennes*, where he talks of distancing himself equally from Habermas and Foucault, and in *Science de la science et réflexivité*, where he specifies the very limited conditions under which Habermas's 'ideal speech situation' might actually apply. To summarise, Bourdieu reads Habermas as envisaging an intellectual exchange subject to the 'strength of the best argument', as opposed to the equation of power and knowledge that is often attributed (with some reason) to Foucault. In other words, while Habermas gives true ideas intrinsic force, Foucault sees knowledge simply as power and imposition.

We might think that these are rather simplistic readings of Habermas's and Foucault's respective positions (and we will take issue with this tactic again when we look at Bourdieu's summary of positions in the field of literary criticism). They do, however, allow Bourdieu to define an evolutionary conception of the historical emergence of scientific fields, in which the progress of reason is tied to social advancement (the accrual of 'symbolic capital'), and which can be understood as a kind of synthesis of Foucault and Habermas. This bi-dimensionality of the scientific field is expressed clearly in the following quotation from *Méditations pascaliennes:*

> Mais qu'on ne s'y trompe pas: on est aussi loin ici de la vision irénique, évoquée par Habermas, d'un échange intellectuel soumis à la 'force du meilleur argument' (ou de la description mertonienne de la 'communauté scientifique') que de la représentation darwinienne ou nietzschéenne de la cité savante qui, au nom du slogan '*power/knowledge*' dans lequel on condense trop souvent l'œuvre de Foucault, réduit brutalement tous les rapports de sens (et de science) à des rapports de force et à des luttes d'intérêt. (...) Les champs scientifiques, ces microcosmes qui, sous un certain rapport, sont des mondes sociaux comme les autres, avec des concentrations de pouvoir et de capital, des monopoles, des rapports de force, des intérêts égoïstes, des conflits, etc., sont aussi, *sous un autre rapport*, des univers d'exception, un eu miraculeux, où la nécessité de la raison se trouve instituée à des degrés divers dans la réalité des structures et des dispositions (*MP*, 131).[44]

---

44 'But we should make no mistake: we are as far here from the irenic vision, evoked by Habermas, of an intellectual exchange subject to the "strength of the best argument" (or from Merton's description of the "scientific community") as we are from the Darwinian or Nietzschian representation of the scientific world which, in the name of the slogan "power = knowledge" into which Foucault's work is too often condensed, summarily reduces all sense relations (and scientific relations) to power relations and to struggles to advance interests. (...) Scientific fields, microcosms

Here we can see not only the double-distance Bourdieu keeps from both Foucault and Habermas, but also his ambivalent attitude towards a scientific field that, on one hand, fails to transcend the usual (and sometimes brutal) structures and mechanisms of human interaction, while, on the other hand, producing knowledge and artefacts of which the truth and usefulness cannot be reduced to their social function, nor to an effect of authority. As we will see in the course of this study, the same pattern of ambivalence also defines Bourdieu's approach to the literary field, which he characterises, in the last lines of the Avant-Propos of *Les Règles*, as again at once the arena of 'l'affrontement souvent impitoyable des passions et des intérêts particuliers'[45], and as a space in which 'les conquêtes les plus hautes de l'entreprise humaine'[46] are produced (*RA*, 16).

Appendix: the composition of *Les Règles de l'art*

As an appendix to this chapter, it is useful to take a closer look at the composition of *Les Règles de l'art*, Bourdieu's major work on literature, in order to give a sense of how it relates to Bourdieu's other texts and articles on literature, and of its internal organisation. This will, it is hoped, help the reader to find inter-texts for particular passages, while also providing some pointers on how to read *Les Règles* itself – a work that requires a quasi-literary reading and re-reading, passing backwards and forwards between passages, and paying close attention to how passages, concepts, and other elements correspond (to what might once have been called its *organic unity*). An initial point to make is that the edition of *Les Règles* this study is using is the 1998 'Nouvelle édition revue et corrigée' in the Seuil 'Points' series, in keeping with the academic convention of referring to the final version of any text. Any revisions seem, however, to have been minimal, the major difference being a useful index of names.

Proceeding through the text, the Prologue, 'Flaubert analyste de Flaubert', including two of the three annexes, 'Quatre lectures de *L'Éducation sentimentale*'

---

which, in a certain respect, are social worlds like others, with concentrations of power and capital, monopolies, power relations, selfish interests, conflicts, etc., are also, *in another respect*, exceptional, some-what miraculous universes, in which the necessity of reason is instituted to varying degrees in the reality of structures and dispositions' (*Meditations*, 109).
45 'the merciless clash of passions and selfish interests' (*Rules*, xx).
46 'the highest achievements of the human enterprise' (*Rules*, xx).

1. *Positions* 35

and 'Le Paris de *L'Éducation sentimentale*' (but not 'Résumé de *L'Éducation sentimentale*'), first appeared in Bourdieu's 1975 article 'L'Invention de la vie d'artiste',⁴⁷ published in Bourdieu's journal *Actes de la recherche en sciences sociales*. The version in *Les Règles* has been considerably re-worked, but contains lengthy verbatim passages taken from the original. The most obvious differences are two lengthy citations from *L'Éducation sentimentale* in the original article, which allow the reader to refer Bourdieu's analysis more readily to the text, and an entertaining game, 'Faites vous-même votre *L'Éducation sentimentale*', which invites the reader to imagine where modern publishers, businessmen, artists, and journalists would be situated in the structure of the social space represented in *L'Éducation sentimentale*.⁴⁸ Yet between this text and *Les Règles* Bourdieu's overall assessment of the value of Flaubert's work had undergone a complete volte face. In his initial 1975 article, Flaubert is described as being deluded as regards his pretensions to stand above the social world, whereas in *Les Règles* this pretension is seen as the key to his objectivity. In the 1975 article, Bourdieu concluded that Flaubert was effectively merely reproducing the deluded ideological viewpoint of the French nineteenth century bourgeoisie. As we will see in Chapter 3, Bourdieu's theory of literary value evolved considerably, along with his notion of autonomy which is not mentioned in 'L'Invention de la vie d'artiste'.

Part one, 'Trois états du champ', contains significant unpublished material, in particular the section in the first chapter 'Baudelaire nomothète'. This section is complemented by a case study of the same author in *Méditations pascaliennes* (*MP*, 101-09). The rest of the first chapter of *Les Règles* is based on Bourdieu's analysis of the French nineteenth-century field, first published in English as 'Flaubert's Point of View' (1988). The second chapter, 'L'émergence d'une structure dualiste', also contains lengthy passages from an older article, this time 'The Field of Cultural Production, or: The Economic World Reversed' (1983), particularly the discussion of Zola. Bourdieu's analysis is more lengthy and elaborate in *Les Règles*. The third chapter, 'Le marché des biens symboliques', should not be confused for Bourdieu's earlier article of the same name, first published in 1971. It is, with only minor changes, his 1977 article 'La Production de la croyance: contribution à une économie des biens symboliques'.⁴⁹ In this case, it is the previously published article that

---

47 Pierre Bourdieu, 'L'Invention de la vie d'artist', *Actes de la recherche en sciences sociales*, 1 (1975), 67-93.
48 'L'Invention de la Vie Artistique', pp. 79; 84; 93.
49 Pierre Bourdieu, 'La Production de la croyance: Contribution à une économie

contains more information and analysis. The 1977 article contains further contemporary examples and exemplifications, including two maps: one showing the geographical groupings of agents and institutions also sharing similar social or institutional characteristics, and the other Parisian theatres and writers' residences.[50]

Part two, 'Fondements d'une science des oeuvres', provides insight into Bourdieu's theory and methods, and would have arguably been better placed before the studies in part one. A prior reading of the section on 'L'espace des points de vue', in particular, and of the second chapter, 'Le point de vue de l'auteur', would allow literary scholars coming to Bourdieu for the first time to situate his theory in relation to more familiar literary theories, and to grasp the fundamentals of his own approach. The first chapter, 'Questions de méthode', contains sections from Bourdieu's article 'The Genesis of the Concept of Habitus and Field', and sections from 'Flaubert's Point of View'. Versions of this last section also appear in the chapter of *Raisons pratiques* entitled 'Pour une science des oeuvres' (first presented in 1986), as well as in Bourdieu's 1991 article (written in 1982) 'Le Champ littéraire'. The version in *Les Règles* is the most complete, although the version in *Raisons pratiques* is more structured and concise. The chapter ends with a rather elliptical and enigmatic discussion of reflexivity, entitled 'Objectiver le sujet d'objectification', of which we can find a better, less dense and more contextualised, version in *Méditations pascaliennes* (*MP*, 141-45). The annex to part two re-works an article on 'Sartre' first published in *The London Review of Books* in 1980. The version in *Les Règles* treats many of the same themes, but what it gains in nuance and theoretical sophistication it loses in readability. The second chapter, 'Le point de vue de l'auteur', re-uses much of the same material published in 'The Field of Cultural Production, or: The Economic World Reversed', and again in 'Le Champ littéraire'. Another annex, 'Effet de champ et formes de conservatisme', is a *précis* of a longer analysis which appears in the main body of 'Le Champ littéraire'.

Part three begins with 'La genèse historique de l'esthétique pure', first published with slight differences as 'The Historical Genesis of a Pure Aesthetic' (1987). The version in *Les Règles* contains a useful analysis of 'Les conditions de la lecture pure', and a discussion of 'La double historicisation', which do not appear in the original. The next chapter, 'La genèse sociale de

---

des biens symboliques', *Actes de la recherche en sciences sociales*, 13 (1977), 3-43.
50 'La Production de la croyance', pp. 11; 36.

l'oeil', is probably of less interest to literary scholars. Identifying parallels between art historian Michael Baxandall's notion of the 'period eye' and Bourdieu's own theory of habitus, it expands on an article written with Yvette Delsaut first published in 1981.[51] The final chapter, 'Une théorie en acte de la lecture', provides an analysis of William Faulkner's short story *A Rose For Emily*. Tucked away towards the very end of the book, and not published elsewhere, this reading has rarely been mentioned by Bourdieu's commentators – but puts a twist in the tale, after five hundred pages of extolling field analysis, by applying Bourdieu's theory and concepts to a literary text without a socio-analysis of the author. The 'da capo', 'L'illusion et l'illusio', re-caps the main themes in the book, and invites the reader to begin again, 'from the beginning' (like a work of modernist literature, which needs to be re-read in light of the ending).

The post-script, 'Pour un corporatisme de l'universel', closes with a call for writers and intellectuals to join forces to defend the conditions of their autonomy. A first and extended version of this text was delivered in 1989 at a lecture in Turin, and published in the American journal *Telos* in 1989.[52] Versions were also published in French in the journal *Politis* in 1992, and in German in 1991.[53] A version also appears in the collection of Bourdieu's political writings *Interventions: science sociale et action politique 1961-2001*, under the title 'Pour des luttes à l'échelle européenne. Réinventer un intellectuel collectif' (I, 257-66).

Three articles that did not make it into *Les Règles* are 'Champ intellectuel et projet créateur', 'Champ du pouvoir, champ intellectuel et habitus de classe',[54] and 'Le Marché des biens symboliques'. Bourdieu describes the first of these as 'à la fois essentiel et dépassé'. It provides a back-drop to the genesis of the French literary field which is only hinted at in *Les Règles*, but Bourdieu admits it contains two errors: 'il tend à réduire les relations objectives entre les positions aux interactions entre les agents et il omet de situer le champ de production culturelle dans le champ du pouvoir, laissant ainsi échapper le principe réel de certaines de ses propriétés'. 'Champ du pouvoir, champ

---

51 Pierre Bourdieu and Yvette Delsaut, 'Pour une sociologie de la perception', *Actes de la recherche en sciences sociales*, 40 (1981), 3-9.
52 Pierre Bourdieu,'The Corporatism of the Universal. The Role of Intellectuals in the Modern World', *Telos*, 81 (1989), 99-110.
53 Pierre Bourdieu, 'Pour une internationale des intellectuels', *Politis*, 1 (1992), 9-15; 'Der Korporatismus des Universellen: Zur Rolle des Intellektuellen in der modernen Welt', trans. Jürgen Bolder et al., *Die Intellektuellen und die Macht* (Hamburg: VSA–Verlag, 1991), pp. 41-65.
54 Pierre Bourdieu, 'Champ du pouvoir, champ intellectuel et habitus de classe', *Scolies*, 1 (1977), 7-26.

intellectuel et habitus de classe', in contrast, situates the cultural field in a 'dominated-dominant' position in the field of power, and takes greater account of the invisible relations between agents, such as the avant-garde and best-selling author, who might never meet – or even avoid each other consciously –, but whose practices remain determined by their opposition to each other. The third article, 'Le Marché des biens symboliques' sets out, as Bourdieu says rather abruptly, the principles that guided his analyses in *Les Règles* (*RA*, 304 n. 17), which are re-iterated in part two, 'Fondements d'une science des oeuvres' and 'Le point de vue de l'auteur'.[55]

A companion work, *The Field of Cultural Production* (1993), contains the original English language translations of 'The Field of Cultural Production', 'Flaubert's Point of View', and 'The Historical Genesis of a Pure Aesthetic'. It also features translations of 'Le Marché des biens symboliques' (original version), of 'La Production de la croyance', and of an article on Manet, 'L'Institutionnalisation de l'anomie'.[56] 'Flaubert's Point of View' has been abbreviated slightly, mainly to avoid the repetition of passages included already in 'The Field of Cultural Production'. Most usefully, *The Field of Cultural Production* contains translations of Bourdieu's lectures during the Christian Gauss Seminars in Criticism at Princeton University in 1986 (chapters 4-6), which are difficult to access in the original French (chapter six is re-printed in a slightly amended form in *Raisons pratiques*). These lectures, which are written in the more accessible style of an oral presentation, offer a good starting point for the newcomer to Bourdieu's work on literature.

---

55 'I owe it to the eventual users of these labours to say that the first of these texts ['Le Marché des biens symboliques'] seems to me essential and yet outmoded. (...) However, it contains two errors which the second article tries to correct: it tends to reduce the objective relations between positions to interactions between agents, and it omits to situate the field of cultural production within the field of power, so it lets slip the real principle of certain of its properties. As for the third ['Champ du pouvoir, champ intellectuel et habitus de classe'], it sets out, sometimes in a rather abrupt form, the principles which served as the basis for the work presented here and for a whole body of research conducted by others' (*Rules*, 185 n. 17).
56 Pierre Bourdieu, 'L'Institutionnalisation de l'anomie', *Les Cahiers du Musée national d'art moderne*, 19-20 (1987), 6-19.

2. Methods

What Bourdieu brings to literature studies is first and foremost a new method for analysing literary texts. The main aim of that method is to connect internal and external levels of analysis, the relation between which has always been problematic, when it has not been ignored, or declared unfathomable. Yet Bourdieu also employs the same general theories and concepts in his studies of sport, philosophy, politics, journalism, linguistics, and education, as he applies in his studies of literature. This was another of Bourdieu's stated methodological aims: to remove the *'statut d'exception'* (*RA*, 10-11)[1] that literature holds traditionally in France, which insists it demands a specific approach. That said, there is a surprising degree of overlap between Bourdieu's sociological theory and more established modes of literary criticism. This chapter will explore these resemblances and differences between Bourdieu's method and more familiar critical approaches, including biography, close reading, and structuralist and Russian Formalist approaches, as a way of introducing Bourdieu's theory to readers from literary backgrounds. It will also look at some of the main criticisms and developments that have been made of Bourdieu's theory, and suggest avenues for further enquiry. First, it is useful to examine the epistemological basis of Bourdieu's theory of fields, which he draws from the philosophy of science of Gaston Bachelard, one of Bourdieu's professors at the ENS. This opening section will explain the basic methodological underpinnings of Bourdieu's method, which attempts to apply the same 'structuralist' or 'relational' principles that are used in the most advanced sciences, such as mathematics and physics, to the study of social phenomena. It will also explain the grounds on which Bourdieu makes his claim to have produced a 'science of works', which we have seen has provoked consternation from critics, who have seen it as a mark of 'reductionism'. This chapter will then serve as a preliminary to the examination, in Chapter 3, of Bourdieu's analysis of the French literary field up to the nineteenth century, and of the central notion of autonomy.

---

1 *'status of exception'* (*Rules*, xvi).

Epistemological preliminaries

In his 1968 work *Le Métier de sociologue* (with Jean-Claude Passeron and Jean-Claude Chamboredon), and the early article 'Structuralism and Theory of Sociological Knowledge',[2] Bourdieu set out to place the human sciences on the same epistemological footing as the natural sciences. This meant, primarily, applying the 'relational' or 'structuralist' mode of thinking to the study of social groups, and secondly establishing certain rules or standards by which 'objectivity' or 'scientificity' could be assessed. This project, Bourdieu claimed, faced particular difficulties when it came to the study of society. The first of these was, paradoxically, the sociologist's immediate familiarity with the object of study, and the apparent obviousness of common-sense explanations of social mechanisms (*MS*, 27). This difficulty was exacerbated, according to Bourdieu, by the fact that sociologists had to compete with other authorities for the legitimate representation and interpretation of social reality: in particular with politicians and journalists, who were disposed to side with popular attitudes and preconceptions (it is how they sell newspapers, and win votes). In *Le Métier de sociologue*, Bourdieu draws a parallel between sociology in the 1960s and the state of the natural sciences in the eighteenth century (according to Gaston Bachelard),[3] when science was a subject for polite conversation, any person of status felt qualified to venture an opinion (often in book form) and 'auteur et lecteur pensaient au même niveau'.[4]

It is in fact from Bachelard, better known by literary scholars as the author of *La Poétique de l'espace*, that Bourdieu derives the fundamental principles by which he defines 'scientific' sociology. Bourdieu condenses these principles into the axiom that *'le fait scientifique est conquis, construit, constaté'* (*MS*, 24). Scientific knowledge is *conquered* against everyday, 'spontaneous', or 'intuitive' knowledge; *constructed* as a formalised model; and *verified* by empirical research and experimentation. This 'experimental cycle' does not take the form of a series of discrete steps, performed in chronological order, but rather sets up a relation and to-and-fro between theory and experience, which support and inform each other. For instance, the construction of the object as a system of intelligible relations is

---

2 Pierre Bourdieu, 'Structuralism and Theory of Sociological Knowledge', *Social Research*, 35 (1968), 681-706.
3 Gaston Bachelard, *La Formation de l'esprit scientifique*, 4th edn (Paris: Vrin, 1965), pp. 24-34, cited in *MS*, 307-15.
4 'the author and the reader thought at the same level' (*Craft*, 233).

inseparably a rupture with visible or 'phenomenal' appearances, which are, however, the basis of verification.

The break with 'spontaneous' or 'intuitive' knowledge is a rupture with the 'substantialism' of primary experience or intuition, with its belief in 'essences' and 'individuals', and which tries to discover the 'inner properties' or 'content' of things. From a scientific perspective, in contrast, Bachelard writes, 'il n'y a pas de phénomène simple, le phénomène est un tissu de relations'.[5] The proper object of science is, therefore, to model this invisible 'noumenal structure' (Bachelard) or 'generative structure' (Bourdieu), which somehow necessitates the observable phenomena, and which is, for Bourdieu as for Bachelard, the 'real' or 'objective' reality. Hence Bachelard's maxim: 'Au commencement était la Relation',[6] and Bourdieu's motto (with a play on Hegel): 'Le réel est relationnel' (RP, 17).[7] The model generated by constructing a system of relations can then be verified against experience, or observable phenomena. In 'Structuralism and Theory of Sociological Knowledge', Bourdieu characterises scientific theory as 'a system of signs organized to represent, through their own relations, the relations among the objects (…) linked to what it symbolizes by a law of analogy'.[8]

The strength of this analogy, and of the principles behind it, is tested by its heuristic value, and corrected in light of the problems or difficulties it encounters. In Bourdieu's words (citing the linguist and philosopher Hans Reichenbach), 'the strength of proof of a relation empirically discovered (…) is a function of those "chains of proofs" that "may be stronger than their weakest link, even stronger than their strongest link", since their validity is measured not only by the simplicity and coherence of the principles employed, but by the range and diversity of the facts considered and by the multiplicity of unforeseen consequences'.[9] It is important to stress the order of this procedure. As Bachelard (cited in Le Métier de sociologue) writes, 'le vecteur épistémologique (…) va du rationnel au réel et non point, à l'inverse, de la réalité au général, comme le professaient tous les philosophes depuis Aristote jusqu'à Bacon' (MS, 54).[10] What happens in

---

5 'there is no simple phenomenon, the phenomenon is a tissue of relations' (trans. J.S.). Gaston Bachelard, Le Nouvel esprit scientifique (Paris: Librarie Félix Alcan, 1937), p. 25.
6 'In the beginning was the Relation' (trans. J.S.), Gaston Bachelard, La Valeur inductive de la relativité (Paris: Vrin, 1929), p. 65.
7 'The Real is Relational' (Practical Reason, 3)
8 'Structuralism and Theory of Sociological Knowledge', pp. 687-88.
9 Ibid., p. 689.
10 'the epistemological vector (…) points from the rational to the real and not, as all philosophers from Aristotle to Bacon professed, from the real to the general' (Craft, 36).

reality is re-interpreted in the light of the constructed model, rather than scientific knowledge being based in the first instance on direct observation (as it is in the positivist tradition). As Vandenberghe writes: 'Paradoxically, it is to render the contact with reality more precise and more penetrating that science is forced to carry out, as Gilles-Gaston Granger beautifully says, "a detour via the realm of abstraction"'.[11]

In *Le Métier de sociologue,* Bourdieu describes the positivist tendency as particularly strong in sociology, partly because of the nature of its object. 'C'est peut-être la malédiction des sciences de l'homme', he writes, 'que d'avoir affaire à *un objet qui parle*' (MS, 56).[12] Sociologists who accept the informants' own explanations and interpretations merely document the preconceptions of the subjects they are studying, and have not yet operated the break with 'common-sense'. According to Bourdieu, an adequate sociological model should be able to account for (without for all that simply reproducing) agents' subjective experiences and representations, by constructing a model of their relative positions and trajectories in social space. The scientist must therefore adopt a particular way of thinking, to which Bourdieu refers, again following Bachelard (but also the German philosopher Ernst Cassirer) as the 'relational mode of thought'.[13] Both Bachelard and Cassirer saw 'relational thinking', as exemplified by mathematics and physics, as one of the cornerstones of modern scientific thought (RA, 298 n. 8). We can appreciate that sociology again encounters particular obstacles when it attempts to apply this ordinary principle to the study of individuals, groups, or institutions, whom or which we are encouraged to think of and treat as distinct and self-enclosed entities, by the full weight of convention, the law, and even morality.

Bourdieu saw the definition of the principles of a 'scientific' sociology as one of the first steps to creating the conditions under which they could be applied systematically. In this sense, he argues, the question 'de savoir si la sociologie est ou non une science, et une science comme les autres', shifts to the question of which 'type d'organisation et de fonctionnement de la cité savante [est] le plus favorable à l'apparition et au développement d'une

---

11 Frédéric Vandenberghe, '"The Real is Relational": An Epistemological Analysis of Pierre Bourdieu's Generative Structuralism', *Sociological Theory*, 17 (1999), 32-67 (p. 38).
12 'It is perhaps the curse of the human sciences that they deal with a *speaking object*' (*Craft*, 37).
13 See Ernst Cassirer, *Substance et fonction* (Paris: Éditions de Minuit, 1977).

recherche soumise à des contrôles strictement scientifiques' (*MS*, 103).[14] Here Bourdieu draws, one last time, on Bachelard, and his image of a 'cité savante homogène et bien gardée' (*MS*, 309)[15] to describe an ideal situation in which social scientists would hold each other collectively to account, and compete solely in the stakes of 'truth' or 'objectivity'. It is only by working towards the creation of these social conditions, which would cultivate and inculcate 'good' scientific practices (to which the statement of the rules that would govern such a scientific community is a contribution) that we can expect the progress and spread of scientific reason.[16] We can notice how Bourdieu's 'constative' definition of science turns by necessity into a 'normative' prescription: by defining the principles of a scientific sociology Bourdieu was also contributing to bring it into being, as he observes in his later work *Méditations pascaliennes*:

> En fait, il n'est pas d'assertion constative concernant ce champ qui ne puisse faire l'objet d'une lecture normative (…). On ne sort pas si facilement de la logique spontanément performative du langage qui, comme je n'ai pas cessé de le rappeler, contribue toujours à faire (ou à faire exister) ce qu'il dit, notamment à travers l'efficacité constructive inséparablement cognitive et politique des classements (*MP*, 139-40).[17]

Bourdieu's indebtedness to Bachelard has become better recognised by Anglophone scholars in recent years, by researchers including Loïc Wacquant, David Swartz, and Frédéric Vandenberghe. Vandenberghe, in particular, gives Bachelard a special position on the long list of authors with whom Bourdieu engages (that is, both builds on and challenges), writing:

> Bourdieu is not a syncretic but a synthetic and heretical thinker. He draws on Durkheim, Marx, Weber, and others but insofar as he critically corrects them, one could as well describe him as an anti-Durkheimian Durkheimian, an anti-Weberian Weberian, or an anti-Marxist Marxist. One could even say that he thinks with Althusser against Althusser and against Habermas with

---

14 'The question of whether sociology is or is not a science, and science like others, therefore has to give way to the questions of the type of organization and functioning of the "scientific city" most conducive to the appearance and development of research that is subject to strictly scientific controls' (*Craft*, 75).
15 'well-guarded scientific city' (*Craft*, 233).
16 See Pierre Bourdieu, 'La Spécificité du champ scientifique et les conditions sociales du progrès de la raison', *Sociologie et sociétés*, 7 (1975), 91-118; 'Le Champ scientifique', *Actes de la recherche en sciences sociales*, 2-3 (1976), 88-104.
17 'One does not easily leave the spontaneously performative logic of language, which, as I have always insisted, helps to make (or make exist) what it says, especially through the inseparably cognitive and political constructive efficacy of classifications' (*Meditations*, 117).

Habermas, but not – and this is probably the only exception – that he thinks with Bachelard against Bachelard.[18]

Yet we should perhaps be more sceptical of Bourdieu's claims to be a faithful disciple, who closely follows Bachelard's epistemological prescriptions. Bourdieu's claims in this respect are undone by his evolutionary conception of the historical emergence of autonomous fields (Bachelard's conception of history was anything but evolutionary) and by his cumulative conception of the history of science (again, this directly contradicts Bachelard's understanding of the history of science).[19] For Bachelard, as later for Thomas Kuhn, whom Bourdieu does criticise on this point, scientific progress takes the form of sudden 'epistemological ruptures' (for Kuhn, 'paradigm shifts'), which cannot be accounted for within the model of a continuous history. As we will see in the next chapter, Bourdieu in contrast emphasises the *continuity and rupture* within any transformation of knowledge, whether in literature or science, and he locates the impetus for such changes not in the disembodied framework of concepts and theories (the Bachelardian 'problematic'), but in the struggle between flesh-and-blood agents with passions and needs.

It is also notable that in their specific works on literature Bourdieu and Bachelard again part company. The apparent universality and transhistoricity of certain cultural works is one of the founding presuppositions in *La Poétique de l'espace*,[20] which Bachelard sets out to discover 'comment (...) cet événement singulier et éphémère qu'est l'apparition d'une image poétique singulière, peut-il réagir – sans aucune préparation – sur d'autres âmes, dans d'autres cœurs'.[21] It would be difficult to find a more perfect expression of what Bourdieu calls the myth of the 'pure gaze', which would be able somehow spontaneously to appreciate and understand works of art and literature. Indeed, in *La Poétique de l'espace*, Bachelard states explicitly his intention to leave his 'habitudes intellectuelles' as a rationalist philosopher of science behind, in order to found 'une phénoménologie de l'imagination' in which, he claims,

---

18 Vandenberghe, 'The Real is Relational', p. 32.
19 On this topic, see Robert J.C. Young, *White Mythologies: Writing History and the West* (London and New York: Routledge, 1990), pp. 84-86.
20 Gaston Bachelard *La Poétique de l'espace* (Paris: Presses Universitaires de France, 1957). The following citations are from pp. 1-5.
21 'how (...) this singular and ephemeral event which is the apparition of a poetic image can arise – without any preparation – in other hearts, in other minds' (trans. J.S.).

'la notion de principe, la notion de "base", serait (…) ruineuse'.[22] As in his philosophy of scientific reason, Bachelard refuses to apply the same principles of probability and causality to the social world that he sees governing the natural world. Bourdieu, in contrast, studies the literary and artistic fields using the same general principles (his theory of fields) that he applies not only in his sociology of science, but also to literature and diverse other fields. In his work on literature, Bourdieu was therefore thinking 'with Bachelard against Bachelard', whose studies of poetry and art were a deliberate departure from his own 'applied rationalism'.

The author's point of view

Bourdieu presents his method of literature analysis as a response to a challenge laid down by the French poet and literary critic Paul Valéry: 'L'objet d'un vrai critique devrait être de découvrir quel problème l'auteur s'est posé (sans le savoir ou le sachant) et de chercher s'il l'a résolu ou non' (RA, 351).[23] He also refers to a problem posed by Gustave Flaubert:

> Où connaissez-vous une critique qui s'inquiète de l'œuvre *en soi*, d'une façon intense? On analyse très finement le milieu où elle s'est produite et les causes qui l'ont amenée; mais la poétique *insciente*, d'où elle résulte? sa composition, son style? le point de vue de l'auteur? Jamais ! (RA, 149)[24]

Bourdieu interprets these challenges as a call to reconstruct the problematic (or 'space of possibilities') as it faced a particular author, and to try to understand, as if from 'the author's point of view', why the author responded in the way (s)he did, given the manifold pressures and constraints (s)he was under.

Bourdieu summarises his analysis as operating on three levels, which are nestled like Chinese boxes fitting one inside of the other. First, Bourdieu opens the biggest box, and analyses the position of the literary field in the 'field of power'. Next, he opens the middle box, and maps the positions of individuals, groups, and institutions in the literary field. Finally, he opens

---

22 'the notion of principle, of a "base", would be ruinous' (trans. J.S.).
23 'The goal of a true critic should be to discover which problem the author posed himself (knowingly or not) and to find whether he solved it or not' (*Rules*, 214).
24 'Where do you know [of] a criticism? Who is there who is anxious about the work in *itself*, in an intense way? They analyse very keenly the setting in which it is produced and the causes leading to it; but as for the unknowing [*inscient*] poetics? Where does it come from? And the composition and style? The author's point of view? Never!' (*Rules*, 87).

the smallest box, and traces the genesis of agents' habitus. To this schema, we need to add the analysis of literary texts in the 'space of works'. It might also be useful to add the transnational dimension of 'world literary space', as developed by Pascale Casanova. Like Bachelard's epistemological check-list, these three steps should not be thought of as discrete stages, or a rigid programme. Each level of analysis needs to take in the information provided by the others, so that the analysis may start at any point along the cycle. Thus, *Les Règles* begins (disconcertingly, from a strict methodological standpoint) with an 'internal' analysis of Flaubert's *L'Éducation sentimentale* (RA, 19-71). Yet from this reading he is able to trace several clues with regard to Flaubert's social position and trajectory, which are corroborated by his sociological research and *vice versa*. In this respect, to borrow an image Pierre Duhem uses to describe structural research more generally (although resisting, for reasons to be explained in Chapter 4, the suggestion of aestheticisation), Bourdieu's model resembles 'a symbolic painting to which incessant retouching gives greater extent and unity (...), while each detail, cut off from the whole, loses any meaning and no longer represents anything'.[25]

The field of power

The first stage of Bourdieu's analysis is to locate the literary field as something like a 'status group' (Weber) in 'the field of power'. The field of power is defined in *Les Règles* as 'l'espace des rapports de force entre des agents ou des institutions ayant en commun de posséder le capital nécessaire pour occuper des positions dominantes dans les différents champs (économique ou culturel notamment)' (RA, 353).[26] Close to the notion of a 'dominant class', it is, however, a 'relational' concept, which tries to move us away from the study of isolated populations, agents, and groups, towards the study of the *structure of the relations* that exist between them. The notion of a field of power also implies a break with the representation of the social world found in some forms of Marxism, which pits the owners of the means of production against the labour force. The field of power is split between competing factions (the fields),

---

25 Pierre Duhem cited by Bourdieu in 'Structuralism and Theory of Sociological Knowledge', p. 688.
26 'the space of relations between agents or between institutions having in common the possession of the capital necessary to occupy the dominant positions in different fields (economic or cultural notably)' (*Rules*, 215).

and polarised between the holders of economic and political power, who are dominant over all, and the holders of 'cultural capital', who are 'dominated dominators': structurally subordinate, but with the (symbolic) power to legitimate or discredit the dominant group.

What Bourdieu describes in his studies of French culture and society, including *La Distinction* and *La Noblesse d'État*, is an *historical* state of the field of power, which took its present form over the second half of the nineteenth century, in Flaubert's time, when 'cultural capital' became almost entirely disassociated from economic capital. Indeed, Bourdieu finds a very accurate depiction of the field of power written into *L'Éducation sentimentale*. At one pole, Bourdieu positions rich bankers like M. Dambreuse, who have very high levels of economic capital and other material assets, but relatively little cultural capital (educational qualifications, cultural knowledge, artistic competence). At the other pole, he positions the artists and intellectuals who gather at the art merchant Arnoux's, who have very high levels of cultural capital, but relatively little economic capital. In the central positions Bourdieu positions lawyers, doctors, and upper-level state bureaucrats, who possess approximately equal levels of both economic and cultural capitals. This is where Bourdieu situates Frédéric (and Flaubert himself).

Yet Bourdieu also claims that the *structure* of the field of power is 'transhistorical' and even 'quasi-universal', surviving in various forms over the centuries, and arising in different cultures and civilisations. Bourdieu follows Georges Duby to find a precedent in the opposition between the *bellatores* (those who fight) and *oratores* (those who pray) in medieval society, and refers to Georges Dumézil's trifunctional hypothesis, which discovers the same triad in Indian society (which splits between the Brahmin and Kshatriya castes), and represented in various mythic systems. The third term refers to the dominated, peasants, commoners, or workers. As well as the forms of power changing, the balance of power varies over time and between national traditions.[27] Indeed, Bourdieu claims that many social struggles and upheavals, sometimes explained by 'class conflict', can better be understood as extensions of the struggles between the dominant over their relative power (or the value of their capitals and their 'rates of exchange'), as the 'dominated-dominant' ally themselves provisionally

---

27 Loïc Wacquant, 'From Ruling Class to Field of Power: An Interview with Pierre Bourdieu on *La Noblesse d'État*', Theory Culture Society, 10 (1993), 19-44 (pp. 22-24).

(and precariously) with the dominated (*MP*, 124). Bourdieu offers few clues, however, how to gauge the position of a literary field in the field of power. According to Bourdieu, the value of the literary field's capital is tied to its autonomy, which can be measured – but how accurately, or consistently? – by writers' ability to resist or ignore external (especially religious, political, and commercial) demands. This resistance can be also seen in the works they produce, by the degree of 'retraduction ou de *réfraction*'[28] they exercise over religious or political representations (i.e., by their degree of 'artistic freedom' over the form), and by their ability to choose their own content (for example, by depicting scenes considered to be 'vulgar', 'ignoble', or merely 'mediocre', according to dominant norms). Finally, the symbolic power and autonomy accorded to writers is also manifested by their ability to contest temporal powers, by invoking their own norms and values ('truth', 'justice', 'beauty', the 'ideal', and so on), against those of the dominant (order, profit, power, etc.) (*RA*, 360-61). These measures seem rather inexact, however, and in practice Bourdieu only locates the position of the French literary field in the field of power in rather an approximate and impressionistic way.

In her study *Literary France: The Making of a Culture*,[29] Priscilla Parkhurst Ferguson identifies a number of variables that can be used more accurately to measure the stock of writers' capital, in comparison with other periods and societies. Ferguson analyses the number of books published and bought each year, and the time spent reading per inhabitant, but also the number of publishers and bookstores, instances of official consecration (writers appearing on bank notes, stamps, monuments and street names, etc.), and press coverage (space allotted to literary topics in newspapers, time given to literature on television programmes).[30] We could observe equally the absence of these: high levels of illiteracy, a weak distribution network (including publishers, libraries, magazines, newspapers), the absence of official instances of consecration, etc., as evidence of a comparative lack of cultural capital.[31]

Positioning the literary field in the field of power (or gauging the symbolic value accorded to the specific capital of the writer) can help

---

28 'translation or of refraction' (*Rules*, 220).
29 Priscilla Parkhurst Ferguson, *Literary France: The Making of a Culture* (Barkeley, CA: University of California, 1987).
30 See Ferguson, *The Making of a Culture*, especially pp. 17-18.
31 See Pascale Casanova, *La République mondiale des lettres* (Paris: Éditions du Seuil, 2008), pp. 35-37.

us understand why particular authors were drawn to the profession and many of their practices and representations once they have arrived there. For example, when we know that the literary field occupies a 'dominated-dominant' position in the field of power, we can understand the ambivalence many writers express or manifest toward both the dominant and the dominated, both in their writings and by their fluctuating political allegiances (*RA*, 353). To different degrees depending on their positions in the literary field, writers seek to define themselves both against the 'vulgar' crowd and the 'philistine' bourgeois, compensating for what they lack in economic capital by accumulating cultural capital.

As Pascale Casanova has shown, the notion of 'cultural capital' (sometimes presented as one of Bourdieu's great theoretical innovations) finds a precedent in the work of the poet and literary critic Paul Valéry.[32] 'Ce capital *Culture ou Civilisation*', Valéry writes, 'est d'abord constitué par des *choses*, des objets matériels – livres, tableaux, instruments, etc., qui ont leur durée probable, leur fragilité, leur précarité de choses'.[33] Valéry's words find an echo in Bourdieu's main theoretical article on 'The (Three) Forms of Capital' (1986),[34] which similarly identifies an '*objectified* state' in which cultural capital can exist: 'in the form of cultural goods (pictures, books, dictionaries, instruments, machines, etc.)'.[35] Cultural capital can also exist in an '*embodied* state; i.e. in the form of long-lasting dispositions of the mind and body', according to Bourdieu.[36] Cultural capital can be internalised in the course of socialisation (whether accompanied or not by a formal education), which inculcates the 'dispositions' and 'schemes of perception and appreciation' necessary to engage in cultural practices. Valéry says much the same:[37]

---

32 Paul Valéry, 'La Liberté de l'Esprit', in *Regards sur le monde actuel*, in *Œuvres*, 2 vols, ed. Jean Hytier (Paris: Gallimard, 1960), vol. 2, pp. 1077-106 (p. 1090).
33 'Of what is this capital called *Culture* or *Civilization* composed? It is constituted first by things, material objects – books, paintings, instruments, etc., which have their own probable lifespan, their own fragility, the precariousness that things have' cited in Pascale Casanova, *The World Republic of Letters*, trans. M. B. Debevoise (Cambridge, MA: Harvard University Press, 2005), p. 14.
34 Pierre Bourdieu, 'The (Three) Forms of Capital', trans. Richard Nice, in *Handbook of Theory and Research for the Sociology of Education*, ed. John G. Richardson (New York: Greenwood, 1986), pp. 241-55 (first publ. as 'Ökonomisches Kapital, kulturelles Kapital, soziales Kapital', in *Soziale Ungleichheiten*, ed. Reinhard Kreckel (Goettingen: Otto Schartz & Co., 1983), pp. 183-98.
35 'The (Three) Forms of Capital', p. 243.
36 Ibid., p. 244.
37 Valéry, 'La Liberté de l'esprit', p. 1090.

> Pour que le matériel de la culture soit un capital, il exige (...) l'existence d'hommes qui aient besoin de lui, et qui puissent s'en servir, – c'est-à-dire d'hommes qui aient soif de connaissance et de puissance de transformations intérieures, soif de développements de leur sensibilité et qui sachent, d'autre part, acquérir ou exercer ce qu'il faut d'habitudes, de discipline intellectuelle, de conventions et de pratiques pour utiliser l'arsenal de documents et d'instruments que les siècles ont accumulé.[38]

Bourdieu adds a third form which cultural capital can take: an '*institutionalized* state (...) which must be set apart because, as (...) seen in the case of educational qualifications, it confers entirely original properties on the cultural capital which it is presumed to guarantee'. Formal acts of accreditation (such as educational credentials, recognised posts, university positions, literary prizes, etc.) guarantee the social value of cultural capital, by providing symbolic recognition and (more or less indirectly) access to economic remuneration.[39]

We know that Bourdieu was familiar with Valéry's œuvre. We can find him citing the poet and writer from his first article on literature,[40] and on several occasions in Les Règles (RA, 351; 523). Without claiming Valéry to be the source for Bourdieu's concept of cultural capital, which was first formulated in his research into the unequal scholastic achievement of children from the different classes and class fractions, and was only gradually elaborated by its use in different empirical contexts, it is possible that Bourdieu had come across Valéry's essay, and been influenced by his metaphor. Which is not one of the places one would usually look for a 'precursor' to Bourdieu.

The literary field

The next step in Bourdieu's analysis is to plot the positions of writers in the 'literary field'. This space is 'relatively autonomous' from the field of power, enclosing the struggle between writers. However, due to the influence of the political and economic fields, the literary field is always divided

---

38 'In order for the material of a culture to constitute capital, it is also necessary that there be men who have need of it and who are able to make use of it (...) and who know, on the other hand, how to acquire and exercise what is necessary in the way of habits, intellectual discipline, conventions, and practices for using the arsenal of documents and instruments that has been accumulated over the centuries', cited in *World Republic*, p. 15.
39 'The (Three) Forms of Capital', p. 243.
40 'Champ intellectuel et projet créateur', p. 874.

between two broad groups or 'sub-fields', which operate according to two opposed and opposite principles. In the case of the French literary field from the nineteenth century up to today, Bourdieu positions, at one pole, writers of bestsellers, whose success is measured by the number of copies sold, and by the popularity of their works with the public and the media. Bourdieu terms these writers 'heteronomous', signifying their state of being beholden to influences, norms, or standards external to the field. At the other pole, Bourdieu positions 'pure' or 'autonomous' writers, who respect no judgement other than that of their peers, and to whom too rapid or great commercial success may even be suspicious. Although these writers tend to be less successful in commercial terms (especially at the early stages of their careers), they receive the specific profits or 'symbolic capital' bestowed by the field (literary prizes, publication with a prestigious editing house, favourable reviews in specialist journals, etc.), through which they can slowly build recognition in the wider community, and perhaps gain the ultimate consecration of the school and university, by being included in the canon and on the curriculum. There is, then, a 'structural homology' between the literary field and the field of power, which is also split between two principles of hierarchy and two competing forms of power (*RA*, 246).

Again, as in the case of the field of power there can be considerable variation between the two 'poles' on the literary field across time and national traditions, in terms both of their relative power and the *form* of their opposition. For instance, 'la même *intention d'autonomie*' Bourdieu writes, 'peut en effet s'exprimer dans des prises de position opposées (laïques dans un cas, religieuses dans un autre) selon la structure et l'histoire des pouvoirs contre lesquels elle doit s'affirmer' (*RA*, 551).[41] Autonomy does not necessarily mean therefore '*l'art pour l'art*', as it appears in the French case, but can take many, sometimes paradoxical forms, depending on the particular constraints and pressures operating on and within the field. In their studies of the literary field in Quebec, for example, Denis Saint-Jacques and Alain Viala found the impulse for literary autonomy coupled with that for political autonomy, and not defined against it.[42] In their struggle to define themselves against both the bordering Anglophone space and

---

[41] 'The same intention of autonomy can in effect be expressed in opposite position-takings (secular in one case, religious in another) according to the structure and the history of the powers against which it must assert itself' (*Rules*, 343).
[42] Denis Saint-Jacques and Alain Viala, 'À propos du champ littéraire: Histoire, géographie, histoire littéraire', in *Le Travail sociologique de Pierre Bourdieu*, ed. Bernard Lahire (Paris: La Découvert, 1999), pp. 59-74 (pp. 67-68).

the French tradition, Quebecois writers have come positively to identify themselves with everything that can distinguish them from their more powerful literary and political neighbours, adopting for instance motifs from Catholicism in an Anglo-Saxon Protestant milieu, and 'regionalist' themes against the 'universalist' French literary tradition. As Maurice Lemire notes, in a contradictory move Quebecois writers submit to the codes and conventions of morality and religion, in order to affirm their independence from cultural domination.[43] This is not to say that Quebecois literature is of any less 'universal' worth than French autonomous literature, which tends to eschew political or religious content in literature. Indeed, its very implication in political struggle could, in a different light, give it more 'universal' appeal than a literature that understands itself to be so (for a full discussion of Bourdieu's notion of 'universality', see Chapter 6 in the present study).

Like the social space as a whole, the literary field also has its dominant and dominated factions. The dominant positions at the autonomous pole are occupied by consecrated authors, who have 'made a name' for themselves by setting a new trend, or by becoming associated with a particular style or genre. These writers have also begun to impose themselves beyond the field, where their growing prestige attracts a wider audience. The dominant positions at the opposite pole are occupied by authors who cater to the dominant faction of the general public. They receive, along with high financial rewards from their affluent and highly literate readership, the benefits of bourgeois consecration (favourable reviews in the bourgeois press, friendships and matrimonial ties, symbols of institutional consecration such as the *légion d'honneur* or a seat at the *Académie*, and so on). Popular writers are doubly discredited, as both mass market and for addressing a lower-class readership. Opposite popular writers stand the new avant-garde: writers who challenge the consecrated avant-garde, in the name of the same values of 'novelty' and 'independence' that had propelled their forerunners into power, or justifying their own revolution in terms of a lost 'purity' or 'return to origins'. Because of the specialised and experimental nature of their work, these authors can have few if any readers beyond the close circle of their peers, and have as yet accumulated little 'symbolic capital'. Also in this dominated position are failed or failing writers, who, behind the times, remain faithful to a

---

43 Maurice Lemire, 'L'Autonomisation de la "Littérature Nationale" au XIXè siècle', *Études Littéraires*, 20 (1987), 75-98 (p. 95).

declining or unsuccessful position. Indeed, there is often some ambiguity as to who belongs in each of these categories: as to who is a misunderstood genius or a second-rate talent (RA, 358).

In *Les Règles,* Bourdieu represents the French literary field at the end of the nineteenth century visually, by means of two sociogrammes. In his diagram of 'Le champ de production culturelle dans le champ du pouvoir et dans l'espace social', Bourdieu represents French society or 'social space' as a rectangle traversed by two axes. The vertical axis measures the total volume of both forms of capital. The horizontal axis measures relative amounts of economic and cultural capitals, which, as we have been seeing, are inversely proportional (i.e., the more cultural capital one has, the less economic capital one has, and *vice versa*). Another box, situated in the top area of the sociogramme, represents the field of power. Within this space Bourdieu locates the field of cultural production on the left towards the cultural pole. Within the field of cultural production itself Bourdieu draws two sub-fields: the sub-field of restricted production, and the sub-field of mass production. The second sociogramme provides a close-up map of these two sub-fields. Bourdieu represents the system of oppositions between literary schools and groups by arrows linking their names, which are placed in the approximate area of the sociogramme corresponding to their positions in the field, defined by the volume and 'structure' (or ratio) of their capitals (RA, 205). Both these sociogrammes are, however, rather impressionistic. Informed by Bourdieu's other studies of fields, they rely less on quantitative data than on wide knowledge and intuition.

In his other major studies of fields, from his 1978 article (with Monique de Saint Martin) 'Anatomie du goût'[44] to one of his last major studies, his analysis of the French publishing field in the 1990s 'Une Révolution conservatrice dans l'édition',[45] but most famously in *La Distinction,* Bourdieu uses Multiple Correspondence Analysis (MCA) as a way of plotting large amounts of data graphically and discerning their patterns.[46] MCA is

---

44 Pierre Bourdieu and Monique de Saint Martin, 'Anatomie du goût', *Actes de la recherche en sciences sociales,* 5 (1976), 5-81.
45 Pierre Bourdieu, 'Une Révolution Conservatrice dans l'Édition', *Actes de la recherche en sciences sociales,* 126 (1999), 3-28.
46 In this discussion of Bourdieu's use of correspondence analysis, I rely on Henry Rouanet, Werner Ackermann and Brigitte Le Roux, 'The Geometric Analysis of Questionnaires: The Lesson of Bourdieu's *La Distinction*', *Bulletin de Méthodologie Sociologique,* 65 (2000), 5-15; and Dianne Phillips, 'Correspondence Analysis', *Social Research Update,* 7 (1995), at http://sru.soc.surrey.ac.uk/SRU7.html consulted on 31/08/11.

primarily a technique for representing the rows and columns of a two-way contingency table (such as an Individuals × Properties table), in a joint plot. The result is a 'cloud' of points, which provides a visual representation of the relationships between the row categories and the column categories in the same two-dimensional space. The calculations and visual representation are usually performed using specially designed computer software (in the original draft of *La Distinction*, however, the simultaneous display of the 'space of individuals' and the 'space of properties' was achieved by layering transparent papers). Bourdieu discovered correspondence analysis from the 'French Data Analysis' school led by Jean-Paul Benzécri, at around the same time he was developing his concept of field in the late 1960s. Bourdieu speaks of 'l'affinité entre cette méthode d'analyse mathématique et la pensée en termes de champ' (*SSR*, 70).[47] It is, he writes, 'essentially a relational procedure whose philosophy fully expresses what in my view constitutes social reality. It is a procedure that "thinks" in relations, as I try to do it with the concept of field'.[48] Since the 1970s, MCA has been used extensively by Bourdieu, his co-workers, and researchers following a similar research method.

MCA has been used by researchers including Jürgan Gerhards, Helmut Anheier, and Gisèle Sapiro in their empirical investigations of literary fields.[49] Gerhards and Anheier use MCA to test Bourdieu's description of the literary field as a relatively autonomous and internally differentiated and stratified social system, in the case of writers in Cologne. Data for the analysis and interpretation was collected by interviews with Cologne writers, conducted with the help of a semi-standardised questionnaire. The authors studied variables such as level of familiarity with the literary work of their colleagues, frequency of informal relationships with other writers, level of assistance received from colleagues preparing manuscripts and establishing contact with publishers, and reference group orientation (measured by their response to the question of whom they would most like to invite to dinner). The authors also collected data on educational level,

---

47 'The affinity between that method of mathematical analysis and thinking in terms of fields' (*Science*, 33).
48 Cited and translated by Henry Rouanet et al., 'The Geometric Analysis of Questionnaires', p. 8.
49 Jürgen Gerhards and Helmut K. Anheier, 'The Literary Field: An Empirical Investigation of Bourdieu's Sociology of Art', *International Sociology*, 4 (1989), 131-46. Gisèle Sapiro, 'La Raison littéraire: le champ littéraire français sous l'occupation', *Actes de la recherche en sciences sociales*, 111 (1996), 3-35.

membership of literary groups or societies, age, and number of books published. This information was then plotted and analysed using MCA and block-model analysis (another relational mode of statistical analysis). The authors concluded that, indeed, the literary field in Cologne is divided between 'legitimate' (autonomous) and 'illegitimate' (heteronomous) groups, and between the elite and junior elite (or the old and new avant-gardes), plus writers on the periphery. One of the frequent criticisms of statistical analyses, of course, is that they expend a great deal of time and effort to tell us relatively little.

Sapiro's article shows how MCA can be used to support, and can even suggest, less expected hypotheses. In her study of 'Le Champ littéraire sous l'Occupation (1940-1944)', Sapiro shows that writers whose positions in the literary field relied on the esteem of their peers (i.e., who were the richest in terms of specific symbolic capital) were also the most likely to resist the German occupation, while those writers more open to heteronomous definitions of literary success (in particular the sanction of the market) were also more likely to collaborate. Not only were autonomous writers in a way adapted already to clandestine activity, which hardly changed their conditions of production (limited print-runs, restricted readership, little remuneration, etc.); they also formed a relatively self-sufficient and close-knit community, oriented by a shared system of values which they collectively supported and reinforced, without need for outside approval or legitimation.[50] Sapiro's analysis supports Bourdieu's hypothesis in *Les Règles* that it is an author's position in the literary field, and the 'interests' attached to it, which determines his or her 'position-takings' (*prises de position*), not only in the literary field, but in the political sphere as well. This finding reverses the more usual assumption that fictional writing reflects or expresses political allegiances and convictions (*RA*, 379-80).

The strong association between MCA and Bourdieusian analysis is likely to be a barrier to literary scholars, who are (at least in the current division of academic skills and labour) unlikely to possess the competence required to perform such complex statistical analyses. However, although he did involve himself at all stages of the collection process, Bourdieu did not always do his own data analysis, but collaborated for this purpose with statisticians including Brigitte Le Roux, Rosine Christin, Alain Darbel, and Salah Bouhedja. It is also worth remembering that Bourdieu himself does not use MCA in *Les Règles de l'art*, but instead relies on discursive

---

50 Sapiro, 'La Raison Littéraire', p. 18.

indicators such as first-hand accounts (in letters and journals), reviews, literary history and criticism, and so on. Indeed, literary scholars may be more practised and skilled in this sort of archive work and close reading than their sociologist colleagues.

The notion of a literary field finds a parallel in the literary tradition in the well-worn notion of a 'Republic of Letters', used since the seventeenth century to designate the community of intellectuals and writers. Bourdieu finds many of the properties of the literary field captured already by this notion, as described by Pierre Bayle (1647-1706): the battle of all against all, the closure of the field upon itself, the freedom encouraged by the field, and so on. Bourdieu argues, however, that this notion has never served as the basis of a rigorous analysis, and warns that, by focusing on the similarities (based on 'une véritable homologie structurale'[51]) between the literary and political fields, it risks reducing literary struggles to the struggle for social power, without recognising the specific profits and interests in the field (RA, 337-38).

Bourdieu also argues against replacing the notion of field with that of a 'literary institution', which, with its Durkheimian connotations, he writes, gives 'une image consensuelle d'un univers très conflictuel',[52] and loses sight of one of the most significant characteristics of the literary field, which is its *'faible degré d'institutionnalisation'* (RA, 379 n. 21).[53] The French literary field has no formal qualifications for entry (such as educational credentials, entry tests, etc.), no universally recognised instance of institutional consecration or arbitration, and few formalised prescriptions for the role or post of the writer. Indeed, idiosyncrasy and rebelliousness are encouraged (RA, 370-71). For similar reasons, Bourdieu finds the concept of field more apt than Louis Althusser's notion of an 'ideological state apparatus' (ISA), with which it is, however, compatible. According to Bourdieu, 'un champ devient un appareil lorsque les dominants ont les moyens d'annuler la résistance et les réactions des dominés' (QS, 136).[54] From this perspective, the French literary field would appear very little like an apparatus, since it has been since the nineteenth century the site of a 'révolution permanente', where a new avant-garde is established every ten or twelve years. Finally, Bourdieu distinguishes his notion of cultural fields from that of Howard

---

[51] 'a true structural homology' (Rules, 204).
[52] 'a consensual image of a very conflictual universe' (Rules, 382).
[53] *'weak degree of institutionalization'* (Rules, 382).
[54] 'a field becomes an apparatus when the dominant have the ability to suppress any resistance and reactions from the dominated' (trans. J.S.).

Becker's 'art world', which he defines as 'consisting of all those people and organizations whose activity is necessary to produce the kind of events and objects which that world characteristically produces'.[55] This 'cooperating network' reduces relations to direct *interactions*, and gives a rather irenic vision of a social field rife with symbolic violence and competition (*RA*, 338-39).

Bernard Lahire warns us, however, that 'tout contexte pertinent d'activité n'est pas un champ'.[56] There may be situations where groupings are more ephemeral, chaotic, or less focused around a unifying problematic than the notion of field implies. In such circumstances less systematic terms, such as 'grouping', 'milieu', or 'space', may be more appropriate. The term 'grouping', for example, may be better for fragile and short-lived micro-structures; while 'space' could be used to describe the macro-relations between more dispersed and disparate groups. Lahire notes that writers, who are often obliged to earn their living from other employment, are more like 'players' who regularly enter and leave the game than stable 'agents' in a field. For this reason, Lahire prefers to speak of a 'literary game' in his book *La Condition littéraire: la double vie des écrivains*.[57] Bourdieu himself switches disconcertingly between the terms *champ* (field), *espace* (space), and *univers* (universe), and also refers to a 'marché des biens symboliques' – without really ever explaining their differences. The point, no doubt, is to encourage his readers to 'think relationally' (*IRS*, 63), and remember that our apparent object (say, a particular writer or group of writers) is always caught in a much wider web of relationships. Bourdieu's use of near-synonyms can be confusing however, especially alongside his strong insistence that the concept of field is irreplaceable with the notions of a Republic of Letters, literary institution, or art world (all of which he can also be found to use).

An important question concerns the limits of the field, or the population to be studied. 'C'est déjà exister dans un champ', Bourdieu writes, 'que d'y produire des effets, fût-ce de simples réactions de résistance ou d'exclusion' (*RA*, 369-70).[58] Jeremy Lane finds this explanation unconvincing, however,

---

55 Howard Becker, 'Art as Collective Action', *American Sociological Review*, vol. XXXIX (1974), 767-76 (p. 774).
56 Bernard Lahire, 'Champ, hors-champ, contrechamp', in *Le Travail sociologique de Pierre Bourdieu*, ed. Bernard Lahire, pp. 23-57 (p. 32). 'Not every pertinent context is a field' (trans. J.S.).
57 Bernard Lahire, *La Condition littéraire: la double vie des écrivains* (Paris: La Découverte, 2006). See also Bernard Lahire, 'Le Champ et le jeu', in *Bourdieu et la littérature*, ed. Jean-Pierre Martin, pp. 143-72.
58 'To produce effects is already to exist in a field, even if these effects are mere

as it seems to beg the question: 'In order to know which agents produce effects in a given field, it would be necessary to know in advance the boundaries of that field, otherwise it would not be possible to assess whether particular agents were producing effects within or beyond its boundaries'.[59] Yet Bourdieu insisted on the need to acknowledge and explain the different and competing definitions of the boundaries of the field, which are in a perpetual state of flux (*flou*). Following and anticipating this historical movement is not the same as knowing the boundaries in advance. Indeed, who is 'in' and 'out' is, in Bourdieu's theory, both constantly evolving and a matter of controversy – and the model should be able to explain and adjust to this change and ambiguity (*RA*, 365).

Anna Boschetti criticises Bourdieu for naturalising the concept of field, which is only a theoretical tool. According to Boschetti, Bourdieu would make the same reifying move 'du modèle de la réalité à la réalité du modèle' (*SP*, 67)[60] for which he criticises Lévi-Strauss and Marxism. Bourdieu finds this error behind both Lévi-Strauss' rigidly rule-bound structuralism, which leaves little room for agency, and the Marxist confusion of classes-on-paper for really mobilised and self-conscious classes. Similarly for Boschetti, Bourdieu makes the mistake of thinking that the literary field really exists in reality. 'It would be better and simpler', Boschetti proposes, 'to wonder if in our object there are aspects that could be explained using Field Theory'.[61] Yet if Boschetti's solution avoids the reifying move from the model of reality to the reality of the model, it risks tipping into the opposite error, that of conventionalism – which, as Frédéric Vandenberghe has shown, is probably the stronger tendency in Bourdieu.[62] Indeed, we may want to side with Vandenberghe on this issue, and argue against Bourdieu (and Boschetti) that 'a theory has to be ontologically bold rather than epistemologically cautious'. Researchers need to make a commitment to the realism of their models, otherwise the referential relation between the model and reality becomes, in Vandenberghe's words, 'ontologically obscure'.

---

reactions of resistance or exclusion' (*Rules*, 225).
59 Jeremy F. Lane, *Bourdieu's Politics: Problems and Possibilities* (London: Routledge, 2006), pp. 89-90.
60 'the model of reality to the reality of the model' (*Logic*, 39).
61 Anna Boschetti, 'How Field Theory Can Contribute to the Knowledge of the World Literary Space', unpublished paper given on 16 May 2009 at *Bourdieu and Literature* conference, University of Warwick.
62 Vandenberghe, 'The Real is Relational', pp. 32-67.

As an alternative, Vandenberghe refers to the British philosopher Roy Bhaskar, whose 'critical realism' keeps a clear concept of independent reality alongside the historicity and relativity of knowledge.[63] In other words, we can claim that something like a field objectively exists, without insisting either that it is an unconscious mechanism, or that its agents are fully or continuously aware of their involvement in the system. Needless to say, Bourdieu contested the charge of conventionalism, and in a reply to Vandenberghe's article claimed that, like Bhaskar (whose works he had read only recently), he had been a 'realist' all along.[64] Notwithstanding Bourdieu's protest, Boschetti's criticism of Bourdieu's apparent 'naturalization' of the notion of field, and Vandenberghe's opposite judgement (that '(at worst) he reduces ontology to epistemology and (at best) he avoids making ontological commitments by resorting to a conventionalist (…) "philosophy of the as if"'), raise a complex point in Bourdieu's theory of sociological knowledge, which we will find also impacts on his conception of literature, to which point we will return in Chapter 4.

Habitus and trajectory

The third stage of Bourdieu's method traces the 'trajectory' of writers, defined as 'la *série des positions* successivement occupées par un même agent ou un même groupe d'agents dans des espaces successifs' (*RA*, 425; *RP*, 88).[65] Here, Bourdieu meets up with traditional biography, with the difference that we should no longer simply be looking at an individual life or career, but also at the system of positions and relations between positions in which the events in an agent's life take place (movements between publishers, genres, groups, etc.). Indeed, Bourdieu is dismissive of ordinary biographical attempts to make sense of a writer's career in terms of the individual alone. He declares:

> Essayer de comprendre une vie comme une série unique et à soi suffisante d'événements successifs sans autre lien que l'association à un 'sujet' dont la constance n'est sans doute que celle d'un nom propre est à peu près aussi absurde que d'essayer de rendre raison d'un trajet dans le métro

---

63 See Vandenberghe, 'The Real is Relational', p. 62 n. 55.
64 See e.g. Roy Bhaskar, *A Realist Theory of Science*, (Hemel Hempstead: Harvester Wheatsheaf, 1975); and *The Possibility of Naturalism* (Hemel Hempstead: Harvester Wheatsheaf, 1989).
65 'the series of positions successively occupied by the same agent or the same group of agents in successive spaces' (*Rules*, 258).

sans prendre en compte la structure du réseau, c'est-à-dire la matrice des relations objectives entre les différentes stations (*RP*, 88; *RA*, 426).⁶⁶

The second key term in these reflections is habitus. Close to the traditional notion of 'character', *Íthos* (familiar already to literary critics), habitus is produced by habit, *ethos*. The spontaneous connotations of these terms, however, should not suggest that we are (always) passive sleep-walkers, running on habit. (Although, who has not experienced a shock when performing quite complex tasks, such as driving a car or brushing one's teeth, even making purchases at the supermarket, when we realise we were not completely aware of what we were doing? Habitus also operates at this 'pre-reflexive' level.) The Latin term *habitus*, which Bourdieu traces both to the Greek *ethos* and to *hexis* (*RA*, 294), is more closely related to *hexis*, which, in Plato's *Theaetetus*, implies the effort of concentration or paying attention.⁶⁷ When we rule out certain courses of action as not being 'true' to ourselves, because we 'know our place' or 'it's not for us'; when we ask ourselves what we 'see ourselves doing' in five or ten years' time, or say certain clothes or haircuts 'suit' us, these are all expressions of habitus. The habitus is, in other words, how we see ourselves in relation to others, what we pay attention to and what we do not habitually pay attention to, and it determines our attitudes towards not only other people, but toward the universe of cultural goods and practices which are formally or potentially available to us – what Bourdieu calls the 'space of lifestyles' (*l'espace des styles de vie*) – all of which are imbued with social significance.

How are our habitus and trajectory determined? According to Bourdieu, we internalise the information inscribed in our social surroundings, beginning at an early age. Indeed, the first 'field' is, for Bourdieu, the family, which has its own physical, economic, and symbolic power relations, measured in terms of affection, trust, age, and so on (all of which are, of course, massively

---

66 'Trying to understand a career or a life as a unique and self-sufficient series of successive events without another link than the association with a "subject" (whose consistency is perhaps only that of a socially recognized proper name) is almost as absurd as trying to make sense of a trip on the metro without taking the structure of the network into account, meaning the matrix of objective relations between the different stations' (*Rules*, 258-59).
67 See Plato, *Theaetetus* (Newburyport, MA: Focus Philosophical Library, Pullins Press, 2004). The primary reference to *hexis*, which is translated into Latin as *habitus*, is at 153 BC. See also Joe Sachs, 'Introduction', in Aristotle, *Nicomachean Ethics*, trans. Joe Sachs, (Newburyport, MA: Focus Philosophical Library, Pullins Press, 2002). I am grateful to Prof. Sachs for help with these references.

determined by social class).⁶⁸ It is in the family that we first gain a sense of 'who we are' and 'where we belong': a stage at which, Bourdieu suggests, sociology could usefully join up with psychoanalysis (*MP*, 199). The process of socialisation continues through various rites of initiation and institution, from the most obvious (a qualification, entrance into a profession, a promotion, a marriage, etc.), to the slightest (a snub or a sign of appreciation), whereby, as if following a path of least resistance (which is not to say without worries and uncertainty, which form part of the process of investiture) we submit willingly to our destiny: doing, and being, what our families, institutions, society, and we ourselves, expect of us (*MP*, 198-99).

In *Les Règles*, Bourdieu applies his theory of habitus, which he had used most famously in *La Distinction* to understand patterns of cultural consumption, to understand the practices, strategies, and choices, of cultural producers. Just as he argued that we exclude goods, groups, places, etc. from which we are excluded, and not only because we do not have enough money (entry to many museums, for example, is free, while many items of clothing that brand individuals as members of the lower-classes cost more than those worn by the middle and even upper-classes), a writer's sense of social identity determines which genres and groups etc. s(he) joins in the field, and his or her subsequent 'position-takings'. The conditions of existence associated with a high birth, for instance, would seem on Bourdieu's understanding to favour dispositions such as audacity and indifference to profit, which orient writers from richer backgrounds towards the most extreme and risky positions (because they out-step demand), but which are also often are the most profitable symbolically and even economically (in the long-run), at least for the first 'investors' who take the credit as 'inventors' (*RA*, 430).

Writers need also, however, to be in tune with the latest developments in the field: to have what Bourdieu calls a 'sense of placement' (*sens du placement*) or 'feel for the game' (*sens du jeu*), which enables them to anticipate where symbolic and economic profit next will fall, not only where they can now be found. This feel for the literary game, Bourdieu writes, 'semble être une des dispositions les plus étroitement liées à l'origine sociale et géographique' (*RA*, 430).⁶⁹ Writers who have been immersed in literary culture, preferably from an early age, internalise not only the sounds and rhythms of prose and poetry,

---

68 Pierre Bourdieu, 'A propos de la famille comme catégorie réalisée', *Actes de la recherche en sciences sociales* 100 (1993), 32-36.
69 'The *sense of placement/investment* seems to be one of the dispositions most closely linked to social and geographical origin' (*Rules*, 262).

but also a sense for the rhythm and changes in the field: a quasi-instinctual awareness that, when positions are becoming too popular or established, they should move on or try something new. These writers also dispose of the 'social capital' (networks of friends and acquaintances), and expertise (awareness of the literary heritage) to know when particular positions are getting crowded, and where undeveloped potential lies. 'À l'inverse', Bourdieu writes, 'c'est un mauvais sens du placement, lié à l'éloignement social ou géographique, qui incite les écrivains issus des classes populaires ou de la petite bourgeoisie et les provinciaux ou les étrangers à se porter vers les positions dominantes au moment où les profits qu'elles assurent tendent à diminuer du fait même de l'attraction qu'elles exercent (…) et de la concurrence intensifiée dont elles sont le lieu (*RA*, 431).[70]

Bourdieu identifies two main types or '*familles*' of trajectories within the literary field. The first is limited to one sector of the field, and lies along the same axis of consecration, which moves through negative, zero, to positive. These are descending, static, or ascendant trajectories, within a same sector of the field, measurable in terms of a greater or lesser accumulation of cultural and economic capital. The second type of trajectory implies a change of sector, and the re-conversion of one kind of specific form of capital into another. In Bourdieu's example, as Symbolist poetry began to lose its prestige, precisely because of the attention and profits it was attracting, its most culturally aware practitioners, grouped around Paul Bourget, switched to the psychological novel, also avoiding naturalism, which they considered too commercial (*RA*, 431). Symbolic capital can also be converted or 'cashed in' for economic capital, as in the case of a passage from poetry to theatre, or still more clearly, to cabaret or serialised fiction. An artist who has achieved renown in one area often attracts public interest when (s)he switches to a more profitable style or genre (although, this is usually at the cost of discredit in terms of symbolic capital) (*FCP*, 65 n. 44; *RA*, 426-27). In much the same way, Bourdieu distinguishes several general categories of *intergenerational* trajectories to the literary field: *directly ascendant* from the popular classes or lower middle-class; *diagonal* from the petite bourgeoisie of shop owners and

---

70 'Conversely, it is a bad sense of placement/investment, linked with social or geographic distance, which sends writers from the working class or the petite-bourgeoisie, provincials or foreigners, towards the dominant positions at the moment when the profits they provide tend to be diminishing due to the very attraction they exercise (…) and due to the intensified competition focused on them' (*Rules*, 262).

artisans or peasantry; *transversal* or horizontal (but in a sense declining) from the business side of the field of power or from its central positions (the 'professions', lawyers, doctors, etc.). Finally, there are cases of pure reproduction, when the children of writers become writers themselves (Kingsley to Martin Amis): '*déplacements nuls*' (*RA*, 247).[71]

The sense a writer has of his or her own position, and 'mission' or 'vocation', Bourdieu calls the 'projet créateur'. Far from a fixed and unitary intention, like Sartre's 'projet originel', or the implicit assumptions behind most traditional biographies, the 'projet créateur' is a practical response to the pressures, tensions, and forces in a field which is itself in constant flux, seen from a particular position on the cusp of a trajectory, embodied as the durable dispositions of habitus. The writer's 'projet créateur' is capable of quite radical changes and reversals. For instance, in 'Champ intellectuel et projet créateur', Bourdieu argues that Alain Robbe-Grillet's understanding of his own work (switching from the statement, in 1953, that '*Les Gommes* est un roman descriptif et scientifique',[72] to the opposite view, in 1961, that the descriptions in *Le Voyeur* and *La Jalousie* 'sont toujours faites par quelqu'un',[73] that these descriptions are 'parfaitement subjectives',[74] and that this subjectivity is and has always been the essential characteristic of the 'Nouveau Roman'), was informed and even transformed by the image projected by critics of his work, which changed how the author himself conceived of his work, and so also its future development.[75] Conversely, it is also possible for writers to modify the dominant interpretation of their work. Indeed, Bourdieu argues, many works might never have been written, or at least not the way they were, if their authors had been recognised from the outset for the qualities for which they are celebrated in retrospect (*RA*, 382). In this way, an artist's 'creative project' is variable, depending on the state of the field and the reception (s)he receives. It is enough to imagine, Bourdieu suggests, what Zola, Barcos, or Flaubert, might have written, had they been transported to an earlier or later state of the field, and found a different occasion to express their dispositions (for instance, if Flaubert had encountered the theory of the novel which meets modern writers, and which his work has done much to inspire), to see that their 'projet créateurs' – and so their entire œuvres – would have been entirely different (*RA*, 385).

---

71 'nil displacements' (*Rules*, 260).
72 '*The Erasers* is a descriptive and scientific novel' (trans. J.S.).
73 'are always made by someone' (trans. J.S.).
74 'perfectly subjective' (trans. J.S.).
75 'Champ intellectuel et projet créateur', pp. 877-80.

The space of possibilities

Bourdieu's most ambitious claim is to be able to see the logic not only of writers' social position-takings (between publishers, groups, genres, etc.), but also that behind their construction of literary works. For this, we will need to introduce a final level of analysis, left out from Bourdieu's three-point scheme, which is what Bourdieu calls the 'space of works' (*espace des œuvres*). Similar to the more familiar notion of intertextuality, which sees works as *referring* to one another (by way of refusal, negation, parody, emulation, etc.), Bourdieu's 'space of works' sees texts as 'position-takings' corresponding to particular positions, and to how writers relate to each other in the field. As a point of method, Bourdieu sees this theory of a correspondence or 'homology' between the 'space of positions' in the field and the system of differences in the 'space of works' as a way of overcoming the problematic opposition between 'internal' and 'external' levels of analysis. Either the work is treated for itself and in itself (or at best, like the Russian Formalists, as a node within a system of related inter-texts), cut off from any biographical or historical context, or it is read as a sort of allegory for the social or biographical context (or alternatively, critics ignore the question entirely, or attempt a sort of fudge between the two). In contrast, Bourdieu reads the inter-textual differences between texts as expressions of the relations of force, struggle and competition between authors – as 'position-takings' directed against other authors and their ways of writing – making the history of changes in the space of works and the history of the struggles between writers, in the words Bourdieu borrows from the philosopher Baruch Spinoza, 'deux versions de la même phrase'.[76]

Bourdieu maintains a distinction between these two levels of analysis, the 'space of positions' and the 'space of works', each of which provides information and insight regarding the other. Micro-textual analysis and macro-social analysis are thereby linked in a sort of hermeneutic circle (not a term Bourdieu uses), in which our understanding of the 'part' (here, a singular text, defined within a web of intertextual relationships, the 'space of works') is informed by our understanding of the 'whole' (the author's position, again defined relationally in the literary field and in the field of power), which in turn increases with our understanding of the 'part', and so on. Bourdieu writes:

---

76 Claude DuVerlie and Pierre Bourdieu, 'Esquisse d'un projet intellectuel: un entretien avec Pierre Bourdieu', *The French Review*, 61 (1987), 194-205 (p. 204). 'two versions of the same phrase' (trans. J.S).

> Armée de l'hypothèse de l'homologie entre les deux structures, la recherche peut, en instaurant un va-et-vient entre les deux espaces et entre les informations identiques qui s'y trouvent proposées sous des apparences différentes, cumuler l'information que livrent à la fois les œuvres lues dans leurs interrelations et les propriétés des agents, ou de leurs positions, elles aussi appréhendées dans leurs relations objectives: telle stratégie stylistique peut ainsi fournir le point de départ d'une recherche sur la trajectoire de son auteur et telle information biographique inciter à lire autrement telle particularité formelle de l'oeuvre ou telle propriété de sa structure (*RA*, 383).[77]

Bourdieu insists that the relation between these two structures is neither direct nor mechanical. Otherwise, we can see that his theory of 'homology' would quickly collapse into tautology, of the sort 'the author did this because of that, and that because of this'. In between, so to speak, is the 'space of possibilities' (*espace des possibles*), which we can think of as including *potential* courses of action and works which were never in fact realised. Bourdieu describes the space of possibilities as 'un espace orienté et gros des prises de position qui s'y annoncent comme des potentialités objectives, des choses "à faire", "mouvements" à lancer, revues à créer, adversaires à combattre, prises de position établies à "dépasser", etc'. (*RA*, 384).[78] The analyst's task is then to comprehend the writer's work as the product as a sort of 'compromise formation' (the phrase is borrowed from Freud), produced by a unique configuration of social forces and relations coupled with the author's dispositions. Bourdieu takes issue on this point with Russian Formalism, and also with Michel Foucault's theory of *épistème* (*RA*, 326). In his 1968 article 'Réponse au Cercle d'Épistémologie',[79] Foucault insists on the 'existence indépendante'[80] of the 'champ des

---

[77] 'Equipped with the hypothesis of a homology between the two structures, research – by setting up a to-and-fro between the two spaces and between identical data offered there under different guises – may accumulate the information which delivers works read *at the same time* in their interrelations, and the properties of agents, or their positions, also apprehended in their objective relations. A stylistic strategy of this sort may thus furnish the starting point for a search for the author's trajectory, or some piece of biographical information may incite us to read differently some formal particularity of the work or such a property of the structure' (*Rules*, 234 trans. modified J.S.).
[78] 'things "to be done", "movements" to launch, reviews to create, adversaries to combat, established position-takings to be "overtaken" and so forth' (*Rules*, 235).
[79] Michel Foucault, 'Réponse au cercle d'epistémologie', *Dits et Écrits 1954-1988*, 4 vols, ed. Daniel Derfert and François Ewald (Paris: Gallimard, 1994), vol. 1, 696-731 (first publ. in *Cahiers pour l'Analyse*, 9 (1968), 9-40). The quotations which follow are from p. 727.
[80] 'independent existence' (trans. J.S.).

possibilités stratégiques',[81] and, taking the case of science, condemns as an *'illusion doxologique'*[82] any attempt to explain what is produced from it by reference to anything other than 'des points de choix qu'il laisse libre à partir d'un champ d'objets donnés, à partir d'une gamme énonciative déterminée, à partir d'un jeu de concepts définis dans leur contenu et dans leur usage'.[83] Indeed, in what may be one of the few inter-textual references to Bourdieu in Foucault's work, Foucault excludes explicitly all attempts to relate scientific systems (whether biology, economics, or linguistics) 'aux divergences d'intérêts ou d'habitudes mentales chez les individus',[84] or to 'du non-scientifique (du psychologique, du politique, du social, du religieux)'. Bourdieu, who had been formulating at the time his theory of habitus, admits to feeling targeted (*RA*, 326).

Likewise, Bourdieu criticises Russian Formalist attempts to explain changes in the 'literary system' in terms of a 'dialectic' of 'banalisation' and 'debanalisation' (*ostrenanie*), which would appear to operate under its own impetus. Like Foucault, Russian Formalism neglects the social dimension, or confuses and conflates the 'space of works' and the 'field' of producers. Bourdieu finds this confusion exemplified by the ambiguity of the Russian Formalists' notion of *ustanovka*, which can mean either 'intention' or 'orientation', understood as 'positioning oneself in relation to some given data' (*RA*, 333).[85] It is unclear who – or what – the 'subject' or 'agent' this process is, and change seems to be attributed to a strange capacity for auto-transformation within the 'literary system' itself.

Bourdieu, in contrast, locates the impetus behind the evolution of the 'space of works' squarely in the dynamic relations and struggle between writers in the field. For Bourdieu, there is nothing mechanical in this process, which is not driven by the 'exhaustion' of existing modes of expression which would prompt the invention of new genres or techniques, but by the influx of new writers, carrying their own social properties, who are looking to define themselves in relation to each other and to writers of the previous generation: to 'make a name' for themselves, either by

---

81 'field of strategic possibilities' (trans. J.S.).
82 'doxical illusion' (trans. J.S.).
83 'the points of choice that it leaves free within a given field of objects, within a determined range of enunciations, within a play of concepts defined in their content and their usage' (trans. J.S.).
84 'to the diverging interests or mental habits of individuals' (trans. J.S.).
85 Bourdieu's reference is to Peter Steiner, *Russian Formalism: A Metapoetics* (Ithaca, NY: Cornell University Press, 1984), p. 124.

conforming to established forms or by inventing new and distinctive modes of production. The analyst's task is then to explain why particular authors have adopted particular strategies, which have propelled them on various trajectories (for example, to one or the other of the field's two 'poles', and to a dominant or dominated position within one of the two 'sub-fields'), always in relation to the strategies of others around them. Included in such strategies (alongside manifestos, choices of publisher, etc.), are literary works themselves, which also contain many 'position-takings' relating to form and subject-matter. Works can then be understood as the expression, translated or 'mediated' into a literary form, of the author's social position and history, and by implication as an objectification of the social structure.

Although they are largely independent *in their principle* (i.e., in the relations of force which determine them), the *outcome* of the struggles in the literary field always depend on 'external' factors, according to Bourdieu. For instance, he observes, the successive waves of romanticism, naturalism, and symbolism, drew support from the new categories of consumers who occupied homologous positions in the social field, and whose interests (defined against those of different social groups) disposed them to be receptive to their products. It follows that a change in the relations of force between consumers (the most dramatic example being a political revolution) can also affect the balance of power in the field. For example, during the last years of the July Monarchy, the swing to the socialist left gave provisional weight to 'social art', so that even Baudelaire spoke of the 'puérile utopie de l'art pour l'art', which slid into a dominated third position (*RA*, 102). Similarly, a global elevation in the level and period of instruction can give a rise to so-called 'intellectual' literature, as larger numbers take part in cultural practices corresponding to their 'educated' social status (*RA*, 416-18 n. 58).

Yet Bourdieu resists the temptation to draw a direct connection between external changes (such as political revolutions, technical innovations, plagues, or economic crises), and the production of works. Here, Bourdieu crosses swords with Marxist literary theorists including György Lukács and Lucien Goldmann, whom he accuses of what he describes as a '*court-circuit*' error. Marxist critics, Bourdieu claims, attempt to relate works and changes in the space of works directly to the social class and political beliefs of their authors or their readers, or both, whose world-visions, values and truths, they purportedly express. Such theories therefore commit the equal and opposite error to those of Foucault and the Russian Formalists, by losing sight of the literary field as a 'world apart' with its own history, capable of enforcing its own norms to the extent of its autonomy.

Bourdieu offers the metaphor of 'refraction' to counter the theory of 'reflection' or mirroring of reality he sees behind Marxist theories, by which he does not mean simply 'distortion' but a *retranslation* of the broader social struggle into the terms of the literary debate. For example, it is too simplistic, Bourdieu argues, to relate the depictions of rustic and petit-bourgeois life in the works of nineteenth-century realist writers and artists such as Champfleury or Courbet directly to their social origin in the peasantry and petite-bourgeoisie. The dispositions that led them to embrace everything that could define them against the 'bourgeois artists' they opposed both socially and politically would have been expressed differently in another historical state of the field, when their opposition would also have changed (*RA*, 436). The effect of 'refraction' is clearest, however, according to Bourdieu, when bankers, businessmen, or politicians turn their hands to writing, and are obliged to give at least lip-service to the field's official norms – for example, by avoiding the crudest forms of self-publicity, professing a love of art, and by modifying their usual discourses by adopting certain stock themes, and paying at least minimal attention to form (*RA*, 362).

We can pause to notice Bourdieu's use of other theorists as tools to think with and against. Bourdieu explores the various positions in the field of criticism, tries to find their background assumptions or their 'principes fondateurs explicites ou implicites' (*RA*, 319),[86] and to overcome their apparent contradictions. Yet it can lead to reductionist and misleading portrayals of other theorists.[87] Foucault's essay from his early structuralist phase, for example, is unlikely to be of the most interest or use to literary scholars (see e.g. his later genealogical model, in which discourse analysis is linked to a theory of power/knowledge, and which implicates discourse in a ubiquitous network of power relations).[88] And Marxist theoreticians had already by the 1970s rejected the conception of literature as 'a material reflection (…) of objective reality', and begun themselves to speak about

---

86 'explicit or implicit founding principles' (*Rules*. 193)
87 Here I am transposing to the field of literary theory a critique first made of Bourdieu's readings of the field of social theory in Rogers Brubaker, 'Social Theory as Habitus', in *Bourdieu: Critical Perspectives*, ed. Craig Calhoun, Edward LiPuma and Moishe Postone, pp. 212-34.
88 See Simon During, *Foucault and Literature: Towards a Geneology of Writing* (London: Routledge, 1992).

'relative autonomy' and 'refraction'.[89] Indeed, Bourdieu sounds at times very much like the structuralist Marxist Louis Althusser – one of several critical theorists and social historians he does not cite. Jean-Louis Fabiani's comment that 'la référence aux études littéraires [dans les *Règles de l'art*] n'existe que pour faire valoir l'originalité et la puissance théorique de la sociologie de l'auteur' is probably unfair.[90] But his instrumental use of other theories to construct his own position does at times do them injustice, while he ignores others which do not fit his purpose.

This is how Bourdieu responds to the challenges laid down by Flaubert and Valéry, 'de découvrir quel problème l'auteur s'est posé (sans le savoir ou le sachant) et de chercher s'il l'a résolu ou non'; and to understand the 'composition' and 'style' of the work from 'le point de vue de l'auteur'. By identifying mentally with the author's position, and in the light of his or her social origin and trajectory, we should be able to see 'ce qui rend l'œuvre d'art *nécessaire,* c'est-à-dire la formule informatrice, le principe générateur' (*RA,* 15),[91] which is nothing other than the basic pattern of action provided by the writer's habitus, as a result of social history, expressed through the grammar of the 'space of possibilities'. Of course, this 'rational' theoretical understanding must be distinguished from the practical understanding of the author, who may have had no clear idea of where this research was leading, but who was driven by the desires and emotions attached to his or her position in the literary field (this is how Bourdieu interprets Flaubert's enigmatic notion of a 'poétique *inscient*').

It is not difficult to see why this phase of Bourdieu's analysis has been so rarely repeated. For one thing it demands an enormous amount of work, as Bourdieu admits: 'que l'on fasse tout ce que font les adeptes de chacune des méthodes connues (lecture interne, analyse biographique, etc.), en général à l'échelle d'un seul auteur, et tout ce qu'il faut faire pour construire réellement le champ des oeuvres et le champ des producteurs et le système des relations qui s'établissent entre ces deux ensembles de relations' (*CD,*

---

89 See Etienne Balibar and Pierre Macherey, 'On Literature as an Ideological Form' in *Untying the Text: A Post-Structuralist Reader,* ed. Robert J.C. Young (Boston: Routledge, 1981), 79-99.
90 'the reference to literary studies [in *The Rules of Art*] is only there to show off the originality and theoretical power of the author's sociology' (trans. J.S.). Jean-Louis Fabiani, 'Les Règles du champ', in *Le Travail sociologique de Pierre Bourdieu,* ed. Bernard Lahire (Paris: La Découverte, 1999), pp. 75-91 (p. 82).
91 'what makes the work of art *necessary,* that is to say, its informing formula, its generative principle' (*Rules,* xix).

176).⁹² In practice, Bourdieu himself only sketches the broad lines of these two spaces, in his analysis of Flaubert and the field of his contemporaries: often offering only the father's profession as a marker of social origin, and characterising the different genres and schools according to very generic properties. Nor do we need to construct the 'space of possibilities' from scratch, from purely bibliographical data and archive research, if we follow Bourdieu's lead. Bourdieu finds numerous representations of the literary field (and sometimes realised or unrealised plans for action), in writers' letters, diaries, notebooks, and even in literary works themselves, as well as in more conventional literary histories. Still, in order to achieve the standards of 'scientific' objectivity Bourdieu sets, we need to be careful to not simply to trust an individual writer's account, but to place its author in the wider space of positions and points of view in the field, in order to account for the author's representations and to see what (s)he excludes from his or her personal account.

In more than one respect, Flaubert and *L'Éducation sentimentale* can seem too easy as targets for this kind of analysis. Not only does Flaubert provide a voluminous correspondence, in which he shows high levels of reflexivity, commenting explicitly on his attempts to keep his distance from contemporaries and immediate precursors, he also provides in *L'Éducation sentimentale* a very accurate, and Bourdieu claims 'quasi-scientific', depiction of the nineteenth-century social world in which it was written, including its author's social position, and even the literary field itself (see Chapter 4 of the present study). John Guillory, for one, finds Bourdieu's choice of *L'Éducation sentimentale* 'altogether too fitting, which is to say that it lends itself too easily to Bourdieusian analysis'.⁹³ Certainly, Bourdieu's analysis reverses his more usual strategy of arguing *a fortiori* (i.e., choosing the *least* favourable example by which to establish a general principle), and places a question mark over the more general applicability of his method. As it stands, the link between 'internal' and 'external' analysis of the 'space of works' and 'space of positions' remains weak, and it is left to later literary researchers to test whether other authors and works are amenable to this method of analysis.

---

92 'that you do everything done by the adepts of each of the methods known (internal reading, biographical analysis, etc.), in general on the level of one single author, and that everything that you must do in order to really construct the field of works and the field of producers and the system of relations established between these two sets of relations' (*Other Words*, 196, trans. modified J.S.).
93 John Guillory, 'Bourdieu's Refusal', in *Bourdieu: Fieldwork in Culture*, ed. Nicholas Brown and Imre Szeman, pp. 19-43 (p. 34).

World literary space

Having reached the end of the method Bourdieu outlines in *Les Règles de l'art*, it may be useful to look in some detail at a major extension of Bourdieu's theory to the transnational level of 'world literary space'. In the context of cultural studies, translation studies, world-system theories, and post-colonial studies, Bourdieu's theory seemed to ignore how literary cultures relate to and influence each other. A first tentative attempt to engage with these issues was in fact made in Bourdieu's 1985 article 'Existe-t-il une littérature belge? Limites d'un champ et frontières politiques'.[94] Bourdieu studied the relations between the French and Belgian literary fields, and arrived at the controversial conclusion that a Belgian literary field did not, in fact, exist. Arguing that the boundaries between political and literary spaces do not necessarily correspond, Bourdieu claimed that Belgian literature was almost entirely dominated by Parisian literary fashions, and that so-called 'Belgian literature' was, in reality, merely a sub-field of the encompassing French literary field. In a 1997 interview with Jacques Dubois, Bourdieu admitted he had 'beaucoup accentué'[95] the influence exerted by French over Belgian literature, and had underestimated Belgian literature's power of resistance.[96] In the light of more recent research, by Pascale Casanova and others, he came to see Brussels as a sort of 'capitale de la deuxième chance' and as a counter-power against the dominant Paris, while Belgian writers also served as role-models for Irish, Norwegian and other small nations who were similarly dominated by more powerful neighbours.

It was in fact Casanova who, most notably, developed a theory of 'world literary space' that could be coupled with Bourdieu's theory, in her 1999 publication *La République mondiale des lettres* (a book Bourdieu himself described as 'important'[97]). Casanova's conception of an 'espace littéraire mondial' builds explicitly on Bourdieu's theory of fields, but also transposes Fernand Braudel's notion of an 'economy-world' to the literary realm. 'World literary space', as defined by Casanova, is in some respects a field like any other, but it has its own mode of operation, its own laws

---

[94] 'Existe-il une Littérature Belge? Limites d'un champ et fontières politiques', *Études de lettres*, 4 (1985), 3-6.
[95] 'overemphasised' (trans. J.S.).
[96] Jacques Dubois and Pierre Bourdieu, 'Champ Littéraire et Rapports de Domination', *Textyles*, 15 (1998), 12-16 (p. 13).
[97] For Bourdieu's comments on Casanova, see 'Champ Littéraire et Rapports de Domination', p. 13.

of canonisation and capital accumulation, and its own history, which is relatively independent of – but bound by mutual influence to – economic and political history. The notion of a world literary space is useful to understand more precisely the 'influence' one literary culture can have over another, and their disparities in terms of prestige and the power of consecration: considerations which (as Casanova shows convincingly in case studies of Kafka, Joyce, and Samuel Beckett) can also determine individual writers' perceptions and strategies.

Casanova observes a link between the prestige or 'nobility' of a nation's literature and its age. The first nations to enter the competition for 'cultural capital' are also the most endowed with literary and linguistic capitals, which survive faster-paced fluctuations in relative economic wealth and political power (this explains the fact that cultural prestige and influence and political power and even autonomy do not necessarily correspond). In the eighteenth century, France emerged as the provisional winner, and Paris as 'world literary capital' – able to exert its influence over the entire world literary space, and to define literary 'modernity' (what Casanova calls the 'Greenwich meridian' of literature).[98] Other cities and countries, such as Rome and Madrid in the seventeenth century, and Ireland and Brazil today, have similarly earned levels of literary prestige which are disproportionate with their political and economic standing. Casanova suggests using the 'cultural indicators' devised by Priscilla Parkhurst Ferguson and discussed above to compare literary practices in various countries and their respective stocks of literary capital. To the number of books published each year, time spent reading per inhabitant, etc., and signs of symbolic consecration, Casanova adds the number of translations made of books from a particular language. Casanova also proposes the creation of an index or measure of the strictly literary power and authority of a language and literary tradition. 'Cet indice', Casanova writes, 'prendrait en compte l'ancienneté, la 'noblesse', le nombre de textes littéraires, écrits dans cette langue, le nombre de textes reconnus universellement, le nombre de traductions…'.[99] Yet her own book contains little quantitative data, and Casanova makes no attempt to make such an index herself. In practice, much of the evidence, and many of the examples, in *La République mondiale des lettres* are anecdotal

---

98 Casanova, *La République mondiale des lettres*, pp. 135-55.
99 Casanova, *La République mondiale des lettres*, p. 42. 'Such an index would incorporate a number of factors: the age, the "nobility", and the number of literary texts written in a given language, the number of universally recognized works, the number of translations, and so on'. *World Republic*, p. 20.

and intuitive: based less on 'hard' (quantitative, numerical) data than on 'subjective' impressions and accounts. Which, in a social universe where so much depends on *opinion* and *belief* ('nous sommes', writes Valéry, 'ce que nous croyons être et ce que l'on croit que nous sommes'[100]) may be less of a problem than it appears.

More conspicuous is the absence of China and the Soviet Union from Casanova's account of literature in the twentieth century. How did these competing spheres of cultural influence, centred on Beijing and Moscow, contribute to structure world literary space?[101] Nor does Casanova's book have much to say about the international circulation of texts (the processes of selection and capital accumulation, how national provenance, translation, or changes of publisher, etc.) determines their reception, beyond noting that the careers of writers including Joyce, Nabokov, and Burgess were launched by their publication in Paris. The link Casanova posits between writers' individual strategies and the structure of world literary space is also tenuous, as it must be filtered through so many mediations (the national field of power and literary field, and the writers' social histories). This weakness is gravest in Casanova's textual analysis, which is never really able to connect the internal structure and properties of texts to macroscopic determinations. Many of these problems relate to economies of scale. In a work that aims at nothing less than to provide a radical remapping of world literary space, simplifications and omissions are inevitable. It is telling that in a later article Casanova suggested that a transnational literary history 'demanderaient, évidemment, des recherches collectives'.[102] Researchers applying a similar method could more easily divide their labour and integrate their results, allowing for greater complexity and detail than Casanova achieves in her study.

Several works have taken this challenge, notably by the research collective ESSE (Pour un Espace des Sciences Sociales Européen), set up after Bourdieu's death with the mission of encouraging the international circulation of ideas in the European social sciences, the first step being

---

100 'Fonction et Mystère de l'Académie', in *Regards sur le monde actuel, Œuvres*, 2 vols, ed. Jean Hytier (Paris: Gallimard, 1960), vol. 2, pp. 1119-27 (p. 1120). 'we are what we believe ourselves to be and what others believe we are' (trans. J.S.).
101 Here I follow and build on suggestions by Joe Cleary, in 'Review: The World Literary System: Atlas and Epitaph', *Field Day Review*, 2 (2006), 196-219.
102 Pascale Casanova, 'La Littérature Européenne: Juste un degré supérieur d'universalité?', in *L'Espace culturel transnational*, ed. Anna Boschetti (Paris: Nouveau Monde Édition, 2010), pp. 233-47 (p. 234 n. 2). 'would obviously demand collective research' (trans. J.S.).

to analyse the conditions in which such a European intellectual space could be created, and the barriers that prevent it from coming into being. From 2004 to 2009, ESSE brought together researchers from various countries within and outside of Europe. Several of its conferences and publications addressed issues related to the modes of production and the usages of culture, literature, and science, and the international circulation of ideas.[103] The comparative method followed by these works, facilitated by the use of a shared theoretical framework, also refutes the claim that Bourdieu's system is restricted to the particular case of France. Bourdieu's theory of literary fields has also been used to analyse writers in different national fields and traditions. Researchers using Bourdieu's concepts and theories have studied the literary fields in Quebec, South Africa, China, and Germany, and particular authors such as Apollinaire, Mallarmé, Beckett, and Borges. These cross-national transpositions are the best evidence that Bourdieu's method is not limited to France, nor to the national level.[104] Then again, and as Bourdieu explained to an audience in Japan in 1989, the fact that his theory is transposable to different national traditions does not mean that it loses sight of the particularities and differences between cultures. What Bourdieu proposes is a *'comparatisme de l'essentiel'* (RP, 29),[105] which would be able to define the basic principles and mechanisms that regulate societies and which, due to a mix of geographical, economic, and social determinations, have evolved in divergent ways. Testing structural principles far from their initial place of conception, where they can be seen in other possible variations, can validate its scientific universality, or reveal gaps and inconsistencies that can then be rectified. In this sense, Bourdieu's theory remains a 'work in progress', which continues to develop in pace with the accumulation of empirical knowledge.

---

103 See e.g. Gisèle Sapiro, ed. *L'Espace intellectuel en Europe: de la formation des États-nations à la mondialisation, XIXe-XXe siècle* (Paris: Éditions du Nouveau Monde, 2009); and Anna Boschetti, ed. *L'Espace culturel transnational*.
104 See Anna Boschetti, 'Bourdieu's Work on Literature: Contexts, Stakes and Perspectives', *Theory, Culture & Society*, 23 (2006), 135-55 (p. 147).
105 *'comparativism of the essential'* (*Practical Reason*, 13).

Appendix: reflexivity and reading

With increasing insistence from the 1980s, Bourdieu presented his sociology as 'reflexive', a word that appears in the titles of two of his most 'theoretical' works, *Science de la science et réflexivité* and *Invitation to a Reflexive Sociology*. For Bourdieu, reflexivity does not mean the reflection on the individual person of the researcher which became fashionable, particularly among literary scholars but also sociologists, especially in the 1980s and 1990s, but involves instead objectifying one's own social universe, its history, structure, and mechanisms, and using what we discover to understand our own habitual processes and responses. When Bourdieu studied his native region of Béarn in *Le Bal des célibataires*, the French system of *Grandes Écoles* which he attended to in *La Noblesse d'État*, or even French culture in general, in *La Distinction*, he was simultaneously analysing the society and culture of which he was a product, and to which he owed his own system of dispositions, thoughts, and perceptions (i.e., habitus). This 'reflexive return' is no less operational in an historical work such as *Les Règles*. Bourdieu was part of the intellectual tradition of Flaubert, Zola, and Sartre, whose precedents he followed, and in many of whose values he believed. Then again, his involvement in that intellectual universe also made him subject to all sorts of blind-spots, prejudices, and unspoken interests, which sociological study, conceived as a form of 'auto-socio-analysis', brought to light. Like Proust excavating lost time and memories, Bourdieu's study of the history of the intellectual field was also partly a work of 'unforgetting', or *anamnesis*, digging up his own 'historical unconscious': the story of how his own position as an intellectual, the associated dispositions, categories, concepts, interests, etc. (which he shared with his antecedents), how the works he read and the institutions that surrounded him, etc., came into being.

Bourdieu believed that reflexivity could provide some measure of control over the 'structures of thought and action' he and others had internalised from the experience of inhabiting a particular intellectual field and position, and that this would give him a 'margin of liberty' and critical distance from the dispositions and determinations which, if ignored, could lead to errors biases in his research. For example he claims that reflexivity enabled him to avoid the double danger of positivism and relativism, by historicising the knowledge (and the social conditions of that knowledge) which sociology produces, and which makes sociology possible, without for all that losing the ability to differentiate between better and worse (i.e., more or less accurate) models and theories. Theories and knowledge are seen as cumulative and historical, and as requiring particular conditions for their creation and transmission (which it is, in part, the task of a reflexive sociology to analyse). This runs counter to both the positivist way of looking at statements and labelling them true or false, and the relativism which, recognising how knowledge is determined by social and historical factors, places all modes of thought, concepts and theories, on the same level. Instead, the researcher becomes aware of the social conditions of possibility of his or her own research practice, which sustain a particular way of looking at and thinking about the world, which can be called rational or scientific. Bourdieu writes:

> Cette forme tout à fait insolite de réflexion conduit à répudier les prétentions absolutistes de l'objectivité classique mais sans condamner pour autant au relativisme: en effet, les conditions de possibilité du sujet scientifique et celles de son objet ne font qu'un et à tout progrès dans la connaissance des conditions sociales de production des sujets scientifiques correspond un progrès dans la connaissance de l'objet scientifique, et inversement. Cela ne se voit jamais aussi bien que lorsque la recherche se donne pour objet le champ scientifique lui-même, c'est-à-dire le véritable *sujet* de la connaissance scientifique (RA, 343).[106]

When one is aware of one's relationship to the object of study, including one's differences and similarities (and perhaps especially what Bourdieu calls one's 'similarity in difference', based on homology), then every discovery also raises the researcher's self-awareness (while inversely, every increase in reflexivity also allows the researcher to achieve greater insight into the lives of others). And of course, these relationships will be stronger the closer to the object of the research we are in time and social space.

Reflexivity, on Bourdieu's understanding, is also part of what enables the sociologist to do better science: by maintaining a state of 'epistemological vigilance', which guards against the sort of errors the research identifies and exposes in others. These include, most prominently, 'historical anachronisms' (imposing modern categories, concepts, and knowledge on past societies and cultures), 'mirror traps' (when two competing schools or

---

106 'This totally unprecedented form of reflection leads to repudiating the absolutist pretensions of classical objectivity, but without being then condemned to relativism. In effect, the conditions of possibility of the scientific subject and those of its object are one and the same; to any progress in the knowledge of the social conditions of production of scientific subjects corresponds progress in the knowledge of the scientific object, and vice versa. This is never as well observed s when research takes as its object the scientific field itself, that is to say, the veritable *subject* of scientific knowledge' (Rules, 208).

theorists also oppose each other on the terrain of theory, when a solution to their theoretical skirmishes is possible), and 'scholastic bias' (when the researcher assumes that everyone observes and analyses the world in the way that (s)he does). Of course, it is a truism that it is easier to find fault in others than in ourselves, and that we should try to learn from others' mistakes. It is also commonplace to attribute people's beliefs and attitudes to their class, race, and gender. It is more unusual, perhaps, to look for the source of bias and misunderstanding (and also of the will and capacity to overcome them) in terms of one's implication and position in a particular intellectual field. But researchers have long been aware of belonging to academic disciplines and traditions; that, for instance, established academics are often less receptive to change than younger researchers (in whose interest it is to overturn the dominant paradigm); and that, more generally, we tend to defend the ideas which are our own. In these respects, Bourdieu's project for a 'reflexive' social science may be less 'unprecedented' than he claims.

Finally, Bourdieu asks for his own texts to be read 'reflexively': for his readers to turn back and examine their own points of view, using the method demonstrated in his works, before turning away or pronouncing judgment (RA, 342). What this means concretely for literary researchers, is that they can apply the knowledge and concepts contained in Bourdieu's work to their own particular case, looking for parallels and correlates in their own experience (or if they do not find them, correcting the research and methods accordingly). Bourdieu again contrasts this approach to 'theoretical' readings, which compare texts only with other texts, or which judge them only on their internal consistency. As a point of interest, Bourdieu traces the preponderance of this approach in France to the once dominant literary tradition of 'close reading', with its internal analysis and inter-textual comparisons (which may also explain why literary researchers tend to find this kind of 'empirical' research inimical). As we have been seeing, there is not necessarily an opposition between 'internal' and 'external' modes of reading, although we should be wary of imposing the theoretical idealisations of the model onto the reality, or of making a 'short-circuit' by interpreting the text directly in terms of the reality to which it refers or represents. These cautions should apply whether we are concerned with literary or scientific writing and with representations of the natural or social worlds. The question of the 'realism' and 'referent' of literary and sociological texts, and of the difference between them, is raised in a surprising way in Bourdieu's analysis of Gustave Flaubert's classic novel *L'Éducation sentimentale*, and will be examined more closely in Chapter 4. First, we will see how Bourdieu's tripartite method of literature analysis, which moves from the field of power to the mapping of the literary field, to the tracing of individual writers' trajectories and the genesis of their habitus, is used in *Les Règles* to produce an expansive social history of the literary field, and of the position of the writer in French culture.

3. Autonomy

Having set out Bourdieu's theory and method of literature analysis and introduced its latest developments, this chapter explores Bourdieu's under-examined but central concept of autonomy, as the point at which the concepts of field, habitus, and capital intersect. The concept of autonomy is fundamental to Bourdieu's thinking about literary fields, because it is through an historical process of autonomisation and differentiation that fields become constituted. It is also this process that leads to the constitution of the dispositions characteristic of the 'pure' writer, motivated by literary ends alone, and to the birth of the literary 'intellectual', first embodied, Bordieu argues, by Zola. Autonomy is also bound inseparably to 'symbolic capital' (the respect given to the literary vocation, the sacredness of literary texts and idols), which gives force to the field's norms and injunctions, and also to 'cultural capital', as one of the conditions of the production and transmission of specialist cultural knowledge and know-how.

This chapter begins by tracing Bourdieu's account of the emergence of the literary field as a long process of differentiation and symbolic capital accumulation. It does this in three phases. First, we will follow the evolution of the literary field through its main stages up to 1830, which Bourdieu identifies as a critical moment when a faction of writers turned their back on the buying and reading public and began a competition according to their own rules and standards. This section compares Bourdieu's version of events to those of other literary critics and historians, and addresses some of the criticisms that have been made of it. The next section examines the opposition between art and money, which established itself, in the second phase of autonomisation, as one of the field's fundamental 'mental structures' and 'structuring principles' in the years between 1830-1880. The third phase spans Zola's intervention in the Dreyfus affair, the point at which, in Bourdieu's account, writers broke out from their self-imposed isolationism, and brought the French literary field to what he describes as the high-point of its autonomy. We will then study the relations between autonomy and value, and follow Bourdieu's attempts to build a more reasoned case for valuing literary works produced with an autonomous intention. The chapter closes with Bourdieu's account of the reversals of autonomous gains occurring in the French literary and publishing fields, which, he warns, have now entered a period of 'restoration' and 'involution'.

The evolution of the literary field

'Au fondement de la théorie des champs', Bourdieu writes, 'il y a le constat (qu'on trouve déjà chez Spencer, chez Durkheim, chez Weber...) que le monde social est le lieu d'un processus de différenciation progressive' (*RP*, 158).[1] Beginning with tribal communities characterised, according to Durkheim, by an original state of homogeneity and the pervasiveness of religion, human societies have evolved into highly differentiated nation states, in which politics, economics, religion, and so on form separate 'spheres of activity' (Weber). Picking up in particular from Weber, the second key term Bourdieu uses to understand this process is *autonomisation*. Insofar as each field becomes differentiated from the others, it imposes its own (auto-) *nomos* on its members: *nomos* signifying the 'fundamental law' or 'rules of the game' which determine the relative positions and possible position-takings of all the agents involved in each particular field.[2] Bourdieu offers as particularly striking examples of alternative *nomoi* the artistic and economic fields, where the hierarchy in each is almost the opposite of that found in the other. The field of cultural production is 'un monde économique à l'envers',[3] in which writers can succeed according to its standards only by ignoring or flouting the demands of the market (*RA*, 139; 356).

In several texts, Bourdieu sketches the history of French literature as part of this much vaster process of differentiation-autonomisation, which has proceeded at different rates and rhythms in different national traditions.[4] In early societies, literary art was unified within 'un spectacle

---

[1] 'At the very foundation of the theory of fields is the observation (which is already found in Spencer, Durkheim, Weber...) that the social world is the site of a process of progressive differentiation' (*Practical Reason*, 83).
[2] Bourdieu translates *nomos* (derived from the Greek νομός) in the usual way as 'law', but also as 'constitution', which reminds his readers of its historical institution, and as 'principle of vision and division', which is closer to the original etymology (*MP*, 116).
[3] 'an economic world reversed' (trans. J.S.).
[4] Pierre Bourdieu, 'Le Marché des biens symboliques'; 'Champ intellectuel et projet

total et immédiatement accessible [unissant] toutes les formes d'expression, musique, danse, théâtre et chant'.[5] Art was then a communal enterprise, and there was a fluid distinction between the 'performers' and the 'audience', whose roles were interchangeable.[6] The first cultural field to form a specialist corps was probably Greek philosophy, in the fifth century B.C. Its social separation from the politico-religious field was accompanied by a mental shift 'de la raison analogique (celle du mythe et du rite) à la raison logique (celle de la philosophie)' (*MP*, 27-28).[7] After a hiatus in the Middle Ages, the process began again with the Renaissance in fifteenth-century Florence, where the fields of art, literature, and science separated from philosophy and religion.[8] It was interrupted again by two centuries of absolutist rule by the European monarchies and the Counter-reformation. It was during this period, however, that writers received a measure of social recognition (above manual labourers, but without being integrated in the dominant class), which both fixed and consolidated their social position. In France, a significant gain was the establishment of the *Académie française* in 1635, which gave writers their own central authority, endowed with a specific literary legitimacy. Yet Bourdieu contests Alain Viala's thesis, in *Naissance de l'écrivain,* that it was at this moment that the figure of the 'writer' definitively appeared.[9] 'En effet', Bourdieu writes, 'ce processus reste longtemps ambigu, voire contradictoire, dans la mesure où les artistes doivent payer d'une dépendance statutaire à l'égard de l'État la reconnaissance et le statut officiel qu'il leur accorde' (*RA*, 193 n. 1).[10] It was not until the second half of the nineteenth century, on Bourdieu's time-line, that the French literary field reached a degree of autonomy it has not exceeded since, with the almost total separation of cultural power from the state and the market.

---

créateur'; *MP*, 30-32.
5 'a total spectacle [unifying] each of the forms of expression, music, dance, theatre and song' (trans. J.S.). Bourdieu, 'Le Marché des biens symboliques', p. 67.
6 Bourdieu cites in support of this contention a long list of ethnographers and their work, including John Greenway, *Literature among the Primitives* (Hatboro, PA: Folklore Associates, 1964) and Raymond Firth, *Elements of Social Organization* (Boston, MA: Beacon Press, 1963).
7 'from analogical reason (that of myth or rite) to logical reason (that of philosophy)' (*Meditations*, 18).
8 Bourdieu's reference here is Ernst Cassirer, *Individu et cosmos* (Paris: Éditions de Minuit, 1983).
9 Alain Viala, *Naissance de l'écrivain* (Paris: Éditions de Minuit, 1985).
10 'In effect, for a long time this process remains ambiguous, even contradictory, to the extent that artists must pay with a statutory dependence on the state for the recognition and official status that it accords them' *(Rules,* 114 n. 1).

Pascale Casanova embellishes and extends this account in her study of *La République mondiale des lettres*. World literary space was created, to follow Casanova's schema, in the sixteenth century, when Joachim du Bellay's *La Deffense et illustration de la langue française* declared that French was the equal of Latin, and sparked a competition for linguistic prestige between nations that has not ceased to spread since literary capital is one of the main stakes. This competition played an important part in the construction of national consciousness and identities (what Benedict Anderson calls 'the revolutionary vernacularizing thrust of capitalism'), which led at once to the linguistic and political unification of nation states.[11] Literature became a source of national pride, and the 'classics' part of a nation's common culture. Since then, however, Casanova's thesis is that the struggle for literary prestige (or capital) has proceeded relatively independently of the struggles for world economic and political power, and that literature therefore constitutes a relatively autonomous field of competition and interests.

This is also a point emphasised by Bourdieu from one of his earliest articles on literature and art, 'Le marché des biens symboliques'. By an apparent paradox, the ending of writers' dependency on the state and aristocracy was made possible by the appearance of an expanding market, itself tied to rising levels of literacy, advances in printing, and to the concentration of large populations in ever-expanding cities. In response to this new market, the population of writers expanded, diversified, and professionalised, to cater to the new classes and categories of reader (for example women, the urban middle classes, and later the working class). There was also a proliferation of publishers, newspapers, reviews, literary magazines, salons, academies, and learned societies, which decentred the circuits of legitimisation and opened multiple channels for dissemination.[12] Despite imposing new rules and demands on writers (particularly those of the market), this diversification also opened new possibilities for artistic liberty, as the market offered an alternative source of income and a new principle of legitimisation, freeing writers from direct patronage and restrictive commissions, and from the thematic and linguistic limits imposed by the obligation of catering to the particular tastes and expectations of the aristocracy. Yet writers could not fail to notice, Bourdieu surmises, that

---

[11] See Benedict Anderson, *Imagined Communities: Reflections on the Origin and Spread of Nationalism* (London: Verso, 1983), p. 39.

[12] Bourdieu, 'Le Marché des biens symboliques', p. 52.

3. Autonomy   83

they now faced an anonymous and impersonal market, whose judgments could be more pitiless than those of their paternalistic patrons, and could create between them unheard-of disparities. It was partly in reaction to the appearance of so-called 'industrial' literature, which followed successful formulas and was produced on demand, that a fraction of writers began a competition between themselves in the stakes of 'originality' and 'independence', which did not respond to some external order, but took its cue from its own history, in a rupture that was inseparably a rupture with political and moral authority. For these writers, literature became a battle against conventions – with the result that they succeeded in alienating the vast majority of readers, and formed their own restricted market.

By dating the moment of rupture to the years around 1830, Bourdieu agrees with literary critics and historians including Sartre and Barthes.[13] Yet there has been some controversy over what Bourdieu meant by proposing this apparently uncontentious cut-off point. Denis Saint-Jacques and Alain Viala point to the 'contradiction' between Bourdieu's mention in *Les Règles* of antecedents to literary bohemia (such as those identified by Roger Darnton in the eighteenth century), and his affirmation that what occurred in the nineteenth-century was 'sans précédent' (*RA*, 98).[14] These authors find the same 'confusion' and 'discrepancy' between the first and second parts of the book.[15] On my reading of *Les Règles*, Bourdieu is quite clear on this point (and in both parts):

> S'il est vrai que l'on peut repérer le moment où le lent processus d'*émergence* (comme dit, très justement, Ian Hacking) d'une structure subit la transformation décisive qui semble conduire à l'accomplissement de la structure, il est tout aussi vrai que l'on peut situer en chacun des moments de ce processus continu et collectif l'émergence d'une forme provisoire de la structure, déjà capable d'orienter et de commander les phénomènes qui peuvent s'y produire, et contribuer ainsi à l'élaboration plus accomplie de la structure (*RA*, 222-23).[16]

---

13 Jean-Paul Sartre, *Qu'est-ce que la Littérature?* (Paris: Gallimard 1964); Roland Barthes, *Le Degré zéro de l'écriture* (Paris: Éditions du Seuil, 1953).
14 'without precedent' (*Rules*, 63).
15 Saint-Jacques and Viala, 'À propos du champ littéraire', in *Le Travail sociologique de Pierre Bourdieu*, ed. Bernard Lahire, pp. 59-72.
16 'Though it is true that one can locate the moment when the slow process of emergence (as Ian Hacking rightly says) of a structure undergoes the decisive transformation that seems to lead to the fulfilment of the structure, it is just as true that one may place at each of the stages in this continuous and collective process the emergence of a provisional form of that structure, already capable of influencing and controlling the phenomena that may be produced there, and thus

In the case of the literary and artistic fields, Bourdieu writes:

> Si l'on doit admettre que c'est seulement à la fin du XIXe siècle que parvient à son accomplissement le lent processus qui a rendu possible *l'émergence* des différents champs de production culturelle et la pleine reconnaissance sociale des personnages sociaux correspondants, le peintre, l'écrivain, le savant etc., il ne fait pas de doute qu'on peut en faire remonter les premiers commencements aussi loin que l'on voudra, c'est-à-dire au moment même où des producteurs culturels font leur apparition, qui luttent (presque par définition) pour faire reconnaître leur indépendance et leur dignité particulière (*RA*, 423 n. 61).[17]

There is thus a double error to be avoided: the illusion of first beginnings ('never before'), encouraged by the cult of originality, and the illusion of constancy ('nothing new'), encouraged by the rigid signifiers 'field', 'avant-garde', 'writer', etc. What is new in the nineteenth century is the position or post of the 'pure' autonomous writer and the associated dispositions of disinterest (indifference to the verdicts of the market), moral neutrality (not immorality), and political independence (and, since Zola, an independent 'political' authority): a social position and personage *inconceivable* to earlier epochs and in previous states of the field. Yet although new, the position of the modern writer, and the corresponding dispositions, did not emerge from nowhere. They were the product of a long collective process, which continued without field autonomy being at all times its immediate, eventual, or even conscious aim, *but through writers' struggles for social legitimacy and distinction.*

We can pause to assess what Bourdieu brings to literary history, which has for a long time stressed the evolutionary character of literary production. Bourdieu himself claims that there has been a veritable 'amnesia' of literature and art's historical genesis, requiring a sociological work of 'anamnesis' to bring these historical conditions back into awareness. As is sometimes the unfortunate case with Bourdieu, this gives an excessively dim view of literary scholarship, and casts his own work in too favourable light. The history sketched by Bourdieu himself is

---

of contributing to the more finished elaboration of the structure' (*Rules*, 133; trans. modified J.S.).

17 'Although it has to be admitted that the slow process which made possible the emergence of different fields of cultural production and the full social recognition of corresponding social figures (the painter, the writer, the scholar, etc.) reached its culmination only at the end of the nineteenth century, there is no doubt that one could push back its first manifestations as far as one likes, to the moment when cultural producers first appeared, fighting (almost by definition) to have their independence and particular dignity be acknowledged' (*Rules*, 387).

only skeletal, and reaches a significant degree of detail only in his studies of the French literary field in the nineteenth century. For this period, however, we have already the studies by Sartre and Barthes, mentioned above, as well as innumerable others, by which Bourdieu's account would be complemented. Indeed, it is hard to escape the feeling that Bourdieu's historical analysis fails to live up in practice to the hubris of his theory (or at least to his self-commentary). Perhaps, we can suggest, it is both more realistic and useful to use Bourdieu's account as a potted-history or thumb-nail account, which provides a broad outline in which to situate any particular object, but needs to be supplemented with wider reading, as well as more detailed scholarship. The trouble with Bourdieu's rhetoric is that he seems at times to hardly encourage such an approach, although he does at others stress the 'unfinished' and 'open' character of his work (*RA*, 303). Critics need to be wary of simply repeating Bourdieu's self-commentary, while researchers need to know they need always also to look further afield than Bourdieu.

Art and money

At the end of the second phase of the constitution of the literary field, between the years 1830-1880, the literary field settled down into a 'structure dualiste', split between a 'pure' or autonomous pole and 'commercial' or heteronomous pole. This split fixed itself in people's minds as 'une des structures fondamentales de la vision du monde dominante': the opposition between art and money (*RA*, 156).[18] For Bourdieu, the imposition of this 'principle of vision and division' (*nomos*) was a major step on the road to autonomy. Literature no longer needed to justify itself in terms of public popularity or political or religious approval. The field could now produce its own value and legitimisation, deemed to be 'disinterested' and 'irreducible' to monetary value. Yet Bourdieu argues this mental shift (Thomas Kuhn, in another context, would have spoken of a 'paradigm shift'), which saw the value of art for its own sake, was achieved at the cost of a wholesale repression of economic interest by everyone involved in literary production, who could no longer admit – perhaps even to themselves – any motivation other than their self-effacing dedication to Art. Indeed, Bourdieu sees a sort of generalised 'euphémisation' pervading both the literary and artistic fields, which exclude systematically economic vocabulary and all mention of money:

---

18 'one of the fundamental structres of the dominant vision of the world' (*Rules*, 91)

> le marchand de tableaux se dit plutôt directeur de galerie; éditeur est un euphémisme pour marchand de livres, ou acheteur de force de travail littéraire (au XIXe siècle, les écrivains se comparaient souvent à des prostituées...) L'éditeur dit à un jeune auteur aux fins de mois difficiles: 'Regardez Beckett, il n'a jamais touché un sou de ses droits d'auteur !' Et le pauvre écrivain est dans ses petits souliers, il n'est pas sûr d'être Beckett et il est sûr qu'il a la bassesse de réclamer de l'argent... (RP, 198).[19]

The discussion of money, especially the economic cost and value of artistic works, became somehow shameful or taboo, as art and money became 'compartmentalised' (opposed in people's minds). Indeed, economic logic, which makes money the ultimate aim of all practices, was for a time inverted (a state that was by no means eternal or inevitable). For 'pure' writers, money became a means to an end, but art was an end in itself.

Yet if writers sacrificed economic profit, they received a different form of 'symbolic' capital, which offered its own rewards and gratifications, and which could even provide access to economic remuneration. Bourdieu defines symbolic capital 'comme capital "économique" dénié, reconnu, donc légitime, véritable crédit, capable d'assurer, sous certaines conditions et à long terme, des profits "économiques"' (RA, 235).[20] Indeed, Bourdieu sees a sort of 'loi de la conservation de l'énergie sociale' (RA, 284),[21] according to which 'profits in one area are necessarily paid for by costs in another (so that a concept like wastage has no meaning in a general science of the economy of practices)'.[22] The investment of not simply money but, in the final instance, of *time and energy* (labour-time) – which is, however, always linked to economic expenditure due to the inter-convertibility of time and money – produces a *symbolic* form of capital, which can later be 'converted' at varying rates and with various levels of difficulty (involving further loss or expenditure) into an economic form. This work is performed not just by the individual writer or artist, but by all those who have a hand in raising the value of the work, including critics, authors, enthusiastic booksellers,

---

19 'the art dealer calls herself a gallery director; publisher is a euphemism for book dealer, or buyer of literary labour (in the nineteenth century, writers often compared themselves to prostitutes...) The publisher says to a young writer at the end of a difficult month, "look at Beckett, he has never touched a penny of his royalties!" And the poor writer feels ashamed, he is not sure he's a Beckett, but he is sure that unlike Beckett he is base enough to ask for money' (*Practical Reason*, 11).
20 'a kind of "economic" capital denied but recognized, and hence legitimate – a veritable credit capable of assuring, under certain conditions and in the long term, "economic" profits' (*Rules*, 142).
21 'the law of conservation of social energy' (*Rules*, 170).
22 Bourdieu, 'The (Three) Forms of Capital', p. 253.

and readers: 'tous ceux qui s'y intéressent, qui trouvent un intérêt matériel ou symbolique à la lire, la classer, la déchiffrer, la commenter, la reproduire, la critiquer, la combattre, la connaître, la posséder' (*RA*, 286).²³ It can be compressed into a period of frenetic activity, as was the case, for instance, with *Madame Bovary*, which provoked a public scandal and a full-scale defence. Too rapid or easy success, however, is often seen as something suspicious, as if the ritual had been reduced to give-and-take (*RA*, 345-46). As in a gift exchange, it is the *interval of time* and the *apparently gratuitous expenditure of effort* (the paper, the bow...) that separate the initial act of creation from its economic remuneration, and allow the writer to experience his motivation as entirely 'disinterested'. Bourdieu writes:

> Il est à la fois vrai et faux, on le voit, de dire (avec Marx par exemple) que la valeur marchande de l'oeuvre d'art est sans commune mesure avec son coût de production: vrai, si l'on prend en compte seulement la fabrication de l'objet matériel, dont l'artiste (ou du moins le peintre) est seul responsable; faux, si l'on entend la production de l'oeuvre d'art comme objet sacré et consacré, produit d'une immense entreprise d'*alchimie symbolique* à laquelle collaborent, avec la même conviction et des profits très inégaux, l'ensemble des agents engagés dans le champ de production (*RA*, 284).²⁴

In the interval between the production of the autonomous artwork and its imposition on the market, writers of course needed to find some way to survive. Bourdieu provides a useful snapshot of the sorts of strategies that nineteenth-century writers used to win greater social status and financial security. Some of these, he admits, were paradoxical or counter-intuitive. For instance, the new positions in the culture industry, in journalism or publishing, provided writers to whom the profession would previously have been closed with the means (if no doubt meagre) to support their writing. This was the case with Théophile Gautier (often credited with having invented the phrase *l'art pour l'art*), and Émile Zola. Of course, the obligation to earn a living was still a hindrance, and in this and other respects writers like Flaubert with

---

23 'all those who have an interest in it, who find a material or symbolic profit in reading it, classifying it, decoding it, commenting on it, reproducing it, criticising it, combating it, knowing it, possessing it' (*Rules*, 171).
24 'it is both true and false to say (with Marx, for example) that the market value of the work of art has no common measure with its cost of production: true, if one takes into acount only the fabrication of the material object, the responsibility of the artist (or at least the painter) alone; false, if one means the production of the work of art as a sacred and consecrated object, product of an immense enterprise of symbolic alchemy involving the collaboration, with the same conviction but very unequal profits, of a whole set of agents engaged in the field of production' (*Rules*, 170).

a private income (or like Virginia Woolf, with money and a room of her own) had a significant advantage: allowing for the sort of single-minded dedication and resistance to compromise for which the author of *Madame Bovary* has become celebrated as a sort of ideal. As Gautier commented with undisguised envy to Ernest Feydeau, Flaubert 'a eu plus d'esprit que nous, (…) il a eu l'intelligence de venir au monde avec un patrimoine quelconque, chose qui est absolument indispensable à quiconque veut faire de l'art'.[25]

Bourdieu finds another unexpected source of material and symbolic support for writers in the salon of Napoleon's niece Princess Mathilde. Mathilde's patronage and protection may have been less enlightened than political. Posing as a liberal guardian of French culture and the arts was a way for Mathilde to distinguish herself from the Empress Eugénie, the unpopular Spanish wife of Napoléon III. Yet the most autonomous writers of the day, including Flaubert, Sainte-Beuve, Taine, George Sand, and Gautier (whom Mathilde appointed her librarian and cultural advisor in 1868, releasing him from his crippling journalistic work) were able to benefit from the struggles among the dominant to secure their positions both economically and socially: an appointment to the senate for Sainte-Beuve, the prize of the *Académie française* for George Sand, the *Légion d'honneur* for Taine and Flaubert (this against Flaubert's rather offhand remark that 'les honneurs déshonorent') (*RA*, 91-93). The literary field could also create its own symbolic capital, by holding its own celebrations (public readings, award ceremonies, meetings, etc.), creating positive representations of artists in literary works themselves, and by publishing treatises and criticism which swung between the normative and the descriptive, by defining literary 'quality' and 'value'. Bourdieu cites as examples Murger's *Scènes de la vie de bohème* and Balzac's *Traité de la vie élégante*, which contributed to create the social reality they described: i.e., the writer and artist as a recognisable figure, and the artist's way of life as a respectable – and 'possible' – social role (*RA*, 99-100). In particular, these works contributed to transform the material and economic hardship of the 'struggling artist' or *poète maudit* (otherwise imposed by the law of the market) into an elected ideal (cf. *MP*, 127). 'Les voies de l'autonomie sont complexes', Bourdieu writes, 'sinon impénétrables' (*RA*, 92),[26] involving symbiotic and sometimes double-edged relations between opposing interests.

Bourdieu's theory of the relation between art and money treads a fine

---

25 Théophile Gautier cited by Bourdieu in *RA*, 142-43 '[Flaubert] was smarter than us, [...] he had the intelligence to come into the world with some patrimony, a thing which is absolutely indispensible to anyone who wants to make art' (*Rules*, 84).
26 'the routes of autonomy are complex, if not impenetrable' (*Rules*, 52).

line between the cynical view of economic self-interest, and the idealisation of literary life. Sometimes he slips. Bourdieu has a particular tendency to idealise Flaubert, whom he raises to a sort of paragon of artistic purity and disinterest. Certainly, Flaubert showed supreme dedication to his work. The 'hermit of Croisset' never married (although he later regretted it), was a noted perfectionist and spent long hours searching for 'le mot juste'. Yet Flaubert was not perhaps as impervious to the demands of publishers and the public as Bourdieu suggests (and as Flaubert himself liked sometimes to pretend, especially to other writers) (*RA*, 144-45). Bourdieu forgets to mention, for instance, that Flaubert was *contractually obliged* by his publisher Michel Lévy to write another 'modern' novel after *Salammbô*, to reprise the success of *Madame Bovary*, the result of which was the second *L'Éducation sentimentale*.[27] And the little attention given by Bourdieu to *Salammbô* also overlooks its considerable commercial success. Given that Flaubert is in many ways a sort of alter-ego for Bourdieu (who sometimes writes of Flaubert as if he were writing about himself), we might even see this idealisation as part of an unquestioned assumption, running throughout *Les Règles* (as indeed through his entire output), that when Flaubert (or Bourdieu) does something, he does it for purely conscious and laudable motives, whereas when other intellectuals do something, they do it for hidden or unconscious reasons relating to their positions in the intellectual field – reasons that only Bourdieusian sociology can lay bare. This seems to amount to a rather significant unquestioned epistemological bias in Bourdieu's work, and indicates the limitations of really existing reflexivity as practiced by Bourdieu.

Zola and the Dreyfus affair

After the initial 'conquête de l'autonomie' and 'émergence d'une structure dualiste', Émile Zola's intervention in the Dreyfus Affair brought the evolution of the literary field in the direction of autonomy to its end (*RA*, 216). Zola might seem an unlikely hero in the history of the process of autonomisation. In his time, Zola was the most commercially successful author in French history.[28] Yet while Zola's books found an expanding

---

27 Pierre-Marc de Biasi, 'Préface', in Gustave Flaubert, *L'Éducation sentimentale* (Paris: Librairie Générale française, 2002), pp. 7-38 (p. 22).
28 See Joseph Jurt, 'Gattungshierarchie und Karrierestrategien im XIX. Jahrhundert', *Lendemains*, 36 (1984), 33-41 (p. 35); and 'Autonomy and Commitment in the French Literary Field: Applying Pierre Bourdieu's Approach', *International Journal of Contemporary Sociology*, 38 (2001), 87-102.

market of readers eager for new products, he also earned the respect of his field. Bourdieu identifies three factors which together combined to protect Zola from the field's emerging logic. Zola's vision of determinism and social conflict (which we might link to his social background and position in the ascendant fraction of the petite bourgeoisie) found resonances with modern science and medicine, with Darwinism and the clinician's gaze, at a time when the scientist was becoming an emblematic social figure in France. According to Bourdieu, Zola explicitly associated his theory of the 'roman expérimental' with the scientific method of Claude Bernard, in order to avoid the suspicion of vulgarity raised by the 'low' social milieus depicted in his novels and by the wide public readership they attracted. At the same time, Zola made himself the spokesman and theoretician of artistic liberty, most notably in his defence of Manet, but asserting simultaneously his own independence.[29] Even in the stylistic features of his works, Bourdieu argues, Zola affirmed the difference and dignified distance of the Man of Letters from the crowd, maintaining a distinction between the language of his working-class characters and that of the narrative voice, to which he gives the rhythms, syntax, and techniques, of high literature (RA, 198).

Yet Zola may not have continued to avoid the discredit to which the volume of his sales exposed him, had he not intervened in the Dreyfus Affair, and succeeded in changing, at least partially, the 'principles of perception and appreciation' by which writers' positions are evaluated (RA, 215). In the short-term, Zola was ruined, his name was blackened, and he was forced into exile. But his intervention proved decisive in shifting public opinion in support of the disgraced Jewish officer; and when Dreyfus was reinstated, Zola emerged a hero, of whom no-one could doubt the integrity and independence.[30] According to Bourdieu, Zola's action released writers from the self-imposed isolation and insularity they had accepted as the price of their autonomy; yet his intervention was also founded upon that autonomy. Zola did not convert into a politician, like François Guizot or Alphonse de Lamartine. Nor did he try to compete with his political masters at their own game, like Rousseau writing a Constitution for Poland. Instead, Zola intervened in the political sphere *as an intellectual*, in the name of the values and principles in operation in his own field – which ruled out the possibility of abdicating his authority and conviction in favour of

---

[29] Émile Zola, *Le Roman expérimental* (Paris: Garnier-Flammarion, 1971).
[30] See Christophe Charle, *Naissance des 'intellectuels' 1880-1900* (Paris: Éditions de Minuit, 1990), pp. 28-36.

political expediency or social approval. At the same time, Zola's action reinforced the autonomy of his field, by affirming the independence of the mandatories of those values from every particular interest, even the interests of state or the private interests of the individual. Bourdieu writes:

> Le 'J'accuse' est l'aboutissement et l'accomplissement du processus collectif d'émancipation qui s'est progressivement accompli dans le champ de production culturelle: en tant que rupture prophétique avec l'ordre établi, il réaffirme, contre toutes les raisons d'État, l'irréductibilité des valeurs de vérité et de justice, et, du même coup, l'indépendance des gardiens de ces valeurs par rapport aux normes de la politique (celles du patriotisme par exemple), et aux contraintes de la vie économique (*RA*, 216).[31]

Bourdieu rejects the idea that intellectuals lose their political power as they gain in autonomy. In fact, he sees a qualitative change in the form of that power, which is no longer dependent on political legitimacy, but is able to provide a rival authority (*RA*, 217 n. 19). Similarly, he challenges the assumption that intellectuals sacrifice their autonomy when they intervene in political affairs. By an apparent paradox, it is by affirming their right to transgress the most sacred values of the state – those of patriotism, for example, with Zola's incendiary accusations against high figures in the army (or later, during the war in Algeria, with the call to support the enemy), that intellectuals can assert their independence to the highest degree (*RA*, 550).

Bourdieu's celebration in *Les Règles* of Zola's 'inaugural' intervention, which 'invented' the new figure and conception of the 'intellectual', may seem to imply that he had fallen victim to the very the illusion of 'first beginnings' against which we have seen him warn his readers. Elsewhere, however, Bourdieu does acknowledge 'precursors' to Zola, in Victor Hugo, who published political pamphlets in exile under the authority of his literary fame; in Edgar Quinet, who combined literary writing with activism; and as far back as Voltaire, who, in the entry under 'l'homme de lettres' in the *Dictionnaire philosophique* already had opposed the 'engagement' of the 'philosophes' to the scholasticism of the 'doctes' in the universities and academies (*I*, 258). Yet whilst acknowledging this lineage, Bourdieu also insists that Zola was the first to have finally transcended the alternative between commitment

---

31 '*J'Accuse* is the outcome and the fulfilment of a collective process of emancipation that is progressively carried out in the field of cultural production: as a prophetic rupture with the established order, it reasserts against all reasons of state the irreducibility of the values of truth and justice, and, at the same stroke, the independence of the guardians of these values from the norms of politics (those of patriotism, for example) and from the constraints of economic life' (*Rules*, 129).

and withdrawal, two options between which intellectuals had swung like a pendulum throughout history. The 'commitment' of the 'philosophes' was continued by the 'men of letters' during the French Revolution, then followed by the Romantic withdrawal, and back again to engagement in a reaction to the Restoration. Disillusioned by the defeat of the revolutionary movement of 1848 and the establishment of the Second Empire, Flaubert and Baudelaire's generation retreated again, this time into an elitist rejection of contemporary art and society. This ivory tower provided Zola, however, with a platform from which to launch his political campaign. Indeed, Zola's action worked to enshrine political engagement in the very definition of the 'intellectual' which, Bourdieu reminds us, asserted itself as a category during the Dreyfus Affair. The role of the intellectual in France has since been essentially two-dimensional, defined by a combination of autonomy and commitment: a tradition continued by prominent French intellectuals including Sartre, Foucault, and Bourdieu.

Yet Bourdieu also warns us that Zola's model of autonomous engagement is not set in stone. Cultural producers can always 'regress' towards one side or another of the alternative between the ivory tower and the political actor (journalist, politician, or expert) (*RA*, 551). It is also possible, however, for the model to be improved – and it may need to be, as the traditional forms of intellectual intervention (petitions, open letters, public declarations, etc.), which have hardly developed since Zola's time, lose their symbolic force and efficacy in competition with new forms of communication, control, and censorship. As we will see in Chapter 5, this was the backdrop to Bourdieu's appeal for the establishment of an '*intellectuel collectif*', which could summon the combined symbolic capital of the intellectual community in support of political ventures, one of the organisational bases he envisaged for which was the International Parliament of Writers. It was also behind his call for the invention of new forms of symbolic action, which would be able to compete with the dominant representations of social reality spread in newspapers, films, radio and television: for intellectuals, including literary authors, to use their specific skills as weapons in a cultural politics.

Reversals

Reading *Les Règles* and Bourdieu's earlier writings on the French literary and artistic fields, we can fall under the impression that they have been building their autonomy progressively over the centuries, until the 1800s when they finally broke free from direct dependency on the state, market, and religion, from which point their histories have proceeded according to their own internal logics. And we can be surprised when we reach Les Règles's post-script, only to be told that we have now entered a period of 'restauration'. At one stage, Bourdieu describes the history of the literary field as 'réellement irréversible' (RA, 398).[32] Each new generation can pick up where the previous generation left off, 'les nouveaux entrants (...) peuvent faire les économies des ruptures plus ou moins héroïques du passé' (RA, 424),[33] so that there seems to be an internal momentum towards ever greater autonomy. References to contemporary 'regressions' are few and far between. As its 'sub-' or perhaps its 'real' title indicates, Les Règles is concerned above all with understanding the 'genèse et structure du champ littéraire', and has little to say about the reverse process of 'involution'. This, however, would seem from the post-script to be what was required more urgently: 'on peut se demander si la division en deux marchés, qui est caractéristique des champs de production depuis le milieu du XIXe siècle (...) n'est pas menacée de disparition (...). Il faudrait analyser les nouvelles formes de mainmise et de dépendance, comme celles qu'instaure le mécénat, et contre lesquelles les "bénéficiaires" n'ont pas encore développé de systèmes de défense appropriés', and so on (RA, 554-55).[34]

In fact, Bourdieu's only major contribution to this programme of research is one of his final published pieces of empirical research, 'Une Révolution conservatrice dans l'édition',[35] which maps the French publishing field, and analyses the ways editorial policies are determined by factors from the delegation of decisions to 'reading committees' to private investment by shareholders or parent companies. His far greater involvement was through his more punctual and publicised political interventions, where Bourdieu lent his symbolic capital as professor at the

---

32 'truly irreversible' (Rules, 242).
33 'new entrants (...) may skip over the more or less heroic sacrifices and ruptures of the past' (Rules, 257).
34 'One could ask whether the division into two markets characteristic of the fields of cultural production since the middle of the nineteenth century (...) is not now threatening to disappear (...). It would be necessary to analyse the new forms of stranglehold and dependence, like the ones introduced by sponsorship, and of which the "beneficiaries" have not yet developed appropriate systems of defence since they are not fully aware of their effects' (Rules, 345).
35 Pierre Bourdieu, 'Une Révolution conservatrice dans l'édition', Actes de la recherche en sciences sociales, 126 (1999), 3-28. Further references to this article will be abbreviated to RC followed by the page number and included in the text.

prestigious *Collège de France*, and his scientific credibility, to the growing number of voices in France who were already warning against the effects on the French cultural field of commercialisation and of American cultural hegemony. In this he was acting on his insight that academic research has no intrinsic impact, and that the struggle to reveal the truth must also be accompanied by a social struggle to be believed. 'Nous sommes dans une situation catastrophique', Bourdieu declared, referring to the Greek *katastrophē*, which he translates as 'renversement', 'dans laquelle nous avons besoin plus que jamais, de redonner de la force à la critique intellectuelle' (*I*, 471-72).[36]

The picture that emerges from Bourdieu's political writings and more fully worked out analyses is certainly bleak, and goes against much of what we are usually told about the expansion of the culture industry, with its increased choice and availability, and economies of scale. In the 1970s, the French publishing industry had entered a phase of rapid concentration, which culminated in the creation, in the 1980s and 1990s, of two publishing giants, Hachette and Havas. Owned by corporations with nothing, historically, to do with literature (on one hand, Mécanique Avion Traction, or Matra, specialists in the aeronautics and armaments industry; on the other, Vivendi Universal, formed in a merger of *Presses de la Cité* and *La Compagnie générale des eaux*), these corporations comprised scores of imprints, and managed annual turnovers of hundreds of millions of French francs (*RC*, 7). According to Bourdieu, the sheer scale of these enterprises determined their editorial policies, demanding quick returns on their capital to cover overheads and a rapid succession of titles to keep the cogs of the machine turning (cf. *RA*, 243-44). Of course, some publishers resisted commercialisation, notably *Les Éditions de Minuit*, which, along with scattered provincial and often fledgling publishers, represented (by 1999) one of the last bastions of literary-editorial autonomy (*RC*, 26). Of particular concern to Bourdieu, however, was the disappearance of the specialist bookstores upon which these specialist publishers relied (along with avant-garde critics and reviews) to give a start to their most inventive and controversial new signings, as supermarket chains such as Leclerc and media mega-stores like Fnac entered the book-selling trade (*RC*, 14). According to Yves Surel, as a direct consequence of their aggressive pricing policies the market share of traditional bookstores

---

36 'We are in a catastrophic situation, in which it is more necessary than ever to give new strength to intellectual criticism' (*Political Interventions*, 385).

3. Autonomy   95

fell from 51% in 1968 to around 31% in 1981: replaced by chain-stores locked in competition for profit, and with little interest in promoting non-commercial, experimental literature.[37]

Bourdieu was also concerned by the rise of powerful new instances of literary consecration, notably on television (of which the paradigm was the discussion programme *Apostrophes*). These self-proclaimed authorities were challenging traditional authorities, such as the school, literary prizes, journals, etc., and increasingly acted as gatekeepers to the public sphere. Of course, cultural journalists would still doff their caps at established authors, and profess their appreciation for the Classics. But they also praised as the heirs and equals of great writers authors whose work presented little that was new, and whose work might even mark a regression in comparison to the achievements of the past. According to Bourdieu, the much bemoaned 'crise du roman français', and much celebrated 'retour au récit', were symptoms of this 'restoration' of commercially successful forms and genres (adventure stories, crime fiction, horror, fantasy, children's fiction made reputable for adults, all in their most facile forms) to the top of the literary hierarchy. Bourdieu says, 'ce brouillage des frontières auquel les producteurs dits 'médiatiques' sont spontanément inclinés (comme en témoigne le fait que les palmarès journalistiques juxtaposent toujours les producteurs les plus autonomes et les plus hétéronomes) constitue la pire menace pour l'autonomie de la production culturelle' (although surely only in some respects...) (*RA*, 556-57).[38] Through it, commercial standards were being imposed within the Republic of Letters.

Bourdieu was not the only one sounding the alarm. From the 1970s, an increasing number of editors led by Jérôme Lindon (post-war owner and editor at Minuit) began to mobilise opposition under the banner *'le livre n'est pas un produit comme les autres'*[39] to prevent commercially-driven distributors from offering vast reductions on editorially set prices, and from stocking their shelves almost exclusively with bestsellers. This lobby eventually won the support of the new Minister of Culture, Jack Lang, who in 1981 introduced the so-called 'Loi Lang', setting the principle of

---

37 See Yves Surel, 'Le Destin de la loi Lang du 10 août 1981', in *Le Prix du livre 1981-2006, La loi Lang*, ed. Olivier Corpet (Paris: IMEC, 2006), pp. 9-29.

38 'This blurring of boundaries to which so-called "media-oriented" producers are spontaneously inclined (as shown by the fact the journalistic lists of hits always juxtapose the most autonomous and the most heteronomous producers constitutes the worst threat to the autonomy of cultural production' (*Rules*, 347).

39 'books are not just products' (trans. J.S.).

a single fixed price for books, chosen by their editors, and to be respected by all distribution outlets. The subject had also attracted the attention of social scientists. In 1992, François Rouet's *Le Livre: mutations d'une industrie culturelle* highlighted the fragile state of small and medium-sized publishers, and the destruction of the network of bookstores.[40] 'Le livre est non seulement en crise', Rouet warned, 'mais il est maintenant en danger'.[41] And in 1995, Jean-Marie Bouvaist, in *Crise et mutations dans l'édition française*,[42] had documented with great detail the history and evolution of the French publishing industry, which he describes as overrun by commercial logic.

Bourdieu did not foresee the rise of internet publishing, blogs, e-books, and so on. But we can imagine he might have been sceptical of the promises often made in their name. Social-networking sites can take the place of cafés and bookshops in which artistic communities used to congregate; writers can publish their own material on-line and reach an international readership with unimaginable ease and speed; the digital medium allows for an unprecedented freedom of expression, linking text, film, graphics, and so on. Yet there might also be no more nightmarish vision of what is happening, if literary life is reduced to this ethereal and ephemeral existence, where writers and critics have to compete for position on popular-search engines, where symbolic capital is reduced to the number of anonymous clicks, where there is no prospect of economic profit, even in the long-term, and where the boundary between the artist and the general public is becoming once again indistinct.

Autonomy and value

Bourdieu does not stop at objectifying into a model the genesis and structure of the literary field, and the logic of its changes. He seems at times to *endorse* its judgments – i.e., to suggest that works written with a 'pure' or 'autonomous' intention are indeed more *valuable* than those influenced by external or 'heteronomous' demands. Bourdieu usually stands back from questions of value in his 'scientific' works, which aim for a sort of neutrality or 'double-negativity', which treats both sides of any opposition

---

40 François Rouet, *Le Livre: Mutations d'une industrie culturelle* (Paris: Documentation française, 1992).
41 'The book industry is not only in crisis, it is now in danger' (trans. J.S.).
42 Jean-Marie Bouvaist, *Crise et mutations dans l'édition française* (Paris: Cercle de la librairie, 1993).

with the same 'quasi-Flaubertian irony' (Ahearne).[43] Indeed, he insists on the difference between the post-script to *Les Règles*, when he comes out finally in support and defence for autonomy, from the chapters it follows, in that it expresses an explicitly 'normative' position (*RA*, 545). Yet arguably there is a bias throughout *Les Règles* in favour of non-commercial literature, which is clearest in the choice of terms he uses. Bourdieu refers persistently in *Les Règles* to 'pure' and 'bourgeois' art, the polemical labels of the nineteenth century, while even the more technical concepts of 'autonomy' and 'heteronomy' are hardly value-free.

This tendency to valorise works written with an autonomous intention cannot be reduced to the difficulty which faces all social and cultural analysts of how to distinguish between the systems of hierarchisation they observe in practice and their own value judgments (so that, as Bourdieu comments, 'quand je dis que la bande dessinée est un genre inférieur (…) il faut que je dise à la fois que c'est comme ça, mais que ce n'est pas moi qui le pense' (*CD*, 67).[44] In several places, Bourdieu hints that his theoretical model justifies the privilege of autonomous culture. This suggestion first appears in Bourdieu's discussion of Flaubert and his ascetic dedication to his craft:

> Peut-être tient-on là, pour ceux qui le réclament, un critère assez indiscutable de la valeur de toute production artistique et, plus largement, intellectuelle, à savoir l'investissement dans l'œuvre qui peut se mesurer aux coûts en efforts, en sacrifices de tous ordres et, en définitive, en temps, et qui va de pair, de ce fait, avec l'indépendance par rapport aux forces et aux contraintes qui s'exercent de l'extérieur du champ ou, pire, de l'intérieur, comme les séductions de la mode ou les pressions du conformisme éthique ou logique avec, par exemple, les problématiques obligées, les sujets imposés, les formes d'expression agréées, etc (*RA*, 145).[45]

---

43 Ahearne, Jeremy, *Between Cultural Theory and Policy: The Cultural Policy Thinking of Pierre Bourdieu, Michel de Certeau, and Régis Debray* (University of Warwick: Centre for Cultural Policy Studies, 2004), p. 69.
44 'when I say that comic strips are an inferior genre, you might imagine I really think that. So I have to say at one and the same time that's how it is, but that it isn't my opinion' (*Other Words*, 52).
45 'Maybe there is here, for those who want it, a rather indisputable criterion of value for all artistic production, and, more generally, for intellectual the investment in a work which is measurable by the cost in effort, in sacrifices of all kinds and, difinitively, in time, and which goes hand in hand with the consequent independence from the forces and constraints exercised outside the field, or, worse, within it, such as the seductions of fashion or the pressures of ethical or logical conformism – for example, the required themes, obligatory subjects, conventional forms of expression and so forth' (*Rules*, 85).

Here, Bourdieu ties the artistic value to the labour-time the creator has put into work, which would seem to be greater in the case of works that break rather than follow conventions, and which could presumably have been spent in more pleasurable or profitable activities (in the accumulation of social capital, economic capital, or symbolic capital, all of which also take time), making labour-time, according to Bourdieu, 'un critère assez indiscutable' of cultural value. The first problem, of course, is that not every ground-breaking work requires great labour on the part of the artist or author. Indeed, at this point Bourdieu seems still not to have broken completely with what he himself calls the myth of 'créateur incréé'[46] (or the 'fétiche du nom du maître',[47] after Walter Benjamin), which credits the author as the sole producer of the work and its value (cf. *RA*, 312-13; 376; 473), and even to have swapped one self-legitimating myth or 'sociodicée' for another – for it is no more true that intellectuals and artists are all self-sacrificing workaholics than that they are all naturally gifted geniuses. We may also be hearing a personal and rather plaintive note here from Bourdieu himself, the largely self-taught petit-bourgeois from the provinces, who admits, 'je ne me suis jamais vraiment senti justifié d'exister en tant qu'intellectuel' (*MP*, 16).[48] It is likely that Bourdieu, who had to learn the hard way, would have identified with Flaubert's well-documented suffering ('les affres de l'Art'), and we can imagine he felt that his personal efforts in some way justified what he always considered to be the extremely privileged position he occupied.

Bourdieu's nascent labour-theory of value is undermined most prominently by his own discussions of Marcel Duchamp. If Flaubert was something of an alter-ego, Duchamp was Bourdieu's polar opposite: 'Issu d'une famille d'artistes – son grand-père maternel, Émile-Frédéric Nicole, est peintre et graveur, son frère aîné est le peintre Jacques Villon, son autre frère, Raymond Duchamp-Villon, est un sculpteur cubiste, l'aînée de ses sœurs est peintre – Marcel Duchamp est dans le champ artistique comme un poisson dans l'eau' (*RA*, 406).[49] Immersed in artistic culture from his earliest days, Duchamp was a virtuoso who had been through

---

46 'uncreated creator'(trans. J.S.).
47 'the fetishism of the master's name' (trans. J.S.).
48 'I have never really felt justified in existing as an intellectual' (*Meditations*, 7).
49 'Born of a family of artists – his maternal grandfather, Émile-Frédéric Nicolle, is a painter and engraver, his elder brother is the painter Jacques Villon, his other brother Raymond Duchamp-Villon is a Cubist sculptor, his oldest sister is a painter, Marcel Duchamp is in the field like a fish in water' (*Rules*, 246, trans. modified J.S.).

all the artistic styles by the age of twenty. Indeed, before giving it up for chess (which obliged a more monastic existence), he seems to have had little difficulty reconciling fine art with fast cars and a busy social life. It is Duchamp's 'ready-mades', however, that present Bourdieu's theory of value with its most immediate difficulty. What could take less time and effort than scribbling *R. Mutt* on a urinal and displaying it on a plinth? And yet *La Fontaine* most definitely broke with 'les problématiques obligées' and 'les sujets imposés' in the field, as it was even rejected by the Society of Independent Artists.

This rather exorbitant critique of what is, after all, only a tentative remark, at least illustrates the need to take a far wider and longer view of the work put into cultural production. Duchamp the individual may not have put a great deal of time or effort into mastering his craft, nor even into producing his works. For him, artistic prowess was an inheritance into which he was born almost as surely as a financial fortune. But the twentieth-century art-world he inhabited 'like a fish in water' (in which he was also a tributary) was itself the product of a long collective labour, and the audacity that cost him little had its precedent in many centuries of struggles for artistic autonomy. Indeed, his works, especially his ready-mades, relied on the existence of an unprecedented array of international institutions and agents involved, full-time or part-time, in the recording, preserving, and analysing of works, and who partake in the *celebration* of works – which, as *La Fontaine* demonstrated in a practical way (almost like a sociological experiment) is the secret of their value (*RA*, 284-88). Bourdieu makes the same argument for Joyce and Faulkner: 'Il a fallu un travail collectif énorme pour arriver à produire des œuvres comme celle de Joyce ou Faulkner, il a fallu des générations et des générations, il a fallu des institutions, des critiques, etc.' (*CP*, 46).[50] And also for writers including Kafka, Beckett and Gombrowicz, who in a sense 'ont été faits à Paris': 'on sait tout le temps qui est nécessaire pour créer des créateurs, c'est-à-dire des espaces sociaux de producteurs et de récepteurs à l'intérieur desquels ils puissent apparaître, se développer et réussir' (*I*, 422-23).[51] In the last two instances, Bourdieu makes this argument in the context of presenting a

---

50 'It required an enormous collective work before works like those of Joyce and Faulkner could be produced, it required generations and generations, it required institutions, critics, etc.' (trans. J.S.).
51 'We know, however, how much time is needed to create creators, i.e. social spaces of producers and receivers, within which they can appear, develop and succeed' (*Political Interventions*, 344).

case for the defence of artistic and literary autonomy, which, he warned, was collapsing under commercial pressure. Yet although intuitively appealing, even Bourdieu's more fully worked out theory of cultural value appears, on closer inspection, hardly 'indiscutable'. Many of us put a lot of time and effort into things which really contribute little to the sum of human happiness (what Bourdieu would in later years call *'l'économie du bonheur'*). In the current climate of anti-intellectualism, aimed particularly at the Humanities, those of us with an interest in literary culture will have to do better than that.

Elsewhere, we will see Bourdieu develops an instrumental vision of cultural value, which appears only marginally and obliquely in *Les Règles* – when he speaks for instance of literary works as 'instruments de production, donc d'invention et de liberté possible' (*RA*, 495 n. 26), or of culture more generally as an 'instrument de liberté supposant la liberté, comme *modus operandi* permettant le dépassement permanent de *l'opus operatum*.'[52] Although Bourdieu does not do so himself, it might even be possible to link these two arguments within a theory of *cumulativity*, and an initial attempt to so has been made in this chapter. Bourdieu already suggests with reference to the evolution of the literary field that 'les produits de cette histoire relativement autonome présentent une forme de *cumulativité*' (*RA*, 398),[53] by increasing the repertoire of stylistic, technical, thematic, etc. possibilities available within the tradition. For example, in the case of Flaubert Bourdieu writes that 'ce qui confère à son œuvre une *valeur* incomparable, c'est qu'il entre en relation, au moins négativement, avec la totalité de l'univers littéraire dans lequel il est inscrit et dont il prend en charge complètement les contradictions, les difficultés et les problèmes' (*RA*, 167).[54] In a series of ruptures – with realism and romanticism, prose and poetry, Balzac the grand precursor and less important writers such as Champfleury and Murger – Flaubert invented an entirely new way of writing the modern novel, which was nevertheless built on what had come before.

---

52 'an instrument of freedom presupposing freedom, as a *modus operandi* allowing the permanent supersession of the *opus operatum*' (*Rules*, 340)
53 'the products of this relatively autonomous history present a kind of *cumulativity* (*Rules*, 242).
54 'what confers on his work its incomparable value, is that it makes contact, at least negatively, with the totality of the literary universe in which it is inscribed and whose contradictions, difficulties and problems he takes complete responsibility for' (*Rules*, 98).

Yet the question of cultural value and its relation to autonomy remains underdeveloped by Bourdieu. Indeed, few commentators have picked up previously on his suggestion that cultural works might have any value at all that was not the product of 'misrecognition' (*méconnaissance*). This may be because the bulk of Bourdieu's work, including the essays included in *Les Règles*, were conceived as critical – that is, they were designed to unseat unfounded 'illusions' and 'beliefs'. It is also no doubt because the high cultural game they exposed had seemed quite secure, and able to survive some deflation during the period in which they were written. Bourdieu's thought seems also to have evolved, especially since his 1975 article 'L'Invention de la vie d'artiste', which concluded that Flaubert was effectively merely reproducing the deluded ideological viewpoint of the French nineteenth-century bourgeoisie.[55] It was only later that Bourdieu started claiming a 'universal' value for Flaubert's work, related to his autonomy. In a 1992 interview, Bourdieu even admits to having thought the artistic field was becoming *more* autonomous, and that he had only changed his mind after his conversations with the German conceptual artist Hans Haacke (whom he first met in 1989[56]), who warned him: 'attention, on retombe dans le mécénat...'[57]

---

55 Pierre Bourdieu, 'L'Invention de la vie d'artiste', *Actes de la recherche en sciences sociales*, 1 (1975), 67-93.
56 Hans Haacke, 'A Public Servant', *October*, 101 (2002), 4-6 (p. 5).
57 Graw, 'Que Suis-Je?' 'we are returning to patronage' (trans. J.S.).

4. Science and Literature

If Bourdieu came to the defence of writers and artists in his political interventions, and even claimed that the sociologist can be the greatest ally of those engaged in the creation and conservation of literary and artistic culture, his analyses have been more often criticised as reductive and destructive of cultural values. A particular bone of contention has been his insistence on the word 'science', which especially jars when it is used to describe Bourdieu's approach to literature, in *Les Règles de l'art* and elsewhere, as 'une science des œuvres'.[1] In this relationship, scientific knowledge and rationality appear to be privileged at the expense of literary expression and imagination. This chapter examines Bourdieu's claim to science in both its social and epistemological contexts, and the opposition he sets up between science and literature. First, it reads Bourdieu's analysis of Flaubert's *L'Éducation sentimentale* as a study of the differences between a scientific and a literary representation of social reality. Next, it assesses the charges of 'reductionism' and 'iconoclasticism' that have been levelled at Bourdieu, and ponders the extent to which they are justified. The chapter then explores the possibilities for 'cross-overs' or exchanges between literature and sociology, as two distinct discourses which, however, still have much to learn from each other. Finally, the chapter compares Bourdieu's position to contemporary post-modern and post-structuralist theories of the relations between literature, science, and reality.

L'Éducation sentimentale

Bourdieu draws on the principles of his theory of sociological knowledge to develop a series of parallels and oppositions between 'science' and 'literature'. Both scientific and literary texts, Bourdieu argues, 'objectify' (copy into an object) the social or psychological structures which regulate experience, usually unseen. Yet whereas scientific discourse agrees to accept what Bourdieu calls

---

1 'a science of works' (trans. J.S.).

'l'arbitrage du "réel"',[2] to submit to the stage of verification, literary fiction does not claim to refer to reality, in fact quite the opposite. According to Bourdieu, the literary work operates 'un euphémisme généralisé' (RA, 69),[3] which 'denegates' (in the Freudian sense of *Verneinung*) the social reality to which it refers, '*mais comme s'il n'en parlait pas*' (RA, 20).[4] In contrast, Bourdieu writes, 'la science tente de dire les choses comme elles sont, sans euphémismes, et demande à être prise au sérieux' (RA, 541),[5] that is, as an accurate representation of reality. Literature also reveals structures in a different way: not as systems of intelligible relations corresponding to the hidden structure of 'reality' by way of analogy, by the use of *demonstrations, exemplifications,* or *evocations,* 'aptes à "parler à la sensibilité" et à obtenir une croyance et une participation *analogues* à celles que nous accordons d'ordinaire au monde réel' (RA, 68).[6] Thus, while sociological theory symbolises the structure of relations that determine and orient our practices, investments, and interests, literature (most obviously, the literature we call 'realist') shows these structures 'in action', in the *form* of concrete characters, with emotions, friendships, ambitions, and desires.

It is above all in his study and analysis of *L'Éducation sentimentale* that Bourdieu elaborates and explores these oppositions between literature and science. According to Bourdieu, Flaubert's novel provides a very accurate (even 'quasi-scientific') representation of the nineteenth-century French social world in which it was written, and even, in Frédéric, an 'objectification' of the author Flaubert himself. Yet Bourdieu resists the temptation to read *L'Éducation sentimentale* either as an autobiography or as a sociological document (which might seem reasonable, given the vast amount of detail that went into Flaubert's works). For Bourdieu, the 'homology' between Frédéric's fictional world and Flaubert's social world is situated at the level of their *structure*. This structure is, however, only visible in the novel (as it is in our everyday reality) by its effects – which goes some way to explaining why it has (or so Bourdieu claims) 'échappé aux interprètes les plus attentifs' (RA, 19).[7]

'Pour dévoiler complètement la structure que le texte littéraire ne dévoilait qu'en la voilant', Bourdieu writes, 'l'analyse doit réduire le

---

[2] 'the arbitrage of the "real"' (*Science*, 70).
[3] 'a generalized euphemism' (*Rules*, 32).
[4] 'as if it did not speak of it' (*Rules*, 3).
[5] 'science tries to speak of things as they are, without euphemisms, and asks to be taken seriously (*Rules*, 336).
[6] 'a belief and an imaginary participation analogous to those that we ordinarily grant to the real world' (*Rules*, 32).
[7] 'eluded the most attentive interpreters' (*Rules*, 3).

récit d'une aventure au protocole d'une sorte de montage expérimental' (*RA*, 69).[8] Taking note of who attends the various soirées, receptions, and reunions, and using the many details Flaubert provides as clues to his characters' social positions, lifestyles, tastes, property and financial assets, etc., Bourdieu divides the twenty protagonists into overlapping groups, which he represents visually by means of a sociogramme. These two main groups are dominated by M. Arnoux and M. Dambreuse, the art dealer and the banker, who hold cultural-and-political power and economic-and-political power respectively, and who attract the weaker characters like the poles of a magnet (*RA*, 24-25). The reader will recognise the structure of the French field of power, with its opposition between cultural and economic poles. Where the characters are positioned in this structure will then determine their conduct in the narrative, each position, embodied as habitus, providing a sort of 'formule génératrice',[9] which orients where their interests lie, and circumscribes their probable attitudes and responses in any given social situation. The 'narrative' then appears in the light of this model as a series of set-pieces, in which Flaubert experiments with different combinations of characters and scenarios: developing 'dans une aventure nécessaire toutes les implications de leurs "formules" respectives' (*RA*, 37-38).[10]

Of course, this is not how one would usually read *L'Éducation sentimentale*. 'Si *L'Éducation sentimentale*, histoire nécessaire d'un groupe dont les éléments, unis par une combinatoire quasi systématique, sont soumis à l'ensemble des forces d'attraction ou de répulsion qu'exerce sur eux le champ du pouvoir, peut être lue comme une histoire', Bourdieu writes, 'c'est que la structure qui organise la fiction, et qui fonde l'illusion de réalité qu'elle produit, se dissimule, comme dans la réalité, sous les interactions entre des personnes qu'elle structure' (*RA*, 38).[11] Just as

---

8 'In order to unveil completely the structure that a literary text could only unveil by veiling, the analysis should reduce the story of an adventure to the protocol of an experimental montage' (*Rules*, 32).
9 'generative formula' (*Rules*, 13).
10 'in a necessary adventure all the implications of their respective "formulas"' (*Rules*, 14).
11 'If *Sentimental Education* – necessarily a story of a group whose elements, united by an almost systematic set of combinations, are subjected to an ensemble of forces of attraction or repulsion exercised over them by the field of power – may be read as a history, it is because the structure which organizes the fiction, and which grounds the illusion of reality it produces, is hidden, as in reality, beneath the interactions of people, which are structured by it' (*Rules*, 14).

in our ordinary experience we do not see the total system of relations between groups and individuals, who seem separated by geographical space and time, so the structure of *L'Éducation sentimentale* is hidden by the characters' actual interactions, which attract our focus. 'Ce qui enlève aux personnages leur allure abstraite de combinaisons de paramètres', Bourdieu continues, 'c'est aussi, paradoxalement, l'étroitesse de l'espace social où ils sont placés' (*RA*, 38).[12] In a closed social universe comprising closely connected networks, and within the confines of the centre of Paris, the protagonists have every possibility to meet, giving an appearance of chance to predictable probabilities.

According to Bourdieu, the extremely close analogy between the structure that propels the narrative, and that which co-ordinates social practices (with the unknowing 'complicity' of agents), is the basis of the particularly intense '*effet de croyance* (plutôt que réel)' it produces. Bourdieu's understanding of this 'belief effect' is rather different from the 'reality effect' of Barthes, for whom it is the 'détails "inutiles"'[13] within a narrative description which, by their apparent contingency and superfluousness, strike the reader as realistic.[14] Indeed, at least in the case of *L'Éducation sentimentale*, what Bourdieu calls 'le travail d'écriture crée (...) un univers saturé de détails significatifs et, par là, plus signifiant que nature' (*RA*, 22),[15] in which every detail – from Deslauriers's beer to Dambreuse's 'grands vins de Bordeaux', passing by the 'vins extraordinaires' served by Arnoux and the champagne at Rosannette's – evokes a recognisable lifestyle and way of being-in-the-world, which makes their actions and responses in different social situations appear coherent and realistic. 'Ainsi', Bourdieu writes, 'la "barbe taillée en collier" de Martinon annonce toutes les conduites ultérieures, depuis la pâleur, les soupirs et les lamentations par où il trahit, à l'occasion de l'émeute, sa peur d'être compromis, ou la prudente contradiction qu'il apporte à ses camarades lorsqu'ils attaquent Louis-Philippe (...), jusqu'au sérieux qu'il affiche, tant dans ses conduites que dans ses propos ostentatoirement conservateurs, aux soirées des Dambreuse' (*RA*, 37-38).[16]

---

12 'What precludes the characters from having the abstract appearance of combinations of parameters is also, paradoxically, the narrowness of the social space in which they are placed' (*Rules*, 14).
13 'useless details' (trans. J.S.).
14 Roland Barthes, 'L'Effet de réel', *Communications*, 11 (1968), 84-89.
15 'the work of writing thus creates a universe saturated with significant details, and therefore more signifying than true life' (*Rules*, 5).
16 'Martinon's neat "beard along the line of the jaw" announces all his subsequent behaviour, from the pallor, sighs and lamentation by which he betrays, on the

4. Science and Literature   107

According to Bourdieu, it is the 'travail d'écriture' or *work on form*, which Flaubert took to new levels, which explains the appearance (albeit veiled) of deep social and psychological structures which usually escape conscious awareness. Bourdieu writes:

> Sous peine de voir l'effet d'une sorte de miracle parfaitement inintelligible dans le fait que l'analyse puisse découvrir dans l'œuvre – comme je l'ai fait pour *L'Éducation sentimentale* – des structures profondes inaccessibles à l'intuition ordinaire (et à la lecture des commentateurs), il faut bien admettre que c'est à travers ce travail sur la forme que se projettent dans l'œuvre ces structures que l'écrivain, comme tout agent social, porte en lui à l'état pratique, sans en détenir véritablement la maîtrise (*RA*, 184).[17]

Flaubert's legendary attention to style enabled him to cut through stereotyped images and associations ('idées reçues'), automaticisms of speech, of rhythm, rhyme, etc., to produce a more penetrating vision of the real than can pass the censorship of ordinary language and representations. Yet it is as if Flaubert *did not mean* to represent these structures in his narrative: they only 'appeared' as a sort of by-product of the work on form, which was the author's sole focus.

Yet it is also through this 'denegated' or 'veiled' reference to reality, Bourdieu claims, that literature is able to 'parfois dire plus, même sur le monde social, que nombre d'écrits à prétention scientifique' (*RA*, 68).[18] The literary form enables the indirect expression and experience of truths which, if confronted in reality, could be 'insupportable' (*RA*, 69).[19] Perhaps the most striking example of this is the relation, often discussed, between Flaubert and Frédéric. Even by writing *L'Éducation sentimentale*, Bourdieu argues, Flaubert repressed the resemblances between himself and Frédéric, of whom a significant characteristic is his *incapacity to write* (*RA*, 57). Flaubert objectified his own previous 'indétermination' in Frédéric, which Bourdieu explains by

---

occasion of the riot, his fear of being compromised, or the prudent contradiction which he offers to his comrades when the attack Louis-Philippe (…) right down to the serious face he puts on, both in his behaviour and in his ostentatiously conservative speeches at the Dambreuse soirées' (*Rules*, 14).
17 'Unless one sees as a sort of completely unintelligible miracle the fact that analysis can discover in the work – as I have for *Sentimental Education*, profound structures inaccessible to ordinary intuition (and to the reading of commentators), it must be acknowledged that it is through this work on form that the work comes to contain those structures that the writer, like any social agent, carries within him in a practical way, without having really mastered them' (*Rules*, 108).
18 'sometimes say more, even about the social realm, than many writings with scientific pretensions' (*Rules*, 32).
19 'unbearable' (*Rules*, 32).

his paradoxical position in the field of power, split between the two poles. Yet Frédéric's hankering for social ubiquity, which means he can never commit to a single woman or career, and so secure his social position and trajectory, Flaubert was able to satisfy in a form of art in which he could 'vivre toutes les vies' (*RA*, 59-60).[20] We can understand that Flaubert had needed fully to be reassured that his own writing was not simply another failed project, with the success of *Madame Bovary* (and, one supposes, *Salammbô*), before he was able to finish Frédéric's story of failure, at the second attempt (*RA*, 57 n. 100).

Bourdieu admits that his analysis of *L'Éducation sentimentale*, which can seem to reduce Flaubert's characters and his narrative to bare bones, 'ait quelque chose de profondément désenchanteur' (*RA*, 69).[21] Several critics have gone further, and seen it and Bourdieu's work on literature more generally as an 'attack' on aesthetic theory, on aesthetic values, and even on the aesthetic itself. One of the more serious of these critiques (because it manages at least to reconstruct portions of Bourdieu's argument), is an article by Jacques Leenhardt, director of studies at the *École des hautes études en sciences sociales* (EHESS), entitled, straightforwardly, 'Les Règles de l'art de P. Bourdieu'.[22] Leenhardt picks up on Bourdieu's use of semi-mystical vocabulary and his talk of *beliefs* (which is a reference in fact to Baudelaire), and by some free-association finds in Bourdieu's analysis an implicit critique of literary knowledge. The 'belief' literature engages becomes, in Leenhardt's mind, a sort of 'opium', the impact of which on the reader is 'd'endormir son désir de savoir'.[23] Alchemy, incantation, and magic suggest 'les contours d'une activité qui tourne le dos à la connaissance',[24] and so on. Leenhardt concludes:

> la position que prend Bourdieu à l'égard de la littérature engage toute une théorie de la connaissance, et son combat *pour* la sociologie prend les allures d'un combat *contre* la littérature dans la mesure où ce qui est en jeu à ses yeux est la sauvegarde de la prééminence du savoir rationnel.[25]

The question Leenhardt puts to Bourdieu is whether there are not

---

20 'live all lives' (*Rules*, 33).
21 'has something profoundly disenchanting about it' (*Rules*, 32).
22 Jacques Leenhardt, 'Les Règles de l'art de P. Bourdieu', *French Cultural Studies*, 4 (1993), 263-70.
23 'suppress his desire to know' (trans. J.S.).
24 'an activity which turns its back on knowledge' (trans. J.S.).
25 Leenhardt, 'Les Règles de l'art', p. 267. 'The position that Bourdieu takes with regard to literature engages a whole theory of knowledge, and his combat *for* sociology takes the appearance of a combat *against* literature insofar as that is at stake in his eyes is to safeguard the preeminence of rational knowledge' (trans. J.S.).

'plusieurs types ou modalités de savoir'[26] – if human knowledge and experience cannot be expressed and communicated in many different ways, which it would be an impoverishment to deny ourselves. 'La littérature ne doit pas être comparée à la science', Leenhardt insists, 'mais lui être juxtaposée, dans une analyse englobante de l'arsenal symbolique que se donnent les sociétés, et singulièrement les sociétés modernes qui tendent à la préférer aux représentations plus statiques que leur fournissaient les mythologies religieuses'.[27] This is, in fact, Bourdieu's position, whose own recourse to the 'symbolic arsenal' of literature will be explored below.

'Le démontage impie de la fiction'

We cannot blame Bourdieu's critics and readers entirely for their misunderstandings and defensiveness, as Bourdieu himself tends to do. It is up to his reader, apparently, 'qu'il dénonce à voir une "attaque" ou une "critique", au sens ordinaire, dans ce qui veut être une analyse' (*RA*, 342)[28] – when, that is, his critics are not trying to earn 'un brevet de vertu culturelle en dénonçant à grands cris, en ces temps de restauration, les menaces que feraient peser sur l'art (ou la philosophie) des analyses dont l'intention iconologique apparaît comme une violence iconoclaste' (*RA*, 305).[29] Bourdieu insists his aim is neither to diminish or destroy literary values and pleasures, but simply to 'understand': in accordance with the maxim he cites often from Spinoza: 'Ne pas rire, ne pas déplorer, ne pas détester, disait Spinoza, mais comprendre', ou, mieux, nécessiter, rendre raison' (*RA*, 448).[30] The problem is that Bourdieu's 'distance objectivante' is not the same as Spinoza's serene detachment, as the bellicose talk of 'conquering' scientific facts might already have suggested. Scientific knowledge can only be won by what Bourdieu calls (echoing Bachelard) 'la polémique de la

---

26 'several tyles or modalities of knowledge' (trans. J.S.).
27 Leenhardt, '*Les Règles de l'art* de P. Bourdieu', p. 270. 'Literature should not be compared to science, but juxtaposed, in an analysis that englobes the symbolic arsenals that societies have developed, particularly modern societies which tend to prefer it to the more static representations of religious mythology' (trans. J.S.).
28 'not to see as an "attack" or a "criticism" (in the ordinary sense) what is intended to be an analysis' (*Rules*, 207).
29 'a certificate of cultural virtue by denouncing loudly, in these days of restoration, the threats made against art (or philosophy) by analyses whose iconological intention looks to them like iconoclastic violence' (*Rules*, 185).
30 '"Do not laugh, do not deplore, do not detest", said Spinoza, "just understand" – or better, make it necessary, give it reason' (*Rules*, 272).

raison': by a generalised *negation* (contradiction and refutation) of 'errors', 'beliefs', 'preconceptions', etc., supported by a social struggle to ensure that the 'truth' wins out. It is difficult not to feel some defensiveness in the face of such an onslaught, especially when it is directed at a form of knowledge that neither claims nor aims for objectivity.

Indeed, even if Bourdieu's 'iconological' intentions are good, we might well wonder if socio-analysis, which is first and foremost a method of 'dismantling' (ana-lysis), may not weaken the strength and sincerity of the beliefs that hold the literary game together. Bourdieu, as we have seen, speaks of sociology requiring a sort of '*épochè*' (suspension) 'de la *croyance* communément accordée aux choses de la culture et aux manières légitimes de les aborder'.[31] More than a simple 'renversement méthodologique', he describes this as 'une véritable *conversion* de la manière la plus commune de penser et de vivre la vie intellectuelle' (*RA*, 305).[32] As Ahearne argues, however, 'it seems likely that some of the belief "suspended" for the purposes of understanding may not return, and that the "credit" accorded to the things of culture may thereby be diminished'.[33]

Bourdieu addresses this issue in his discussions of a brief excerpt from Stéphane Mallarmé's 1895 publication *La Musique et les lettres*.[34] In an interview with Isabelle Graw, Bourdieu admits to having been 'très content d'avoir trouvé ce texte. C'est comme si j'avais trouvé chez Heidegger un passage

---

31 'a sort of epoche of the belief commonly granted to cultural things and to the legitimate ways of approaching them' (*Rules*, 185).
32 'far from a simple methodological overturning: it implies a veritable conversion of the most common manner of thinking and living the intellectual life' (*Rules*, 185).
33 Ahearne, *Between Cultural Theory and Policy*, p. 49.
34 'Nous savons, captifs d'une formule absolue, que, certes, n'est que ce qui est. Incontinent écarter cependant, sous un prétexte, le leurre, accuserait notre inconséquence, niant le plaisir que nous voulons prendre: car cet *au-delà* en est l'argent, et le moteur dirais-je si je ne répugnais à opérer, en public, le démontage impie de la fiction et conséquemment du mécanisme littéraire, pour étaler la pièce principale ou rien. Mais, je vénère comment, par une supercherie, on projette, à quelque élévation défendue et de foudre ! le conscient manque chez nous de ce qui là-haut éclate. À quoi sert cela – À un jeu'. Stéphane Mallarmé, *La Musique et les lettres* (Paris: Didier, 1895), pp. 44-45. 'We know, captives of an absolute formula that, indeed, there is only that which is. Forthwith to dismiss the cheat, however, on a pretext, would indict our inconsequence, denying the pleasure we want to take: for that beyond is its agent, and the engine might say were I not loathe to perform, in public, the impious dismantling of the fiction and consequently of the literary mechanism, display the principal part or nothing. But I venerate how, by a trick we project to a height forfended – and with thunder! – the conscious lack in us of what shines up there. What is it for? A game' (cited and trans. in *Rules*, 274).

où il dise que le monde social explique le conscient'.³⁵ Mallarmé, he notes, 'est d'ordinaire utilisé comme Hölderlin pour défendre l'idée selon laquelle l'art est quelque chose de sacré', following, we might add, examples set by Maurice Blanchot and Jacques Derrida. In this passage from *La Musique et les lettres*, however, Mallarmé appears to say (albeit in highly obscure language, especially as the text was originally presented in French at a conference in England) what Bourdieu attempts to prove in *Les Règles*, which is that the value and interest we think of as inherent to literary works are products of a *social game founded on collective belief*. Bourdieu calls this belief the field's *illusio*, which he defines as 'la croyance collective dans le jeu (*illusio*) et dans la valeur sacrée de ses enjeux [qui] est à la fois la condition et le produit du fonctionnement même du jeu' (*RA*, 376).³⁶ This common agreement, even if there is little agreement on anything else, that the game is worth the time and effort it takes to play (but one should not be flippant: some have paid dearly, including with their lives, to defend a theory or for freedom of expression), is what keeps the game 'interesting' – and of course, the game becomes more interesting with the more interest it attracts.³⁷ Indeed, Bourdieu writes:

> l'*illusio* littéraire, cette croyance dans l'*importance* ou l'*intérêt* des fictions littéraires, est la condition, presque toujours inaperçue du plaisir esthétique qui est toujours, pour une part, plaisir de jouer le jeu, de participer à la fiction, d'être en accord total avec les présupposés du jeu; la condition aussi de l'*illusion* littéraire et de l'effet de croyance (plutôt qu''effet de réel') que le texte peut produire (*RA*, 538).³⁸

The ability of books to attract our attention, and obtain the 'suspension of disbelief' we accord willingly to works in anticipation of gratification, as well as the indissociable pleasure of taking part in the literary game (which is always also, to some extent, the *pleasure of taking sides* (of

---

35 Graw, 'Que Suis-Je?' 'Mallarmé is usually used like Hölderlin to defend the idea that art has something sacred about it (...) I was very happy to have found this text. It is as if I had found in Heidegger a passage in which he explains that the social explains the conscious' (trans. J.S.).
36 'the collective belief in the game (illusio) and in the sacred value of its stakes which is both the condition and the product of the functioning of the 'literary mechanism' (*Rules*, 230).
37 Ahearne, *Between Cultural Theory and Policy*, p. 52.
38 'The literary illusio, that originating adherence to the literary game which grounds the belief in the importance or interest of literary fictions, is the precondition – almost always unperceived – of the aesthetic pleasure which is always, in part, the pleasure of playing the game, of participating in the fiction, of being in total accord with the premises of the game. It is also the precondition of the literary illusion and of the belief effect (rather than the "reality effect" which the text can produce' (*Rules*, 334).

expressing preferences, outrage, etc.)), are all, Bourdieu explains, functions of the literary *illusio*, the fundamental belief in the value and importance of the game and of its stakes. If we follow Bourdieu's argument, Mallarmé was aware of his own involvement in this social game, which 'elevates' works and their authors, 'par une supercherie',[39] to the status of fetishes, endowed with quasi-magical properties. Mallarmé refused, however, in his own words, 'à opérer, en public, le démontage impie de la fiction et conséquemment du mécanisme littéraire',[40] in case this divulgation 'accuserait notre inconséquence, niant le plaisir que nous voulons prendre' – in case, precisely, the statement and explanation of its rules would in Ahearne's terms 'dis-credit (take belief from)' the cultural game.[41] Mallarmé only spoke the truth in such a way that it had little chance of being understood – and has not been, as is shown by the fact, as Bourdieu observes, that 'nul plus que lui n'a été mis au service de l'exaltation de la "création", du "créateur" et de la mystique heideggérienne de la poésie comme "révélation"' (*RA*, 455 n. 101).[42]

We might think all this more than a little hypocritical. Bourdieu's interpretation of Mallarmé's text is almost as obscure as the original. We might want also to find more and less enigmatic evidence that Mallarmé indeed shared something like Bourdieu's sociological vision of the field, to avoid the suspicion that Bourdieu was projecting his own thoughts and theories into the mind of the poet. But Bourdieu saw himself as doing something very different from the poet. Mallarmé himself kept playing along, despite having no illusions regarding the objective value and importance of literary works and authors (including himself). By what Bourdieu describes as 'une sorte de fétichisme décisoire'[43] (we can notice the apparent oxymoron), Mallarmé chose to keep playing along – and not, as we might expect, half-heartedly or cynically, but with the conviction that the 'plaisir que nous *voulons* prendre' (italics added by Bourdieu) justifies 'le leurre' (*RA*, 452).[44] Although Bourdieu admits that he had sometimes regretted 'devant les dénonciations pharisiennes de mes 'dénonciations',

---

39 'by a trick' (cited and trans. in *Rules*, 274).
40 'to perform, in public, the impious dismantling of the fiction and consequently of the literary mechanism' (cited and trans. in *Rules*, 274).
41 Ahearne, *Between Cultural Theory and Policy*, p. 49.
42 'he more than than anyone has been pressed into the service of the exaltation of "creation", of the "creator" and the Heideggerian mystique of poetry as "revelation" (*Rules*, 390).
43 'a sort of deliberate fetishism' (*Rules*, 275).
44 'the pleasure we want to take' justifies the 'cheat' (cited and translated in *Rules*, 274).

(...) de n'avoir pas suivi les traces de Mallarmé qui, se refusant à 'opérer, en public, le démontage impie de la fiction' (...) choisissait de sauver la fiction, et la croyance collective dans le jeu' (*MP*, 15),[45] he claims that he could not have been satisfied completely with following Mallarmé's strategy. 'Prendre le parti de garder le secret, ou de ne pas le dévoiler que sous une forme strictement voilée, comme fait Mallarmé, c'est préjuger que seuls quelques grands initiés sont capables de la lucidité héroïque et de la générosité décisoire qui sont nécessaires pour affronter dans sa vérité l'énigme de la fiction et du fétichisme' (*MP*, 15).[46] Bourdieu's wager is that Mallarmé was wrong not to trust the public's capacity to choose their own cultural icons, once they understand the correct principles of judgement (for instance, the difference between 'autonomous' and 'heteronomous' producers). What Bourdieu describes in an early article as the 'terrorisme du goût',[47] which imposes unconditional recognition for consecrated works, would then give way to a more informed – and democratic – sort of delegation.

If this changed relation to culture impacts at all upon our reading pleasure, Bourdieu claims it would only *intensify* it. Here, Bourdieu returns to Spinoza and his notion of an *amor intellectualis dei*, the intellectual love of God, conceived of by Spinoza not as an individual, a person like ourselves, but 'as the necessary order of things, as the eternal and involuntary cause of everything that exists' (Alfred Weber).[48] Spinoza saw *amor intellectualis dei* as the highest form of knowledge, and even as the key to human blessedness: when the philosopher becomes aware of his place in nature, and nature (God, or 'substance') becomes aware of itself. Taking his cue from the Spinozist sociology of Durkheimians (whose motto 'la société, c'est Dieu'[49] he cites in several places), Bourdieu adapts this notion of *amor intellectualis dei* to his theory of artistic perception and appreciation:

---

45 'faced with the pharisaical denunciations of my "denunciations", I have often regretted not having followed the example of Mallarmé, who, refusing to 'perform, in public, the impious dismantling of the fiction (...), chose to save the fiction, and the collective belief in the game' (*Meditations*, 6).
46 'To opt to keep the secret, or to unveil it only in a strictly veiled form, as Mallarmé does, is to pre-judge that only a few great initiates are capable of the heroic lucidity and willed generosity that are necessary in order to confront the enigma of fiction and fetishism' (*Meditations*, 15).
47 'Champ intellectuel et projet créateur', p. 871. 'Terrorism of taste' (trans. J.S.).
48 Alfred Weber, *History of Philosophy*, trans. Frank Thilly (New York: Charles Scribner's Sons, 1908), chapter 55.
49 'Society is God' (trans. J.S.).

l'analyse scientifique, lorsqu'elle est capable de porter au jour ce qui rend l'œuvre d'art *nécessaire*, c'est-à-dire la formule informatrice, le principe générateur, la raison d'être, fournit à l'expérience artistique, et au plaisir qui l'accompagne, sa meilleure justification, son plus riche aliment. À travers elle, l'amour sensible de l'œuvre peut s'accomplir dans une sorte d'*amor intellectualis rei*, assimilation de l'objet au sujet et immersion du sujet dans l'objet littéraire (qui, en plus d'un cas, est lui-même le produit d'une semblable soumission) (*RA*, 15).⁵⁰

When we understand the logic and history behind an author's habitus, and the space of possibilities from which his work was composed, we can also see the necessity objectified in his work, which in turn appears necessary to us. And as we know from the artist Wassily Kandinsky's saying (also quoted by Bourdieu), 'est beau ce qui correspond à une nécessité intérieure'.⁵¹

Clearly, the question of the impact that socio-analysis exerts on cultural life is more complex than the frequent accusations of Bourdieu's 'reductionism' and 'scientism' suggest. If it seems likely that something is lost in the 'translation' of the structure of the literary field (and of literary works) into sociological concepts and principles, Bourdieu holds out the prospect of a sort of compensation, in the form of a less alienated relation to 'legitimate' culture, and of an *amor intellectualis*, which promises to deepen our sense of participation in literary life, and sense of ownership over works, which will correspond more closely and at several levels to our (perhaps as yet unformulated) expectations.⁵² Yet there is also a process of 'dismantling' that goes on before, which can be disenchanting, and provoke resistances. We need perseverance, and not a little courage, see it though, against the grain of both ritualistic celebrations and the barbarian rage to reduce and destroy (which is to say, frequently against

---

50 'scientific analysis, when it is able to uncover what makes the work of art *necessary*, that is to say, its informing formula, its generative principle, its *raison d'être*, also furnishes artistic experience, and the pleasure which accompanies it, with its best justification, its richest nourishment' (*Rules*, xix).

51 Bourdieu, 'Champ intellectuel et projet créateur', p. 871. 'What is beautiful is that which corresponds to an inner necessity' (trans. J.S.).

52 It is not only in literary and art criticism that this *amor intellectualis* can be felt, according to Bourdieu. He claims to have experienced it when trying to understand the problems and points of view of his interviewees, especially in *La Misère du monde* (*MM*, 914; *RA*, 494 n. 25). Here, however, it would seem to intensify one's empathy, rather than one's aesthetic pleasure. In the case of literature, however, aesthetic pleasure and empathy (identification with the author, or with the characters in a narrative) are perhaps not unrelated.

our own spontaneous dispositions). In this sense, Bourdieu can justifiably speak of 'lucidité héroïque' (*MP*, 15).[53]

Cross-overs

So far, we have kept social science and literature relatively distinct, in our effort to define them. What we can now explore, are the possibilities for what I will call 'cross-overs' between literature and sociology. Bourdieu advises sociologists to avoid trying to compete with writers on their own ground. Not being adequately aware of the exigencies and potentialities inscribed in the logic of the field and the literary heritage, would expose sociologists to the risk of appearing as 'naïve' writers (in the sense that Douanier Rousseau was a naïve painter, who did not really understand the artistic game that was being played with him by Duchamp and his other artist friends). Sociologists can, however, Bourdieu says, 'find in literary works research clues and orientations that the censorship specific to the scientific field tend to forbid to them or to hide from them' (*IRS*, 206), and appropriate instruments from literature's 'symbolic arsenal' to help with specific scientific problems. Bourdieu remembers how, for instance, in his work on Flaubert he had 'stumbled upon many problems – and solutions – that he [Flaubert] had himself encountered, such as that of the combined use of direct style, indirect style, and free indirect style which lies at the heart of the problem of transcription and publication of interviews' (*IRS*, 208). We can find a good example of Bourdieu's use of these techniques in his report on his interview with 'un jeune cadre qui "sait vivre"' in *La Distinction*, in which he switches skilfully between direct citation, reported speech, and periphrasis (*D*, 340-44). Bourdieu's writing style (not often noted for its literary elegance), seems also to have drawn inspiration from Proust, whose complex sentence structures are also crafted to reflect the complexity of reality:

> Je pense que, la qualité littéraire du style mise de côté, ce que Spitzer dit du style de Proust, je pourrais le dire de mon écriture. Il dit que, premièrement, ce qui est complexe ne se laisse dire que de façon complexe; que, deuxièmement, la réalité n'est pas seulement complexe, mais aussi structurée, hiérarchisée, et qu'il faut donner l'idée de cette structure: si l'on veut tenir le monde dans toute sa complexité et en même temps hiérarchiser et articuler, mettre en perspective, mettre au premier plan ce

---

53 'heroic lucidity' (*Meditations*, 15).

qui est important, etc., il faut recourir à ces phrases lourdement articulées, que l'on doit pratiquement reconstruire comme les phrases latines; que, troisièmement, cette réalité complexe et structurée, Proust ne veut pas la livrer telle quelle, mais en donnant simultanément son point de vue par rapport à elle, en disant comment il se situe par rapport à elle, en disant comment il se situe par rapport à ce qu'il décrit (CD, 67).[54]

Bourdieu's writing style and syntax enable him to integrate multiple voices and perspectives, including that of the author, and to symbolise the complexity of the social structures he analyses (the tension between positions, their implication in multiple causal series, the over-determined nature of practices (which do and signify more than we think), etc.), through the associations between words; the layering of thought; 180-degree turns; 'antithèses entre choses parallèles et parallèles entre choses antithétiques' (the formula is one Bourdieu applies to Flaubert, but Bourdieu must have seen it applied equally to himself) (RA, 64).[55]

Literary authors seem also to have inspired Bourdieu's use of 'polyonomasie', the plurality of perspectives on the same person or object, which, especially in Modernist literature (Bourdieu mentions in various places Virginia Woolf, Faulkner, Joyce, Flaubert, but also Cervantes, who in some ways anticipated Modernism), shatters the fixed and unitary gaze of the observer, and according to Bourdieu brings us closer to the reality of co-existing, and sometimes directly competing, points of view (MM, 9-10; HA, 42-43). Similarly, Bourdieu came to see the non-linear narratives of Woolf, Faulkner, Claude Simon, and Robbe-Grillet, as 'closer to the truth of temporal experience', and 'anthropologically more truthful', than the 'life-stories' used usually by sociologists and anthropologists, the conventions of which have themselves been reinforced by the literary tradition (IRS, 207). Literary writers are in a sense ahead of sociologists, in that they have

---

[54] 'I think that, literary and stylistic qualities apart, what Spitzer says about Proust's style is something I could say about my own writing. He says, firstly, that what is complex can only be said in a complex way; secondly, that reality is not only complex, but also structured, hierarchically ordered, and that you have to give an idea of this structure: if you want to hold the world in all its complexity and at the same time order and articulate it, show it in perspective, bring what's important into the foreground and so on, you have to use heavily articulated sentences that can be practically reconstructed like Latin sentences; thirdly, he says that Proust does not want to reveal this complex structured reality just as it is, but to present us simultaneously with the point of view from which he sees it, telling us where he locates himself in relation to what he is describing' (Other Words, 51).

[55] 'antitheses between parallel things and parallels between antithetical things' (Rules, 29).

already broken with chronology, the logical ordering of events, and with unilinear narratives, which, in our subjective memory and experience, can be blurred and ambiguous. 'C'est pourquoi', Bourdieu writes, 'il est logique de demander assistance à ceux qui ont eu à rompre avec cette tradition sur le terrain même de son accomplissement exemplaire' (RP, 83).[56] Writers can give sociologists the tools to listen to and document more accurately actor accounts of memory and experience.

Literature can moreover provide the sociologist with a fresh view of his object, an example of which is Bourdieu's use of Virginia Woolf's novel *To the Lighthouse* to elucidate the structures of domination within families in *La Domination masculine*. As we have seen, Bourdieu's reading of Woolf makes no attempt to analyse Virginia Woolf's 'point of view', position, and trajectory. Indeed, the 'epistemological vector' appears to go in the opposite direction: it is not sociological theory that provides new insight into the literary text, but the literary text that gives the sociologist a fresh perspective on his object. Again, Bourdieu attributes this fact to the strange 'sorcellerie évocatoire' (Baudelaire)[57] of the writer's work on form:

> Il fallait toute l'acuité de Virginia Woolf et l'infini raffinement de son écriture pour pousser l'analyse jusqu'aux effets les mieux cachés d'une forme de domination qui est inscrite dans tout l'ordre social et opère dans l'obscurité des corps, à la fois enjeux et principes de son efficacité (*DM*, 113).[58]

Woolf's formalist research enabled her to break through stereotyped representations (not least the simplistic polemics and slogans about gender that still blight much feminist criticism, including Woolf's own theoretical texts), and to reveal structures of symbolic power and violence that usually remain hidden, misrecognised or denied. As Bourdieu notes, Woolf was aware of this paradox, writing, 'I prefer, where truth is important, to write fiction', or again, 'fiction here is likely to contain more truth than fact' (*DM*, 98 n. 20).

Several critics have made their own comparisons between Bourdieu's work and that of literary authors. Alain Caillé considers Bourdieu's work to

---

56 'this is why it is logical to ask assistance from those who have broken with this tradition on the very terrain of its exemplary accomplishment' (trans. J.S.).
57 'evocatory magic' (cited and trans. in *Rules*, 32; 107; 108; 109).
58 'It took all the insight of Virginia Woolf and the infinite refinement of her writing to pursue the analysis into the best-concealed effects of a form of domination which is inscribed in the whole social order and operates in the obscurity of bodies, which are both the stakes and the principles of its efficacity' (*Masculine Domination*, 81).

be a sort of sociological continuation of Balzac's *Comédie Humaine*.[59] Gérard Mauger makes a comparison with Claude Simon: 'même longueur des phrases, même multiplication des incises – digressions, associations, homologies – même recherche du mot juste et de l'énoncé ajusté au plus près'.'[60] And Jeremy Lane likens Bourdieu's technique of 'discursive montage' (exemplified in *La Distinction*, but often used in his journal *Actes de la recherche en sciences sociales*) – which incorporates different forms of documents, photographs, advertisements, interview transcripts, statistics, reproductions of artworks, snippets from a play – to Mikhail Bakhtin's concept of the 'polyphonic' novel, which in Lane's words juxtaposes 'competing voices and speech genres, each expressing conflicting social, cultural, and political values'.[61]

Literature lovers may shudder at such comparisons, and there are counter-arguments. David Swartz sees Bourdieu's prose style as a reaction 'designed to shatter the notion of excellence as a sort of natural ability' in a country 'where clarity of expression (*la clarté*) is elevated to a national virtue, where it is seen as truly a mark of natural talent and intelligence'.[62] According to this interpretation, Bourdieu's writing style contains an implicit rejection of the politically-laden 'belle prose' taught at the École Normale Supérieure. We can also see Bourdieu's writing style (perhaps more convincingly) as an attempt to demarcate his work from literature, to give it an appearance of scientific rigour and seriousness. This suggestion is supported by an analysis in *Homo academicus*, in which Bourdieu charts reflexively 'l'espace des styles' available to the scientist, historian, philosopher, etc., and in which literature is a central point of reference (*HA*, 45-46). As Bourdieu often cited Spinoza (again) to say, 'bien qu'il n'y ait pas de force intrinsèque de la vérité, il y a une force de la croyance dans la vérité, de la croyance que produit l'apparence de la vérité' (*HA*, 44).[63] Bourdieu felt he needed the legitimacy and recognition that 'science' can provide to give symbolic force to his research, so that it would be treated with the attention and seriousness it requires.

---

59 Alain Caillé, 'Esquisse d'une Critique de l'Économie Générale de la Pratique', *Cahiers du LASA*, 12-13 (1992), 109-220 (p. 113).
60 Gérard Mauger, 'Lire Pierre Bourdieu', *Politis*, 686 (2002), 26-27 (p. 25). 'the same long phrases, the same multiplication of parenthetical clauses – digressions, associations, homologies – the same search for the perfectly appropriate word or phrase for the situation' (trans. J.S.).
61 Lane, *Bourdieu's Politics*, p. 136.
62 Swartz, *Culture and Power*, p. 13.
63 'although truth has no intrinsic force, there is an intrinsic force of belief in truth, of belief which produces the appearance of truth' (*Homo Academicus*, 29).

In the later phases of his career, when his position was established as a professor at the Collège de France and an international researcher, Bourdieu felt secure enough to experiment with more obviously 'literary' forms and language. The most obvious example is the multi-authored work *La Misère du monde*, published in 1993, in which interview transcripts are interspersed with short analyses presented as short stories, where the authors 'set the scene' for the interviews that follow. Written in plain prose, with few mentions of concepts or theories, these brief introductions read like works of realist fiction, and manage to evoke concrete and sometimes shocking realities, which may have been drained of their impact by more abstract analysis. Bourdieu insists, however, that they were informed by sociological theory and analysis, which sensitised the authors to important details (the description of the décor in their houses, their clothing and body language, as well as what they say) that provided the pertinent information on the interviewees. Bourdieu, at least, was happy with the result, which encourages and enables the reader to reflect back on his own experience: 'Le lecteur absorbe presque sans un bruit les instruments de la sociologie pour se comprendre lui-même'.[64]

The interviews in *La Misère du monde* are reproduced at length, if not in entirety, with few corrections or re-workings: a practice that was quite exceptional in contemporary French sociology. Expressing in direct speech the often brutal experiences and poor living conditions of the interviewees, they can reach, as Bourdieu writes, 'une intensité dramatique et une force émotionnelle proche de celle du texte littéraire' (*MM*, 922).[65] Indeed, the format is strongly reminiscent of theatrical scripts. In one of the interviews, 'Avec un dealer portoricain de Harlem' (*MM*, 211-17), there are even what seem like stage directions: 'ce coin en plus est frustrant, tu sais [*aspirant alors de la cocaïne et secouant la tête*]'.[66] Bourdieu claims that hearing, as it were 'directly', from these individuals, whose real voices are rarely heard in published material, can be a first step towards empathy and understanding their situations, by weakening our preconceptions, resistances and hostilities. 'Capables de toucher et d'émouvoir, de parler à la sensibilité, sans sacrifier au goût du sensationnel, [les entretiens transcrits] peuvent entraîner les conversions de la pensée et de regard qui sont souvent le préalable de la compréhension' (*MM*,

---

[64] Graw, 'Que Suis-Je?' 'The reader absorbs almost without noticing the instruments of sociology to understand himself' (trans. J.S.).
[65] 'a dramatic intensity and an emotional force close to those of a literary text' (*Weight of the World*, 623).
[66] 'That place is frustrating you know [*sniffing more cocaine and shaking his head*]' (*Weight of the World*, 433).

922).⁶⁷ Bourdieu seems to have reversed his position here since *Les Règles* where he writes: 'ce n'est pas la sympathie qui conduit à la compréhension véritable, c'est la compréhension véritable qui conduit à la sympathie' (*RA*, 494).⁶⁸ We should probably dialecticise (set up a to-and-fro, backwards-and-forwards) between these two positions: empathy and understanding being complementary, as we have been seeing, through *amor intellectualis*.

La Misère du monde remains, for all that, rather a flat read. As Günter Grass remarked to Bourdieu when they met in 1999,⁶⁹ 'il n'y a pas d'humour dans ce genre de livre. Il manque le comique de l'échec, qui joue un grand rôle dans mes histoires, les absurdités découlant de certaines confrontations'.⁷⁰ Grass does not suggest we should make light of the situations depicted and analysed in *La Misère du monde*, which represent very real human tragedies. Yet Grass argues that tragedy is not incompatible with comedy. Grass cites as examples from the literary tradition Voltaire's *Candide* or Diderot's *Jacques le Fataliste*. '[Ce] sont des livres où les conditions sociales décrites sont également affreuses. N'empêche que même dans la douleur et l'échec, la capacité humaine d'être comique et, dans ce sens, victorieux s'impose'.⁷¹ Laughter in the face of tragedy (what Beckett calls the '*risus purus* (…) the laugh that laughs – silence please – at that which is unhappy'⁷²) is also a form of defiance. Bourdieu, however, appears to resist this idea of employing comic effects in his writing, even implying that it is a sign of the times – and of the 'révolution conservatrice' he believed was in full swing – that intellectuals (including Grass) felt the need to be 'entertainers', as if they had been reduced to the status of court jesters. 'On nous dit: vous n'êtes pas drôles. Mais l'époque n'est vraiment pas drôle ! Vraiment, il n'y a pas de quoi rire'.⁷³

---

67 'Being able to touch and move the reader, to reach the emotions, without giving in to sensationalism, they [the interview transcripts] can produce the shifts in thinking and seeing that are often the precondition of comprehension' (*Weight of the World*, 623).
68 'it is not sympathy which leads to true understanding, but true understanding which leads to sympathy' (*Rules*, 303).
69 Pierre Bourdieu and Günter Grass, 'La tradition "d'ouvrir sa gueule"', *Le Monde*, 3 December 1999.
70 'there is no humour in such books. The comedy of failure, which plays such an important role in my stories, is missing—the absurdities arising from certain confrontations.' Bourdieu and Grass, 'The "Progressive" Restoration', *New Left Review*, 14 (2002), 63-77 (p. 64).
71 'Voltaire's *Candide* or Diderot's *Jacques le fataliste*, for example, are books in which the circumstances of the time are also appalling, and yet the human ability to present a comic and, in this sense, victorious figure, even through pain and failure, perseveres.' Bourdieu and Grass, 'The "Progressive" Restoration', p. 65.
72 Samuel Beckett, *Watt* (New York: Grove, 1959), p. 48.
73 'we're told we lack humour. But the times aren't funny! There's really nothing to

4. Science and Literature   121

Bourdieu's repeated insistence on the scientist's *sérieux* no doubt gives an unduly severe image of his writing, which is not without its amusements: literary puns and plays on words, pervasive irony, paradoxes, and 180-degree turns (as Slavoj Žižek cites Bertolt Brecht to say, 'there is no dialectics without humour: the dialectical reversals are deeply connected to comical twists and unexpected shifts of perspective'[74]). Even Bourdieu's field analyses have a certain – malign? – comedy, for instance when he tracks the exchanges of symbolic capital between writers and intellectuals:

> Mauriac écrivant une préface à un livre de Sollers: l'aîné célèbre écrit une préface et transmet du capital symbolique, et en même temps, il manifeste sa capacité de découvreur et sa générosité de protecteur de la jeunesse qu'il reconnaît et qui se reconnaît en lui (…) Lévi-Strauss écrit une préface à l'œuvre de Mauss par laquelle il s'approprie le capital symbolique de l'auteur de l'*Essai sur le Don*. Je vous laisse réfléchir sur tout ça.[75]

Bourdieu also saw a comedic effect in his reflexive analysis in *Homo academicus*, which puts the author himself on display (like the central character in David Garnett's short story *A Man in the Zoo*, evoked by Bourdieu to illustrate the strange situation of the analyst, who after an argument with his girlfriend offers himself as an exhibit in the local zoo, and is put in a cage with a chimpanzee and with a sign asking visitors 'not to tease the man with personal remarks'). 'Grâce à moi, avec moi', Bourdieu writes, 'l'Homo classificateur est tombé dans ses propres classements. Je trouve ça plutôt comique. Je crois que mon livre devrait faire beaucoup rire' (*I*, 192).[76] Indeed, in a 1989 interview Bourdieu's first – and perhaps best – piece of advice to any aspiring sociologists is to 'have fun!'

> The craft of the sociologist is one of the most pleasant and enriching activities one can indulge in, spanning the whole gamut of intellectual practices and skills, from those of the novelist laboring to create emotions and character to

---

laugh about'. Bourdieu and Grass, 'The "Progressive" Restoration', p. 65.
74 Slavoj Žižek, *Organs Without Bodies* (London: Routledge, 2004), p. 58.
75 Pierre Bourdieu, 'Les Conditions Sociales de la Ccirculation internationale des idées', *Romanistische Zeitschrift für Literaturgeschichte / Cahiers d'Histoire des Littératures Romanes* 14 (1989), 1-10; also published in *Actes de la recherche en sciences sociales*, 145 (2002), 3-8. 'Mauriac writing a preface to a book by Sollers: the famous elder writes a preface and transmits symbolic capital, and at the same time, manifests his talent as a discoverer and generosity as a protector of young writers whom he recognises and who recognise themselves in him (…) Lévi-Strauss writes a preface for a work by Mauss by which he appropriates the symbolic capital of the author of *The Gift*. I leave you to reflect on all that' (trans. J.S.).
76 'Thanks to me, and with me, "Homo classifier" has fallen into his own classifications. I find this somewhat comic, and I believe that my book should raise a good laugh' (*Political Interventions*, 150).

those of the mathematician striving to capture the world in abstract models and equations. We must repel any unilateral, unidimensional and monomaniacal definition of sociological practice and resist all attempts to impose one.[77]

Nonetheless, we have seen that Bourdieu tried consistently to distance himself from writing 'too well', or from giving 'too much' pleasure, in order to conform to certain conventions by which we recognise 'serious' and 'scientific' thought. As Bourdieu commented to Hans Haacke, if philosophers and social scientists make too many jokes, evoke too much pathos, use too colourful language, or make too many references to popular culture, etc., they are immediately assumed (quite often correctly) to be chasing success at the expense of academic standards (cf. *LE,* 111-12).

It is not only that Bourdieu's sociology drew inspiration from literature. Writers have also been inspired by Bourdieu's sociology. Several of the interviews in *La Misère du monde* were indeed adapted for the stage in 1998, by Didier Bezace in *Le Jour et la nuit*. Günter Grass also admits to a temptation to mine *La Misère du monde* for raw material, suggesting that sociological research can form the basis for literary works. If there is a 'Bourdieusian' literary writer, however, it is undoubtedly Annie Ernaux, author of (among other works) *Les Armoires vides, La Honte,* and *La Place*. Ernaux has spoken frequently of Bourdieu's influence on her writing, including in the obituary she wrote for *Le Monde*: 'les textes de Bourdieu ont été pour moi un encouragement à persévérer dans mon entreprise d'écriture, à dire, entre autres, ce qu'il nommait le refoulé social'.[78] This was not a case of direct inspiration, Ernaux explains in a later essay. Her desire to write preceded her reading of Bourdieu. Instead, she says, 'ce que je dois à Bourdieu, (…) c'est une injonction à prendre comme matière d'écriture ce qui jusque-là m'avait paru "au-dessus de la littérature"'.[79] It is as if Bourdieu legitimated the subject-matter and style of Ernaux's books, at a time when she had been drawn to writing an 'experimental' novel, in the genre of the then fashionable *Nouveau Roman*.

In an interview with the sociologist Isabelle Charpentier, Ernaux speaks of discovering what Bourdieu means by *'distance objectivante'* during the writing of *La Place*. We can see what she means when Ernaux reflexively discusses

---

77 Wacquant, 'Towards a Reflexive Sociology', p. 54.
78 Annie Ernaux, 'Bourdieu: le chagrin', *Le Monde,* 5 May 2002. 'Bourdieu's texts have been an encouragement to persevere in my writing project, to speak, amongst other things, what he called the social unconscious' (trans. J.S.).
79 Annie Ernaux, 'La Preuve par Corps' in *Bourdieu et la littérature,* ed. Jean-Pierre Martin, pp. 23-27 (p. 26). 'What I owe to Bourdieu (…) is an injunction to take as my writing-matter what had previously seemed to me "beyond literature"' (trans. J.S.).

her writing practice, taking care, for instance, not to slip into either nostalgia or pathos for her working class origins.[80] In the later essay, she further elaborates that Bourdieu 'm'a aidée à concevoir ce que j'appelle 'l'écriture distanciée' (plutôt que 'plate')'.[81] Ernaux goes so far as to describes her genre of writing as 'autosociobiographie'; and on writing *La Place*, she comments: 'j'ai voulu travailler comme un ethnologue'.[82] Ernaux even uses sociological terms such as 'domination' or 'violence symbolique' in her writing, although she stresses that her works are very much rooted in 'des scènes vécues, des choses vues, des phrases entendues', and are not abstract analyses.[83]

Of course, we could (rather cynically) see a strategy by Ernaux to distinguish her work – with its 'true life' subject-matter and self-conscious 'écriture plate' – from run of the mill 'confessional' autobiographies and from the memoirs of childhood misery which proliferated in the 1990s: much as we have seen Zola try to avoid the suspicion of vulgarity by associating the gaze of the 'romancier expérimental' with the clinical gaze of the physician (cf. *RA*, 197-98). Nevertheless, Ernaux's works and personal biography (which provides its subject matter), resonate strongly with those of Bourdieu, and can complement his more abstract analyses. See for example the characterisation of Ernaux's working-class father in *La Place* – his shame at his accent, his constant fear 'd'être déplacé', his leitmotiv '*il ne faut pas péter plus haut qu'on l'a*':[84] a perfect illustration of Bourdieu's theory of how we internalize as habitus a 'sense of one's place' which leads us to keep our distance from what we consider beneath us and reject what seems beyond our reach (cf. *D*, 549).

Fiction and realism

The question of the relation between literature and science was one of the major problems facing French intellectuals from the mid-1960s. This question was brought into focus by changes in the hierarchies and relations between the scientific and humanistic disciplines in the French university field, and by a

---

80 Annie Ernaux, *La Place* (Paris: Gallimard, 1983), p. 46.
81 Annie Ernaux, 'La Preuve par corps', p. 27. 'he helped me to conceive of what I call "writing from a distance" (rather than "flat")' (trans. J.S.).
82 See Isabelle Charpentier, '"Quelque part entre la littérature, la sociologie et l'histoire…"', *Contextes*, 1 (2006) at http://contextes.revues.org/index74.html consulted on 26/08/11.
83 *Lettres en première autobiographie: 'Ernaux'*, in *L'École des Lettres*, 9 (2002-03), ed. Thierry Poyet and Fabrice Thumerel, p. 25.
84 Ernaux, *La Place*, pp. 58-61. 'don't have an overly high view of yourself' (trans. J.S.).

general educational shift in favour of more 'technological' studies, which were deemed to offer greater employment prospects. At first, the tipping balance of power towards the natural sciences, which were becoming the ideal of academic excellence, inspired scholars in the faculty of letters to try to give their work an air of scientific rigour and legitimacy. According to Bourdieu, this was the explanation behind the popularity of what he calls 'l'effet -logie': as philosophers, literary scholars, and historians began to borrow the techniques and lexicons of the nearby social sciences, in particular structural linguistics and anthropology, and to adopt a scientific-sounding *nom de guerre* ending in *-ique*, *-isme*, or *-logie* (CD, 16). In 1967 Derrida published *De la Grammatologie*, in 1969 Foucault published *L'Archéologie du Savoir*, Barthes launched his 'semiology', and so on. Indeed, for a time the theories grouped loosely under the banner of 'structuralism' were able to postpone the subordination of literary culture to that of science, by combining the prestige and profits (for a long time considered irreconcilable) of the appearance of scientific rigour with those of philosophical *hauteur* and fine writing (HA, 160-61).

The strategy of accumulating both literary capital and scientific capital was matched at the theoretical level by attempts to produce a 'synthesis' of literature and science. Encouraged by academic routines of reading, and by a mechanical transposition of the linguistic structuralism of Ferdinand de Saussure, semiology and structuralism treated any system of signs (for example, *the garment system, the food system, the car system, the furniture system*) as if it were a 'language'. It was only a small step for Barthes (and other theorists associated with the 'linguistic turn', who, around the time, began to say that the 'world is text') to conclude that there 'is' only writing (*écriture*). Indeed, Barthes explains in an article first published in 1968[85] that because literature assumes its 'Being' as language, while scientific language is a language 'qui s'ignore',[86] and because literature already englobes everything that science has ever said ('il n'est certainement pas une seule matière scientifique qui n'ait été à un certain moment traitée par la littérature universelle'[87]), it follows that literature must be *more* scientific than science. According to what would become a standard post-structuralist position, the science of 'literature' must therefore become homogenous with its object if it wishes to remain a science, that is, 'la science deviendra littérature, dans la

---

85 Roland Barthes, 'De la Science à la Littérature' in *Le Bruissement de la langue* (Paris: Éditions du Seuil, 1984), 13-20.
86 'is ignorant of itself' (trans. J.S.).
87 'there is certainly no scientific subject which has not been treated ant some time by universal literature' (trans. J.S.).

mesure où la littérature (...) est déjà, a toujours été, la science'.[88]

As we have seen, Bourdieu avoided involving himself in structuralist and post-structuralist debates, as he worked to establish his own position. It was only in his last course of lectures at the Collège de France in 2001, published as *Science de la science et réflexivité*, that he finally struck out at what he calls the 'délires "post-modernes"'[89] which, he warned, were sapping public confidence in science, and in social science in particular (*SSR*, 5-6). Bourdieu singles out for criticism a book published in 1979 by Bruno Latour and Steve Woolgar, *Laboratory Life: The Construction of Scientific Facts*,[90] which had achieved some prominence in the sociology of science. Citing as authorities Foucault and Derrida, and drawing on Greimas's semiology, Latour and Woolgar present their book as 'a first tentative step towards making clear the link between science and literature',[91] this link being that science is a discourse (and a fiction) among many.

Latour and Woolgar describe scientific facts as 'literary inscriptions' (with reference to Derrida), and 'statements' (with reference to Foucault), with no referent 'out there' in external or objective reality, but which only lead to other 'texts', from which they have also been generated. In this sense, they argue, science is a form of 'literary production'; scientists are 'writers and readers in the business of being convinced and convincing others';[92] their works are 'fictions' in the sense that they do not refer to 'reality'; and 'between scientists and chaos, there is nothing but a wall of archives, labels, protocol books, figures, and papers'.[93] Needless to say, in good 'reflexive' method Latour and Woolgar include their own work in this endless proliferation of texts, concluding that their 'own account is no more than *fiction*'.[94]

In making this case, Latour and Woolgar seem to be denying the existence of any objective reality beyond or 'outside' text (understood

---

88 'science will become literature, insomuch as literature (...) is already, and has always been, science' (trans. J.S.).
89 '"postmodern" rantings' (*Science*, 1).
90 Bruno Latour and Steve Woolgar, *Laboratory Life: The Construction of Scientific Facts* (Princeton, NJ: Princeton University Press, 1979).
91 Ibid., p. 261.
92 Ibid., p. 88.
93 Ibid., p. 245.
94 Ibid. p. 257. The authors also explain that a previous version had admitted that their analysis is 'ultimately unconvincing', but that the publishers had insisted this sentence be removed, because they 'were not in the habit of publishing anything that "proclaimed its own worthlessness"' (p. 284).

as a tissue or web of signifiers referring only to each other). This is what they say: 'the artificial reality, which participants describe in terms of an objective entity, has in fact been constructed by the use of transcription devices'. 'It is not simply that phenomena *depend on* certain material instrumentation; rather, the phenomena *are thoroughly constituted by* the material setting of the laboratory'. For example, 'the molecular weight of proteins could hardly be said to exist except by virtue of the centrifuge'.[95] 'Bref', Bourdieu summarises, with characteristic irony, 'la croyance naïvement réaliste des chercheurs en une réalité extérieure au laboratoire est une pure illusion dont seule peut les débarrasser une sociologie réaliste' (*SSR*, 57).[96] Yet if Bourdieu was concerned in his last series of lectures to affirm the existence of an independent, 'objective' reality, he had himself come dangerously close in the past to affirming a radical constructivist position. When Bourdieu resorts to *'as if thinking'* (cf. *MS*, 72), states that 'les fonctions sociales sont des fictions sociales' (*LL*, 49),[97] or writes that 'ultimately, objective relations do not exist and do not really realise themselves except in and through the *system of dispositions* of the agents, produced by the internalisation of objective conditions',[98] we might well mistake him (as we have seen Vandenberghe does) for a constructivist.

In fact, we can explain Bourdieu's strong and sometimes exclusive emphasis on the 'constructedness' of scientific knowledge in light of the opposition he was up against. Bourdieu indicates with reference to Gaston Bachelard that 'epistemology is always conjunctural: its propositions and thrust are determined by the principal scientific threat of the moment' (*IRS*, 174). In 1968, that threat came from positivist empiricism. 'En sociologie', *Le Métier de sociologue* states, 'l'empirisme occupe, ici et maintenant, le sommet de la hiérarchie des dangers épistémologiques' (*MS*, 95-96).[99] Bourdieu was brought therefore to stress (and sometimes over-emphasise) the steps of 'rupture' and 'construction', against empiricist positivism, which does not operate the break with direct

---

95 Ibid, pp. 64-65.
96 'In short, the researchers' naïvely realist belief in a reality external to the laboratory is a pure illusion, from which only a realist sociology can rid them' (*Science*, 27).
97 'social functions are social fictions' (trans. J.S.). Pierre Bourdieu, *Leçon sur la Leçon* (Paris: Éditions du Minuit, 1982), p. 49.
98 Bourdieu, 'Structuralism and Theory of Sociological Knowledge', p. 705.
99 'in sociology, here and now, empiricism ranks highest in the hierarchy or epistemological dangers' (*Craft*, 69).

experience. Similarly, in the context of the rising supremacy of radical constructivism and post-modernism, Bourdieu was brought more strongly to affirm the relation between the 'model' and 'reality', the existence of which, he claims, is so integral to their undertaking that it forms part of 'l'attitude naturelle' of scientific researchers (SSR, 137), which need hardly be stated. 'Ce postulat ontologique en suppose un autre', Bourdieu writes:

> l'idée qu'il y a du sens, de l'ordre, une logique, bref, quelque chose à comprendre dans le monde, y compris dans le monde social (contre ce que Hegel appelait 'l'athéisme du monde moral'); que l'on ne peut pas dire n'importe quoi à propos du monde ('*anything goes*', selon la formule chère à Feyerabend), parce que tout et n'importe quoi n'est pas possible dans le monde. Ce n'est pas sans quelque étonnement que l'on trouve une expression parfaite de ce postulat chez Frege: 'Si tout était dans un flux continu et que rien ne se maintenait fixé pour toujours, il n'y aurait pas de possibilité de connaître le monde et tout serait plongé dans la confusion (SSR, 137-38).[100]

Against the idea we have found in *Laboratory Life* that there is only 'chaos' beyond the ordering system of language, for Bourdieu the social world, like the natural world, has its own order and sense, and constant patterns in its changes, of which it is the scientist's role to discover the invisible structures, laws, and principles.

Yet as we have seen Bourdieu suggest in his reply to Vandenberghe, we can also find this 'realist' position in Bourdieu's earliest meta-scientific writings. In 'Structuralism and Theory of Sociological Knowledge' (1968), for instance, Bourdieu already cites the introduction to Hegel's *Philosophy of Right* against those who would 'deny the social world the immanent necessity they recognize in the natural one', and the quantum physicist Gustave Juvet, this time, to say: 'in the rushing flux of phenomena, in the ever changeable reality, the physicist observes something permanent'.[101] Like a sort of social physicist, the sociologist's

---

100 'This ontological postulate presupposes another one, the idea that there is meaning, an order, a logic, in short something to be understood in the world, including the social world (as opposed to what Hegel called "the atheism of the moral world"); that one cannot say whatever one likes about the world ("anything goes", in Feyerabend's phrase), because "anything and everything" is not possible in the world. Not without some surprise, one finds a perfect expression of this postulate in Frege: "If everything were in continual flux, and nothing maintained itself fixed for all time, there would no longer be any possibility of getting to know anything about the world and everything would be plunged in confusion"' (*Science*, 69).
101 Bourdieu, 'Structuralism and Theory of Sociological Knowledge', pp. 683; 689.

task, as Bourdieu sees it, is to 'translate' or objectify the structures of reality into systems of intelligible relations and their explicatory principles, through the lens of which we should be able understand and predict observable phenomena.

For all his interest in the 'relations' and 'cross-overs' between literature and science, then, Bourdieu insists that they should not be simply conflated or folded into one another. The crux of their difference is in their relation to the structural or relational reality 'beyond' or 'behind' experiential 'reality'. Whereas in the case of literature this reference is 'denied', 'euphemized' and 'veiled' (in the terms Bourdieu uses), and is given in the form of demonstrations and exemplifications, or better *'evocations'*, science, Bourdieu writes, 'ne vise pas à donner à voir, ou à sentir, mais à construire des systèmes de relations intelligibles capabes de rendre raison des données' (RA, 14),[102] which it accepts to submit to *'l'arbitrage du "réel"'* (SSR, 137).[103] Bourdieu writes:

> Le discours scientifique se distingue du discours de *fiction* – du roman, par exemple, qui se donne plus ou moins ouvertement pour un discours feint et fictif – en ce que, comme le remarque John Searle, il *veut dire* ce qu'il dit, il prend au sérieux ce qu'il dit et accepte d'en répondre, c'est-à-dire, le cas échéant, d'être convaincu d'erreur (HA, 43).[104]

In order for this distinction to hold, we need to maintain a conception of external reality, which has been lost by post-modern and post-structuralist theories, with the result that it has seemed logical to conflate literary and scientific discourses, since texts only referred to each other. This does not mean that Bourdieu falls into the trap of naïve realism or positivism. For Bourdieu, all scientific knowledge is constructed, and our experience of the 'real' is always mediated by the theory (which can continue to develop and progress over time). Nor does Bourdieu's conception of the difference between literature and science lead him to privilege scientific knowledge over the specific form of knowledge that literature can produce and provide. Bourdieu sees a 'resemblance in

---

102 'he aims not to offer (in)sight, or feeling, but to construct systems of intelligible relations capable of making sense of sentient data' (Rules, 18).
103 'the arbitration of the "real"' (Science, 70).
104 'Scientific discourse is distinct from the discourse of *fiction* – from the novel, for instance, which passes itself off more or less openly as a feigned and fictitious discourse – in that, as John Searle remarks, it *means* what it says, it takes seriously what it says and accepts responsibility for it, that is, if the case arises, for its mistakes' (Homo Academicus, 28).

difference' between literature and science, which are able to reveal the patterns and structures of reality in different ways. Bourdieu thus brings a non-reductive response to a problem that, at both the conceptual and institutional levels, had defined his intellectual generation, and which we will see him again confront in his cultural policy proposals for the reform of the education system (see Chapter 6).

5. Literature and Cultural Politics

In the last decade of his career, Bourdieu became a figure on the French political stage, following in the tradition of engaged public intellectuals including Foucault, Sartre, and Zola. This chapter explores the place of literature and literary effects within Bourdieu's wider political-intellectual project. First, it traces what Bourdieu calls 'La production de l'idéologie dominante', and explains the analogies between literary and political discourse, which is open therefore to literary modes of analysis and subversion. Next, it examines literature's function as a vehicle for critical or ideological messages, and the particular force that literature can contribute to symbolic struggles. Thirdly, the chapter explores the reasons behind Bourdieu's own interest in strategies and techniques exemplified in the literary and artistic fields, as we follow him moving towards the deployment of more 'literary' devices in his own sociological writing. Finally, the chapter discusses Bourdieu's attempts to establish or strengthen the organisational structures for collective and collaborative interventions by artists, writers, and intellectuals, including at an international scale – and the reasons for which his most ambitious initiatives (including for an International Parliament of Writers and *Liber*, an international book review) failed.

The production of the dominant ideology

In 1976, Bourdieu and Luc Boltanski published in *Actes de la recherche en sciences sociales,* the review Bourdieu had founded the previous year, a long article entitled 'La Production de l'idéologie dominante'.[1] An early example of what Bourdieu, in *Libre-échange,* would offer as a model for

---
1 Pierre Bourdieu and Luc Boltanski, 'La Production de l'idéologie dominante', *Actes de la recherche en sciences sociales,* 2/3 (1976), 3-73.

politically engaged research, able to 'produire des messages à plusieurs niveaux' (*LE*, 110),² 'La Production de l'idéologie dominante' combines text, photographs, cartoons, statistics, analysis, polemic and ironic humour, in a dissection of the neo-liberal *doxa* which was only just establishing itself as the ruling ideology in France. Although Bourdieu would later come to 'bannir l'usage du mot "idéologie"'³ from his work, as having too many misleading connotations of a theory of consciousness (which would be unable fully to explain embodied forms of practice) (*MP*, 216),⁴ this early text remains key to understanding important aspects of his later political interventions.⁵ For the purposes of this chapter, it can help to explain, in particular, Bourdieu's interest in 'cultural politics': in the role of cultural producers and works, including writers and literary texts, in ideological battles (or in his later terminology, 'luttes symboliques'), over the *sense* (meaning and direction) of social history. The significance and continued relevance of this text were confirmed when Raisons d'Agir, the independent publishing house Bourdieu co-founded in the late 1990s, re-published 'La Production de l'idéologie dominante' in book form in 2008.⁶

La Production de l'idéologie dominante begins with an introduction to the 'dominant discourse', which had reached ideological supremacy in the 1960s, taught and rewarded at elite schools including the *École nationale d'administration* and the *Institut d'études politiques de Paris*. This discourse was generated from a system of classification and schemes of thought and action – something like a 'generative grammar' (Chomsky) – which guided the opinions and judgments of the dominant. This system is what Bourdieu and Boltanski term 'l'idéologie dominante'. The 'dominant discourse' is then built up from elements of this structure, which fit together according to its rules. Thus we get a string of 'commonplaces' and 'received ideas', which the person versed in this discourse can produce quite fluently. The associations which are likely to have been brought to the mind of literary scholars, with the 'commonplace books' kept by students in the Renaissance (a sort of dictionary of beautifully expressed sayings by Classical authors

---

2 'to produce messages on several levels' (*Free Exchange*, 106).
3 'to shun the use of the word "ideology"' (*Meditations*, 181).
4 Lane, *Bourdieu's Politics*, pp. 49-50.
5 References to ideology still seem useful, however, on the basis of familiarity and for the purposes of communication, and so have been retained in this chapter, which will, however, begin to replace them with Bourdieu's preferred language of symbolic violence and symbolic struggle.
6 References will be to this edition.

on stock subjects, for the purposes of rhetorical composition), and with Flaubert's famous impatience with 'idées reçues', are not accidental. In their own work, Bourdieu and Boltanski construct an 'Encyclopédie des idées reçues et des lieux communs en usage dans les lieux neutres' – an evident pastiche of Flaubert's *Le Dictionnaire des idées reçues*, in which Flaubert documents the banalities and automaticised figures of speech that circulated in polite society in the nineteenth century. Bourdieu and Boltanski's 'Encyclopédie' collects exemplary formulations of the most frequently expressed ideas on the most commonly cited subjects in the dominant discourse, organised and cross-referenced in alphabetical order, from several dozen works, interviews, and articles. The 'Encyclopédie' then serves as a point of reference for the rest of *La Production de l'idéologie dominante*, whenever one of the shared preoccupations (commonplaces) and opinions (the 'idées reçues') of the dominant class is mentioned, usually under inverted commas (*ID*, 17-22).

Bourdieu and Boltanski's intention was not only to amuse (although, picking out the most recognisable traits of what is supposed to be a 'discours d'importance' does, they note, produce an almost automatic *effect of parody*). Bourdieu and Boltanski insist on the 'scientificity' of the 'Encyclopédie', to which they give a three-page explanation and a full bibliography. Those it cites belonged to a real group, which was relatively coherent and conscious of itself (as shown by inter-citations and social inter-connections), and the dictionary is an accurate if distilled breakdown of their discourse (*ID*, 19). Clearly concerned that their analysis should not be dismissed as a joke, their protestations cannot hide, however, that the authors were also having some fun – as shown by the gratuitous mock title page, printed in the style of the nineteenth century, complete with crest and date of publication in Latin numerals (*ID*, 15). Then again, even the humour of the 'Encyclopédie' was in a sense 'serious', in that it reinforced its quasi-political purpose – the same, in fact, as that which Flaubert intended for his own *Dictionnaire*. Flaubert's hope had been that 'une fois qu'on l'aurait lu on n'osât plus parler, de peur de dire naturellement une des phrases qui s'y trouvent'.[7] As we will see, Bourdieu also recommended this ability to *resist* words, and resist repeating them, as one of the principal 'instruments of defence' against the dominant discourse and ideology, which draws strength from appearing self-evident.

---

7 Gustave Flaubert, 'Lettre à Louise Colet, 1852', in *Correspondance*, Series 3, 1852-1854 (Paris: Conard, 1927), p. 67. 'once you read it you wouldn't dare to speak, lest you let slip one of the phrases it contains' (trans. J.S.).

According to Bourdieu and Boltanski's analysis, the dominant ideology is structured by a fundamental opposition between the *old* and the *new* (or the past and the future, the traditional and the modern, etc.). Into one or the other of these categories fits each of the other components, forming opposing pairs: 'fermé/ouvert, bloqué/débloqué, petit/grand, clos/ouvert, local/universel, etc.' As a rule, the first term is never evoked positively. This schema can be applied in any circumstances and to any object: the small village and the large town, the grocery story and the drugstore, pre-war and post-war, France and America. 'Quel que soit le terrain auquel il s'applique', Bourdieu and Boltanski write, 'le schème produit deux termes opposés et hiérarchisés, et du même coup la relation qui les unit, c'est-à-dire le processus d'évolution (ou d'involution) conduisant de l'un à l'autre (soit par exemple le petit, le grand et la croissance)' (*ID*, 57).[8] The sequences of noun and adjective produced in this way can then be strung together and elaborated to create a flow of discourse, which (like an improvised narrative) can incorporate several themes:

> Chacune des oppositions fondamentales évoque, plus ou moins directement, toutes les autres. C'est ainsi par exemple que de l'opposition entre le 'passé' et 'avenir' on peut passer à l'opposition entre le 'petit' et le 'grand', au double sens de 'planétaire' et de 'complexe', ou encore à l'opposition entre le 'local', c'est-à-dire le 'provincial' ou le 'national' (et le nationaliste), et le cosmopolite qui, prise sous un autre rapport, s'identifie à l'opposition entre l'"immobile' et le 'mobile' (*ID*, 57).[9]

What Bourdieu and Boltanski present in *La Production de l'idéologie dominante* is an 'ideal' model, which, they admit, may strike their readers as being 'trop beau pour être vrai' (*ID*, 17).[10] Individual habitus may have formed incompatible attachments (for example, to a romanticised vision of village life), and some may have internalised imperfectly the dominant ideology, leading to contradictions within the system; although

---

[8] 'Wherever it is applied, the scheme produces two opposed and hierarchised terms, and at the same time the relation which unifies them, which is to say the process of evolution (or of involution) from one to another (for example the small, the big, and growth)' (trans. J.S.).

[9] 'Each of the fundamental oppositions evokes, more or less directly, all of the others. Thus for example from the opposition between the "past" and "future" one can pass to the opposition between the "small" and "large", in the double sense of "planetary" and "complex", or else to the opposition between the "local", which is to say the "provincial" or the "national" (and the nationalist), and the cosmopolitan which, from another angle, is identified with the opposition between the "immobile" and the "mobile"' (trans. J.S.).

[10] 'too good to be true' (trans. J.S.).

the authors note the extreme homogeneity of the French dominant class, in terms both of social origin and education, reduced discrepancies and discord. To give an image of the shared culture, values and beliefs, of the French political class (which is also part of what gives an elite its supreme *confidence*), *La Production de l'idéologie dominante* includes a photograph of the 'Simone Weil' class of 1974, being led down the stairs of the École Nationale d'Administration by Michel Poniatowski (then Minister of State and Minister of the Interior, and himself an aluminus of the ENA), with his pet... a German short-tailed pointer, and Mlle Florence Hugodot, 26, sole woman in a group of besuited graduates, who seem to be sharing a private joke, ranked in files behind their paternalistic leader, who looks confidently past the camera, as if towards a bright and secure future.

'La Pensée Tietmeyer'

Twenty years later, in a presentation delivered at the University of Freiburg, Bourdieu again drew inspiration from the literary tradition to analse the functioning of the neo-liberal discourse, which was by now massively dominant. Since he was speaking at a university known for its tradition of hermeneutical analysis, Bourdieu borrowed from its tools of textual criticism to analyse an interview published in *Le Monde* with Hans Tietmeyer,[11] then president of the Deutsche Bundesbank. Bourdieu's analysis (which it is useful to cite at some length) attempts to uncover the hidden presuppositions and unspoken implications behind Tietmeyer's apparently anodyne statements, and to expose the rhetorical sleight of hand and automaticised figures of speech which enabled it to appear uncontroversial to the majority of its readers:

> Voici ce que dit le 'grand prêtre du deutsche mark': 'L'enjeu aujourd'hui, c'est de créer les conditions favorables à une croissance durable, et la confiance des investisseurs. Il faut donc contrôler les budgets publics'. C'est-à-dire – il sera plus explicite dans les phrases suivantes – enterrer le plus vite possible l'État social, et entre autres choses, ses politiques sociales et culturelles dispendieuses, pour rassurer les investisseurs qui aimeraient mieux se charger eux-mêmes de leurs investissements culturels. (...) Je continue ma lecture: 'réformer le système de protection sociale'. C'est-à-dire enterrer le *welfare state* et ses politiques de protection sociale, bien faites pour ruiner la confiance des investisseurs (...). 'Démanteler

---

11 Lucas Delattre, 'Le président de la Bundesbank parie sur l'euro en 1999', *Le Monde*, 17 October 1996.

les rigidités sur les marchés du travail, de sorte qu'une nouvelle phase de croissance ne sera atteinte à nouveau que si *nous* faisons un effort de flexibilité sur le marché de travail'. Splendide travail rhétorique, qui peut se traduire: Courage travailleurs ! Tous ensemble faisons l'effort de flexibilité qui *vous* est demandé ! (...) Les travailleurs, s'ils lisaient un journal aussi indiscutablement sérieux que Le Monde, entendraient immédiatement ce qu'il faut entendre: travail de nuit, travail pendant les week-ends, horaires irréguliers, pression accrue, stress, etc. On voit que, 'sur-le-marché-du-travail', fonctionne comme une sorte d'épithète homérique susceptible d'être accroché à un certain nombre de mots, et l'on pourrait être tenté, pour mesurer la flexibilité du langage de M. Hans Tietmeyer, de parler par exemple de flexibilité ou de rigidité sur les marchés financiers. L'étrangeté de cet usage dans la langue de bois de M. Hans Tietmeyer permet de supposer qu'il ne saurait être question, dans son esprit, de 'démanteler les rigidités sur les marchés financiers', ou de 'faire un effort de flexibilité sur les marchés financiers'. Ce qui autorise à penser que, contrairement à ce que peut laisser croire le 'nous' du 'si nous faisons un effort' de M. Hans Tietmeyer, c'est aux travailleurs et à eux seuls qu'est emandé cet effort de flexibilité (CF1, 51-54).[12]

Again, we can notice that there is a humorous effect produced by treating Hans Tietmeyer's text as if were a literary commentary passage,

---

12 'Here is what "the grand priest of the deutsche mark" has to say: "The important thing today, is to create conditions favourable to durable growth, and the confidence of investors. We should therefore control public budgets". Which is to say – and he will be more explicit later on – bury as quickly as possible the State, and among other things, its costly social and cultural policies, to reassure investors who would prefer to take care of their own cultural investments. (...) I'll continue my reading: "reform the system of social protection". Which is to say bury the Welfare State and its policies of social protection, which risk ruining the confidence of investors (...). "Dismantle rigidities on the work market, since a new phase of growth will not be achieved unless we make an effort for flexibility on the employment market". A splendid rhetorical turn of phrase, which can be translated as: Take courage workers! All together lets make the effort for flexibility which is demanded of *you!* Workers, if they read a newspaper which is so undeniably serious as *Le Monde*, would immediately understand what this means: nightshifts, week-end work, irregular hours, increased pressure, stress, etc.. We can notice that "on-the-employment-market" functions as a sort of Homeric epithet which can be stuck on at the end of a phrase, and we might be tempted, to measure the flexibility or the rigidity of Mr. Hans Tietmeyer's language, to speak for example about flexibility or rigidity on the financial markets. The strangeness of this usage in Mr. Hans Tietmeyer's cant allows us to suppose that it would never be question, in his heart, of "dismantling the rigidities on the financial markets", or of "making an effort for flexibility on the financial market". Which also allows us to suppose that, contrary to what is suggested by that "we" in "if we make an effort" from Mr. Hans Tietmeyer, it is from the workers and from them alone that is demanded this effort of flexibility' (trans. J.S.).

appearing to raise its status, but simultaneously deflating its rhetoric, by 'translating' the 'Neoliberal Newspeak' into plain words.[13] The effect of aestheticisation is also to defamiliarise the text, drawing our attention to its *form* and *structure* (as if we were approaching a literary work), when in the course of a distracted and uncritical reading we may simply have followed Tietmeyer's train of thought.

Yet Bourdieu was not, as we know, an adept of hermeneutic analysis, and the first thing he he would have added to theories of reception was to ask how the 'fusion of horizons' (Gadamer) which brings our understanding in line with that of Tietmeyer's text (or with any literary work) occurs. According to Bourdieu, 'si les mots du discours de M. Hans Tietmeyer passent si facilement, c'est qu'ils ont cours partout' (*CF1*, 55).[14] Starting as a drip in the 1930s, formulated in think-tanks and published subsequently in reviews such as *Preuves* and *Der Monat* (affiliated with the Congress for Cultural Freedom, an anti-communist *internationale* of intellectuals founded in 1950 and funded secretly by the CIA, until this link was revealed to scandal in 1967), the neo-liberal *doxa* now saturated the airwaves, and flowed from the mouths of politicians, journalists, 'organic' intellectuals, and simple citizens, until, by a process of *immersion* familiar to language teachers, it could be understood and reproduced more or less fluently almost everywhere, without hesitation or forethought.

According to Bourdieu, the first line of defence against the dominant ideology was therefore to understand how it was produced and disseminated, and by whom. Bourdieu directs us to research in this area which had been going on already, by scholars in Britain, America and France.[15] One of the services which the academic community could provide to the public, Bourdieu suggests, would be to circulate this information widely, and in accessible formats, so that they would see where their ideas come from, and whose interests they express (*CF1*, 34-35). Another instrument of defence, however (and one which has been losing

---

13 Bourdieu makes this reference to George Orwell's *Nineteen Eighty-Four* in the title of his article with Loïc Wacquant, 'Neoliberal Newspeak. Notes on the New Planetary Vulgate', *Radical Philosophy*, 105 (2001), 2-5.
14 'if Mr. Hans Tietmeyer's words come so easily, it is because they are everywhere' (trans. J.S.).
15 Bourdieu's references are: Keith Dixon, 'Les Évangélistes du Marché', *Liber*, 32 (1997), 5-6, expanded into a book by Raisons d'Agir in 1998; and Pierre Grémion, *Preuves: une revue européenne à Paris* (Paris: Juilliard, 1989), and *Intelligence de l'anticommunisme: le Congrès pour la liberté de la culture à Paris 1950-1975* (Paris: Fayard, 1995).

its sense of purpose), is simply the ability to read texts closely, in order to understand how they can affect us at an aesthetic as well as cognitive level – for instance, in Tietmeyer's text and others like it, by playing on the evocative connotations of 'openness', 'flexibility', 'adaptability', 'mobility', etc., which make 'liberalism' sound like the road to universal emancipation (*I*, 351). We can find many of the sharpest tools for this sort of analysis in literary criticism: honed by the study of some of the most powerful and suggestive texts ever written. Standing back from language and examining our immediate responses to it, we open a space for reflection in which we can consider other possibilities. It is little surprise, then, that when asked by Didier Éribon how to oppose the imposition of dominant values, Bourdieu replied by citing the poet Francis Ponge: 'C'est alors qu'enseigner l'art de résister aux paroles devient utile, l'art de ne dire que ce que l'on veut dire. Apprendre à chacun l'art de fonder sa propre rhétorique est une œuvre de salut public' (*QS*, 17).[16]

On aesthetics and ideology

One of the weaknesses of progressive movements against neo-liberalism, according to Bourdieu, was that they had underestimated its symbolic dimension, and lacked the cognitive and expressive instruments with which to combat it. This meant that they were struggling against not only brute domination and exploitation, but also against 'symbolic domination', which controls how people see the world and their place within it: a 'soft' form of domination, which is accepted as part of normal reality by those who suffer it, and who may even resist changes in the *status quo*. As we have seen, the dominant ideology was spread by the media, journalists, and politicians, but it was also spread by experts, who played in an important role in supporting the dominant order. The elite no longer justified its rule by God-given right, but by competence and merit, and backed up their political decisions with science (particularly economics), the new religion. These factors combined, on one hand, to reinforce the confidence of the elite in their own good sense, and on the other to encourage popular disengagement from politics: either on the basis that it was best left to the experts, or from resignation in the face of 'economic realities'.

---

[16] 'This is when teaching the art of resisting words becomes useful, the art of saying only what one wants to say. Teaching everyone the art of founding their own rhetoric is a public service' (trans. J.S.).

5. Literature and Cultural Politics 139

Since ideology, in Bourdieu's view, played such an important part in the maintenance of the social order, he also saw a role for critical intellectuals, including artists and writers, to counteract its effects. Academics and researchers could first of all meet the dominant on the terrain of theory: 'À cette idéologie, qui habille de raison pure une pensée simplement conservatrice', he argued, 'il est important d'opposer des raisons, des arguments, des réfutations, des démonstrations, et donc de faire du travail scientifique' (*CF1*, 60).[17] Particularly close to Bourdieu's heart was the idea of an *'économie du bonheur'*, which would link social and economic policy, by counting the social costs and benefits of economic decisions. Bourdieu even hoped eventually to see a role for the sociologist at the level of political decision-making, in the way that economists are consulted currently (*I*, 354-55). Until then, researchers could expose the suffering caused by neo-liberal policies, and try to spread this information widely (as Bourdieu and his co-workers did in *La Misère du monde*). Indeed, as part of this Bourdieu suggested turning economic arguments back against policy-makers:

> même si cela peut paraître cynique, il faut retourner contre l'économie dominante ses propres armes, et rappeler, que, dans la logique de l'intérêt bien compris, la politique strictement économique n'est pas nécessairement économique – en insécurité des personnes et des biens, donc en police, etc. (...) Qu'est-ce que cela coûtera à long terme en débauchages, en souffrances, en maladies, en suicides, en alcoolisme, en consommation de drogue, en violence dans la famille, etc. autant de choses qui coûtent très cher, en argent, mais aussi en souffrance? (*CF1*, 45)[18]

Neo-liberalism also had its 'organic intellectuals' – like Anthony Giddens, theorist of the 'third way' followed by Tony Blair and Bill Clinton, against whom Bourdieu took a personal stand (*I*, 449; 471) – and it was important for those who had the expertise to confront them on their own ground.

It was not only by opposing rational arguments, though, that intellectuals could help in the struggle against neo-liberalism. As has often

---

17 'Against this ideology, which dresses as reason pure and simple a system of thought that is simply conservative, it is important to oppose reasons, arguments, refutations, demonstrations, and therefore to do scientific work' (trans. J.S.).
18 'even if it can appear cynical, we should turn back against the dominant economy its own weapons, and point out that, according to the logic of well-understood interest, strictly economic policies are not necessarily economical – in terms of insecurity of people and things, so in policing, etc. (...) What will that cost in the long term in job losses, suffering, sickness, suicides, alcoholism, drug-taking, domestic violence, etc. so many things which are very costly, in money, but also in suffering?' (trans. J.S.).

been observed, modern capitalism functions in large part by manufacturing desires, through advertising, films, bestsellers, etc., which celebrate consumer culture, and the materialistic, militaristic and moral values of the dominant. It was also important, therefore, to fight back with counter-discourses which could function at the somatic and perceptual (aesthetic) level, and change the way people think about the direction the world is taking. Bourdieu suggests a particular role in this project for writers: experts in the creation of alternative and future worlds, they could give 'forme visible et sensible aux conséquences prévisibles mais non encore visibles de la politique néolibérale' (*I*, 475).[19] Writers also hold the symbolic power to challenge dominant representations and the system of values they uphold: for instance by giving voice and visibility to the victims of the political and economic order (immigrants, illegal workers, the poor), who are more often blamed for society's woes. 'Les mots', as Bourdieu cites Sartre to say, 'peuvent faire des ravages' (*CD*, 177),[20] and the power to change how we think about and see the world is also a political force. We can find many precedents for this sort of work in the literary tradition, from Zola's series *Les Rougon-Macquart*, which portrays the prostitution, alcoholism, and violence that accompanied the second wave of the industrial revolution, to George Orwell's *Nineteen Eighty-Four*, which has entered the popular consciousness, and provides a constant point of reference – and a beacon of warning – in today's world of surveillance cameras, wars waged in the name of 'peace' and 'freedom', political jargon that narrows the range of thought, and even computer-generated (in the book, mechanically produced) music and novels.

Another of the ways in which writers and artists could contribute to the symbolic struggle was by using the 'symbolic weapons' of comedy, parody, satire, and pastiche, to unsettle our usual confidence and belief in figures of authority. A particular group Bourdieu singled out for such action were journalists, and especially those whom he termed 'media-intellectuals', who used their power over the means of cultural production and consecration (in particular television) to exert considerable influence over French political and cultural life. 'Ces nouveaux maîtres à penser sans pensée', Bourdieu writes, 'monopolisent le débat public au détriment des professionnels de la politique (parlementaires, syndicalistes, etc.); et

---

[19] 'give visible and sensible form to consequences of neoliberal policy that are predictable but not yet visible' (*Political Interventions*, 387).
[20] 'words, said Sartre, can wreak havoc' (*Other Words*, 149).

5. Literature and Cultural Politics   141

aussi des intellectuels', whose traditional function they had replaced (*RA*, 556).[21] But with neither the specialist competence nor the critical acumen to present serious resistance to the powerful and their powerful discourse, even their challenges served to ratify the existing order, as having stood up to scrutiny and debate (*LE*, 58-59). Again, there is a strong tradition of this sort of symbolic action in France, including the caricaturists of the *Ancien régime* in 1789 and Honoré Daumier in the 1830s, *Le Canard enchaîné*, a satirical newspaper founded in 1915, through to the comedian Coluche and the latex puppets on *Les Guignols de l'info*, a Canal-Plus television show.

Of course, art alone cannot change the world, and Bourdieu puts us on our guard against the belief (which gained some currency in the 1960s) that literature is in itself subversive. Most 'symbolic revolutions', Bourdieu notes, remain purely symbolic, leaving social mechanisms and power structures intact (*CD*, 177; *MP*, 156). Yet whereas the dominant ideology tends to close the fan of possible futures, for instance by presenting global 'free-market' capitalism as, if not the best of all possible worlds, then at least the only 'reasonable' and 'rational' path – 'there is no alternative' (Thatcher); 'Es gibt keine Alternativen' (Schröder) – writers and artists could play a significant role in the properly symbolic struggle over the *sense* (direction and meaning) of the social world: of its history, and so also – as George Orwell well knew – of its future. This symbolic struggle can then lead to social struggles, which can change systems and structures. As Bourdieu writes: 'la croyance que tel ou tel avenir, désiré ou redouté, est possible, probable ou inévitable, peut, dans certaines conjonctures, mobiliser autour d'elle tout un groupe, et contribuer ainsi à favoriser ou à empêcher l'avènement de cet avenir' (*MP*, 277–78),[22] and literature and art can contribute to this mobilising effect.

A major weakness of most artistic and literary interventions however, according to Bourdieu, is that, able to show, point, or evoke, they cannot explain or render intelligible (*I*, 380). Indeed, writers and artists who intervene practically in the political and public spheres risk embarrassing themselves when they are asked to explain their actions – bringing them into uncanny proximity with journalists and journalist-intellectuals whom Bourdieu also criticises for out-stepping their field of specialism, and for

---

21 'These new masters of thoughtless thought monopolize public debate to the detriment of professionals of politics (parliamentary legislators, trade union leaders, etc.), and also to the detriment of intellectuals' (*Rules*, 346).
22 'the belief that this or that future, either desired or feared, is possible, probable or inevitable can, in some historical conditions, mobilize a group around it and so help to favour or prevent the coming of that future' (*Meditations*, 235).

presenting simplistic interpretations of complicated problems. Bourdieu therefore thought that different specialists should support each other, combining their expertise – just as he himself supported the candidacy of the comedian Coluche in the 1981 presidential election, which, he explained, was not just a joke, but a way to 'rappeler que n'importe qui peut être candidat',[23] and expose the closure and insularity of the French political field (*CP*, 55-56; *I*, 163). Bourdieu hoped that this kind of collaboration and support could be organised by setting up inter-disciplinary groupings, able to call on the diverse talents of their members.

Bourdieu imagined, for instance, 'une émission critique qui associerait des chercheurs avec des artistes, des chansonniers, des satiristes, pour soumettre à l'épreuve de la satire et du rire ceux qui, parmi les journalistes, les hommes politiques, et les "intellectuels" médiatiques, tombent de manière trop flagrante dans l'abus de pouvoir symbolique' (*I*, 394).[24] And he proposed to the International Parliament of Writers that it should 'orienter et organiser un travail continu et approfondi, associant les écrivains et les spécialistes, sur des problèmes politiques, économiques, culturels importants' (*I*, 290-91).[25] These groupings would be the seeds for Bourdieu's dream of an 'intellectuel collectif, interdisciplinaire et international' (*I*, 474-75),[26] which would be able to co-ordinate joint actions at an international level and mobilise a symbolic force equivalent to that of the mainstream media and public relations industry (which were already operating on a global scale). As we will see, there were considerable barriers to the realisation of these projects, especially their extension to the international level, and Bourdieu's most ambitious plans (including for the International Parliament of Writers) failed. Firstly, however, it is useful to consider how, at the level of individual practice, Bourdieu himself took advice and guidance from writers and artists to give his own political interventions greater symbolic force, and to introduce some of the artists and works he cites as possible models for new forms of symbolic action by intellectuals.

---

23 'anyone can be a candidate' (trans. J.S.).
24 'a critical programme bringing together scholars and artists, singers and satirists, with the aim of putting to the test of satire and laughter those journalists, politicians, and media "intellectuals" who fall in too glaring fashion into abuse of symbolic power' (*Political Interventions*, 323).
25 'orient and organize a continuous and deepening work, associating writers and specialists, on important political, economic and cultural problems' (*Political Interventions*, 239).
26 'a "collective intellectual", interdisciplinary and international' (*Political Interventions*, 387).

A politics of form

In 1999, Bourdieu met with the Nobel laureate Günter Grass in front of an audience of trade-unionists to discuss the role of intellectuals in society, stylistic practices in literature and sociology, neo-liberalism, and other topics. The dialogue was sent out on *Radio Bremen*, and excerpts from their conversation were printed simultaneously in *Le Monde* and the German weekly *Die Zeit*.[27] In 2002, a longer version of their dialogue was published in the *New Left Review*.[28] The title under which the original transcript was published in *Le Monde,* refers to the European 'tradition "d'ouvrir sa gueule"', to speak out against injustice and the abuse of authority. It is also significant that this is a popular expression (not 'prendre la parole'), which suggests their desire to reach a wider popular audience. Bourdieu's meeting with Grass repeated, in some respects, his 1991 collaboration with the German-American conceptual artist Hans Haacke. The edited transcript of their dialogue was published in 1993, under the title *Libre-échange*. This time, the two refer to 'plain-speaking' (*le franc-parler*), which implies both honesty and a will to communicate, again very much in the spirit of 'speaking out', and again with working-class connotations.

What Bourdieu claims to admire in Grass's work is in fact his 'search for means of expression to convey a critical, subversive message to a very large audience'.[29] For instance, in *My Century*, Grass evokes the major events in German twentieth-century history, but from the perspective of ordinary people: a sort of reverse strategy from the more usual sensationalising of Germany's recent past, which, by making wars, massacres, Nazism, and concentration camps seem extraordinary, and strangely unimaginable, allows us to forget that these were part of people's ordinary reality – so that we might also be encouraged to take a clear look at what is happening today, under our own noses.

In his conversation with Haacke, Bourdieu discusses how similar effects could be produced to those created by the artist with the written word. Bourdieu admits to having difficulty finding equivalents to Haacke's artistic practice in the history of philosophy or literature. One he suggests is the Austrian writer, journalist, playwright, and poet Karl Krauss (1874-1936) (*LE,* 11). Krauss's provocations, published notably in his satirical journal *Die*

---

27 Bourdieu and Grass, 'La tradition "d'ouvrir sa gueule"'.
28 Pierre Bourdieu and Günter Grass, 'The "Progressive" Restoration', *New Left Review*, 14 (2002), 63-77.
29 Bourdieu and Grass, 'The 'Progressive' Restoration', p. 70.

Fackel, created veritable 'happenings', which provoked his adversaries to make mistakes, or show themselves up (*I*, 37-38). We can see a comparison with the famous cancellation of Haacke's solo exhibition at the Guggenheim, when Haacke refused to withdraw a piece detailing the business dealings of a New York real-estate company with strong ties to several art institutions [*Shapolsky et al...* (1971)], which demonstrated powerfully that corporate sponsorship restricts what artists and galleries are able to exhibit. Also like Haacke, Krauss turned the forces of his adversaries against them: for example, by using the techniques by which journalism constructs a particular vision of reality (headlines, selected quotations, even what is chosen to be reported or not) against journalism itself (*I*, 377; *LE*, 113). This is similar to a tactic deployed by Haacke, for example in *A Breed Apart* (1978), which re-works an advert for Jaguar cars by British Leyland to 'advertise' the company's support of South Africa's apartheid regime, by selling it police and military vehicles.

Interestingly, Bourdieu also draws another comparison between *Die Fackel* and his own sociological journal, *Actes de la recherche en sciences sociales* (*I*, 375). Each makes use of the technique (which we can also find in Haacke's work) of confronting the reader directly with a fragment of the 'real' (a document, a photograph or an extract from an article), which, pasted into an analytical text (or placed within an artwork or in an art museum), can be compared to and resonate with the texts or other artefacts around it (*I*, 375). In *Libre-échange*, Bourdieu suggests this kind of artistic/literary experimentation, combining different levels or registers of language with visual elements, as one of the ways that critical texts could be made less abstract and more accessible: so that the theoretical text does not present an insurmountable obstacle, but can be easily referred to more tangible elements (of which it also informs our understanding) (*LE*, 110). If we look at *Die Fackel*, we can see that this sort of 'discursive montage' could be taken much further. Whereas *Actes de la recherche en sciences sociales* is very much dominated by sociological texts (many written *à la* Bourdieu), *Die Fackel* uses diverse text types, such as essays, notes, commentaries, poems, aphorisms, drama, and other modes of literary expression (almost all written by Krauss himself). This was one of the directions that *Liber*, the European book review Bourdieu launched in 1989, could have taken, as it announced itself as offering 'aux artistes, aux écrivains et aux savants un forum où ils puissent débattre librement, dans un langage aussi accessible que possible, des "problèmes intellectuels d'intérêt général"'.[30] Although,

---

30 Introductory statement, *Liber*, 1 (1989), 48-72 (p. 48). 'to offer artists, writers, and

5. Literature and Cultural Politics   145

for reasons we will discuss in the next section, it failed to become the collaborative venture that Bourdieu had intended.

Critics might object that Bourdieu's vision for 'une politique de la forme' (*LE*, 89)[31] is too pedagogical: a regression, in fact, to 'social art', or worse, propaganda, comparable to Stalinist or Nazi art. Certainly these criticisms have been directed at Haacke, who is Bourdieu's main inspiration – a 'prophète exemplaire' in the terms Bourdieu borrows from Max Weber (*LE*, 36). Cynthia Freeland, for example, argues that Haacke's work is 'too preachy' and 'ephemeral', risks 'losing its punch when the context alters', and does not therefore qualify as genuinely 'universal' art.[32] In *Libre-échange*, Haacke answers his critics, by noting that all art has always been a response to the politico-social determinations of its age. 'Les œuvres d'art, que les artistes le veuillent ou non, sont toujours des marques idéologiques', Haacke argues – if only insofar as they are always also 'marques de pouvoir et de capital symbolique' (*LE*, 93).[33] Also against the critics exemplified, here, by Freeland, Haacke adds that 'la signification et l'impact qu'a un objet donné ne sont pas fixés à perpétuité. Ils dépendent du contexte dans lequel on l'examine' (*LE*, 94).[34] This is true whether the work in question is a Rembrandt or a urinal.

Another possible criticism is that the attempt to address the general public amounts necessarily to 'dumbing down'. On the contrary, Bourdieu and Haacke suggest that the attempt to find easier ways of expressing ideas and experiences can even lead to new theoretical and artistic discoveries, which had been excluded by the limits of their specialised languages:

> HH: Si on fait attention aux formes et au langage qui sont accessibles au grand public, on risque de découvrir des moyens qui ne font pas partie du répertoire ésotérique mais qui pourraient bien l'enrichir.
>
> PB: Donc, contrairement à ce qu'on dit, l'intention de divulgation, loin de mener *en tous les cas* à des compromis ou des compromissions esthétiques, à abaisser le niveau, etc. peut être source de découvertes esthétiques (*LE*, 111).[35]

---

scholars a forum in which to debate freely and as accessibly as possible "intellectual problems of general interest"' (trans. J.S.).
31 'a politics of form' (*Free Exchange*, 84).
32 Cynthia Freeland, *But is it Art? An Introduction to Art Theory* (Oxford: Oxford University Press, 2001), p. 113. Cited in Lane, *Bourdieu's Politics*, p. 135.
33 'Whether artists like it or not, artworks are always ideological tokens (…). As tokens of power and symbolic capital (I hope my use of another of your terms is correct) they play a political role' (*Free Exchange*, 89).
34 'the meaning and impact of a given object are not fixed for all eternity. They depend on the context in which one sees them' (*Free Exchange*, 89).
35 'HH: If one pays attention to the forms and the language that are accessible to an

Finally, Bourdieu was not unaware of the social barriers to this sort of interdisciplinary work. First of all, Bourdieu admits that the combination of artistic talent and critical intelligence embodied by Haacke is extremely rare. 'Les intellectuels sont très mauvais dans ce domaine', Bourdieu says, speaking of the aspect of *performance*. 'Il n'y a pas non plus beaucoup d'artistes qui soient à la fois porteurs d'une vue intelligente, non-naïve et critique, et qui en même temps possèdent des instruments d'expression ayant une force symbolique'.[36] Personal encounters such as those between Bourdieu and Haacke and Grass are also the exception. As Grass commented when he met Bourdieu, 'il est plus fréquent que les philosophes se rassemblent dans un coin de la pièce, les sociologues dans un autre et les écrivains, en froid les uns avec les autres, dans l'arrière-boutique'.[37] This is why Bourdieu worked particularly over the 1990s to mobilise intellectual and cultural groupings that could bring together the symbolic skills and capital in the field that are currently dispersed and divided. Yet these initiatives ran into their own difficulties.

For a collective intellectual

In May 1989, Bourdieu presented a paper in Turin which marks the start of a period of more intense political activism on his own part, and during which he called consistently upon others in the academic and artistic communities to join him and mobilise collectively. Bourdieu calls for the creation of an interdisciplinary and international 'intellectuel collectif', which would constitute 'un pouvoir international de critique et de surveillance, voire de proposition' (RA, 558),[38] and restore the intellectuals' role as 'un des derniers contrepouvoirs critiques capables de s'opposer aux forces de l'ordre économique et politique' (RA, 545).[39] At least (but as we will

---

uninitiated public, one can discover things that could enrich the esoteric repertoire. PB: Therefore, contrary to what is said, the intention of reaching a broad public, far from leading in all cases to concessions of aesthetic compromises, to lowering the level, may well be a source of aesthetic discoveries' (*Free Exchange*, 107).
36 Graw, 'Que Suis-Je?' 'Intellectuals are very bad in this domain. Nor are there many artists who have an intelligent, critical and non-naïve perspective, and who are also equipped with instruments of expression with symbolic force' (trans. J.S.).
37 Bourdieu and Grass, 'La tradition "d'ouvrir sa gueule"'. 'Here, the philosophers sit in one corner, the sociologists in another, while the writers squabble in the back room. The sort of exchange we're having here rarely occurs.' Bourdieu and Grass, 'The "Progressive" Restoration', p. 63.
38 'an international power of criticism and watchfulness, or even of proposals' (*Rules*, 348).
39 'one of the last critical countervailing powers capable of opposing the forces

see in Chapter 6, the two things could be connected), intellectuals should join forces, he urged, to defend their own social conditions of existence, which (as we began to see in Chapter 3, and will examine more closely in Chapter 6) Bourdieu considered under threat from the commercialisation of the book trade and the publishing industry, from new forms of State patronage, and from the massive domination of journalism and television over cultural life, in France and elsewhere (*RA*, 558).

Bourdieu had some experience of establishing such networks. In the wake of May 1968, Bourdieu set up the *Centre de sociologie de l'éducation et la culture* (CSEC), to reflect on the reform and democratisation of education and cultural institutions. In 1975, he established his own sociological review, *Actes de la recherche en sciences sociales*, around which he focused his research group. Bourdieu also presided over *l'Association de réflexion sur les enseignements supérieurs et la recherche* (ARESER), set up in 1992 to give voice to the views of academics on the direction of French higher education. Bourdieu was also involved in the *Comité international de soutien aux intellectuels algériens* (CISIA), created in 1993 to support Algerian intellectuals who, since the beginning of the civil war, had been victims of violence and executions (see *I*, 293-95). And in the mid-1990s Bourdieu helped to launch Raisons d'Agir, which announced itself as 'un intellectuel collectif autonome', 'destiné à mettre les compétences analytiques des chercheurs au service des mouvements de résistance aux politiques néolibérales, pour contrebalancer l'influence des *think-tanks* conservateurs' (editors' comment, *I*, 331). [40]

Bourdieu's attempts to create organisations on an international scale, however, met with less success. Bourdieu's grandest project was, as it happens, a fundamentally 'literary' project: *Liber*, a European book review, which launched in October 1989.[41] Bourdieu envisaged *Liber* as a way of uniting Europe's intellectuals around a shared project. It was also envisaged that it would 'contribuer à créer les conditions d'une circulation libre des idées',[42] by working to overcome the linguistic barriers, slowness of translations, and inertia of scholastic institutions, which impede communication between European cultures. The review had an initially

---

of economic and political order' (Rules, 339).
40 'designed to place the analytical skills of researchers at the service of movements resisting neoliberal policies, and thus counterbalance the influence of conservative think-tanks' (*Political Interventions*, 273).
41 This discussion of *Liber* is based on Peter Collier's article 'Liber: Liberty and Literature' in *French Cultural Studies*, 4 (1993), 291-304.
42 'contribute to create the conditions of a free circulation of ideas' (trans. J.S.).

strong start. It found a clutch of institutional sponsors, and was carried as a free supplement in national newspapers in Britain, Spain, Italy, France, and Germany. Yet it soon ran into difficulty. The review faltered after just the first few issues, as financial backers and host publications pulled out one by one, and as the structure of its organisation disintegrated – leaving, in the end, only Bourdieu and one other running the entire operation (*CP*, 79). Already by the seventh issue, *Liber* had retreated to the French language, and between the covers of *Actes de la recherche en sciences sociales*, although it retained its pan-European coverage. The review was quietly disbanded just before its tenth anniversary.

Another cautionary tale concerns the International Parliament of Writers, established in 1993 by writers and intellectuals including Bourdieu, Beryl Bainbridge, Toni Morrison, Jacques Derrida, Christopher Hitchens, and Salman Rushdie. In a manifesto statement, 'A Declaration of Independence' (1994), Rushdie describes the purpose of the parliament as being to 'fight for oppressed writers and against all those who persecute them and their work, and to renew continually the declaration of independence without which writing is impossible; and not only writing but dreaming; and not only dreaming, but thought; and not only thought, but liberty itself'.[43] Key among its practical initiatives was the creation of a network of Cities of Asylum, which provided safe-haven and support to writers fleeing censorship and persecution. While clearly endorsing these aims and initiatives, Bourdieu proposed a far more ambitious programme for the Parliament, in a rejoinder to Rushdie's manifesto first published in *Libération*.[44] Bourdieu envisaged giving the International Parliament of Writers a far more organised administrative structure, including secretariats, commissions, regional meetings, etc., from which to launch simultaneous press-conferences, demonstrations, and petitions, etc.; and proposed expanding the parliament's remit, to include the defence of autonomous instances of distribution (publishing houses, magazines, translation policy), which, as we have seen, are also crucial components in the production of literary texts. Clearly with his own vision for an 'intellectuel collectif' in mind, Bourdieu also saw the writers' parliament working with other specialist groupings to produce 'livres blancs présentant les résultats du travail de "commissions de

---

[43] Salman Rushdie, 'A Declaration of Independence: For the International Parliament of Writers', in *Liber*, 17 (1994), p. 29.
[44] Pierre Bourdieu, 'Un parlement des écrivains pour quoi faire?', *Libération*, 3 November 1994. Reprinted in (*I*, 289-92).

spécialistes" (accompagnées de contributions d'écrivains) et servant de base à des revendications ou des recommandations pratiques qui seront défendues collectivement dans la presse' (*I*, 292).⁴⁵ Bourdieu's proposals went unheeded, however, and he scaled back his involvement. Even in its more limited capacity, the International Parliament of Writers was always a fragile and fractious grouping. It was also dissolved after a decade, and without much comment.

Perhaps, as Bourdieu suggested in a 1989 interview, Europe's intellectuals were 'not yet ready' for the sort of collaboration and joint commitment he was trying to encourage – which was without precedent in any national tradition, and which ruled out a certain number of pre-established roles.⁴⁶ The notion of an 'intellectuel collectif' was intended to overcome the opposition, particularly strong in English-speaking countries (which do not have the tradition of Voltaire, Zola, and Sartre), between scholarship and politics, or between the 'pure' and 'committed' intellectual. But it was also constructed against the Sartrean model of engagement on every possible issue, which exposed intellectuals to the risk of out-stepping their field of competence. As Loïc Wacquant suggests, it may perhaps be understood best as a sort of synthesis of Sartre's 'total intellectual' and Foucault's 'specific intellectual', who limits his or her political activity to a particular area of expertise (*IRS*, 190). Bourdieu wanted to 'rassembler des "intellectuels spécifiques" au sens de Foucault, dans un "intellectuel collectif", interdisciplinaire et international' (*I*, 474-75),⁴⁷ able to roam across a broad range of issues, and to produce a wide variety of forms of intervention by drawing on the specialist skills and expertise its members. At least with *Liber*, Bourdieu admits to having wanted to 'aller trop vite et trop haut'. As he came to see, it takes time to invent and consolidate a new position in the cultural field: 'on doit préparer ce genre de choses très lentement pour que cela soit réel et puisse durer'.⁴⁸

---

45 'the International Writers' Parliament should promote the publication of White Papers presenting the results of the work of 'commissions of specialists' (accompanied by contributions from writers) and serving as a basis for demands or practical recommendations that are collectively defended in the press' (*Political Interventions*, 240).
46 Loïc Wacquant, 'From Ruling Class to Field of power: An Interview with Pierre Bourdieu on *La Noblesse d'État*', *Theory Culture Society*, 10 (1993), 19-44 (p. 38).
47 'bring together those whom Foucault referred to as "specific intellectuals" into a "collective intellectual", interdisciplinary and international' (*Political Interventions*, 387).
48 Graw, 'Que Suis-Je?' 'these things must be prepared very slowly so that they

Yet there are also more practical reasons why Bourdieu's dream of an 'international of intellectuals' appears unrealistic. As the *Liber* project proved, any organisation requires a steady source of funding, and demands high levels of commitment, especially if it is voluntary, in which case the symbolic reward becomes paramount. It is difficult to see where such an *internationale* would find sponsors, especially if two of its targets were to be transnational media enterprises and governments. In his plans for the International Parliament of Writers, Bourdieu seems to suggest it would run on pure generosity. The Parliament should be 'capable de demander et d'obtenir un dévouement militant, c'est-à-dire des contributions (cotisation, don de temps et de travail) sans contrepartie (anonymat, travail collectif) et respectueux des singularités' (I, 290).[49] Bourdieu's own sociology however suggests this is a near impossible request: that reserves of goodwill will soon run dry if individuals do not receive anything in return for their 'gifts'. The idea of imposing organisations and bureaucracies is also unlikely to appeal to artists and writers, who (as Bourdieu again suggests) are drawn to the field of cultural production precisely because of its extremely *low degree of institutionalisation*, and the degree of freedom and independence it not only permits but encourages. Intellectuals might unite around particular issues, but their campaigns are most often *ad hoc*, and they disperse soon afterwards.

As Ahearne writes, 'the odds, clearly, would always be against such a potentially nebulous pole, liable always to rescatter, and whose only substantial capital is cultural and symbolic'.[50] Yet we may also be reminded of Bourdieu's analysis of the nineteenth-century literary and artistic fields in France, in light of which, as Ahearne suggests, Bourdieu may be seen to have been attempting something 'homologous' to the proponents of *l'art pour l'art*. Oppressed and stifled by the cultural climate of the Second Empire, which was awash with 'industrial' literature serialised in the expanding press, and dominated by the most conventional and compliant of artists and writers, who were celebrated with commissions and pensions from Napoleon III, in which anti-intellectualism was rife, and economic values or 'le règne de l'argent' (RA, 87) prevailed, artists and writers including Flaubert, Baudelaire, and Manet, worked to create a new

---

become real and last' (trans. J.S.).
49 'a movement able to demand and obtain an an activist commitment, i.e., contributions (subscriptions, gifts of time and work) that are unrewarded (hence anonymity, collective work) and respectful of singularities' (*Political Interventions*, 239).
50 Ahearne, *Between Cultural Theory and Policy*, p. 68.

position and 'possibility' in the cultural field. Refusing both the 'bourgeois' art of the dominant class and the 'social art' of the realists, which they judged to be aesthetically inferior, these artists seceded from all existing authorities, and created their own 'empire within an empire', subject to its own *nomos* – imposing a new system of values and dispositions in the intellectual body (RA, 122-25). Certainly it helped, then as now, to have a private income or assured inheritance. But writers also found material and symbolic support from unlikely sources, such as Princess Mathilde, and even from competing interests in the culture industry, which opened up new ways of making a living, through publishing and journalism. Bourdieu admits this 'empire' was in its formative phase apolitical and 'radicalement élitiste' (RA, 549). But within a few decades its structure was strong enough that it could be used by Zola and his fellow 'intellectuels' as a platform from which to launch their protest against the injustice of Dreyfus's imprisonment, combining intellectual autonomy and political engagement. 'In a homologous fashion', Ahearne writes, 'Bourdieu could be seen as seeking to help into being a new position in the cultural policy field that could alter the play of forces within that field'.[51] Faced with new forms of patronage and censorship, more subtle and insidious than in the past, Bourdieu sought to reaffirm and strengthen cultural autonomy, by creating more organised and institutionalised groups/platforms than had existed previously. In which case, we should be able to use the same words to describe Bourdieu's projects for a 'collective intellectual' as he uses to write about *l'art pour l'art:*

> plus qu'une position toute faite, qu'il suffirait de prendre, (...) [c']est une *position à faire*, dépourvue de tout équivalent dans le champ du pouvoir (...). Ceux qui prétendent l'occuper ne peuvent pas la faire exister qu'en faisant le champ dans lequel elle pourrait trouver place, c'est-à-dire en révolutionnant un monde de l'art qui l'exclut, en fait et en droit (RA, 131).[52]

---

51 Ahearne, *Between Cultural Theory and Policy*, p. 68.
52 'Rather than a ready-made position which only has to be taken up (...) [it] is a *position to be made*, devoid of any equivalent in the field of power. Those who would take up that position cannot make it exist except by making the field in which a place could be found for it, that is, by revolutionizing an art world that excludes it, in fact and in law' (*Rules*, 76).

6. Literature and Cultural Policy

Bourdieu usually avoided making 'normative' proposals, especially in his 'scientific' work. Even in his political interventions, he warns against 'le piège du programme', arguing 'il y a bien assez de partis et d'appareils pour ça' (*CFI*, 62).[1] In Bourdieu's view, researchers are better off keeping to what they are good at: providing information and analysis, rather than programmes and prescriptions. On several prominent occasions, Bourdieu did, however, engage directly in the cultural policy debate, most notably in two reports commissioned by the French government on the reform of education.[2] This chapter examines the points at which Bourdieu's cultural policy reflection impacts or intersects with cultural policy issues related to literature in education and society. Firstly, it tries to dispel the belief that Bourdieu reduces the value of literature to its uses in strategies of social distinction, which would hardly seem to justify State subsidy and protection, or literature's place in a modern education system. Next, it explores the apparently contradictory role of the State within Bourdieu's cultural policy reflection, which argues both for greater State support for literature and the arts and on cultural producers more actively to oppose undue State interference. The chapter closes with Bourdieu's call, included as the post-script to *Les Règles*, 'Pour un corporatisme de l'universel', in which he urged writers and intellectuals to pursue a *Realpolitik de la raison* in their own interests and in the general interest.

---

1 'the trap of [suggesting] programmes (…) there are well enough parties and apparatuses for that' (trans. J.S.).
2 In the general discussions of Bourdieu's work on cultural policy in this chapter, I draw extensively on Ahearne, *Between Cultural Theory and Policy*, especially chapters one and two.

DOI: 10.11647/OBP.0027.07

Reproduction and distinction

Literature appears in Bourdieu's sociological critiques of contemporary French society in his work on education and in his analysis of patterns in French cultural consumption and tastes. In this section, we will begin with Bourdieu's critiques of how literature was effectively deployed within existing State educational/cultural policies, and then move on to consider how these mesh with his critiques of its uses in more generally distributed strategies of cultural/social distinction. We will then see if Bourdieu, especially when he switches to an explicitly 'normative' mode in his proposals for educational reform, indicates any more positive reasons for teaching or conserving non-commercial literary culture. To do so, we will need to distinguish between the intrinsic 'use value' of literature and its 'exchange value' within social fields as an instrument of cultural distinction.

At the time of writing *Les Héritiers* and *La Reproduction*, published in 1964 and 1970 respectively, literary values were still dominant in the French education system. In *La Reproduction*, Bourdieu and Passeron describe 'la valeur éminente que le système française accorde à l'aptitude littéraire, et, plus précisément, à l'aptitude à transformer en discours littéraire toute expérience, à commencer par l'expérience littéraire, bref ce qui définit la manière française de vivre la vie littéraire – et parfois même scientifique – comme une vie parisienne' (*R*, 143-44).[3] In *Les Héritiers*, this situation is described as playing into the hands of students from privileged, especially Parisian, backgrounds. Such students were more familiar with the bookish language used in the classroom, because it was the language used in the home, meaning that they could follow and reproduce the lessons more easily. Even if there was no direct pressure from their families to read, they acquired from their parents habits and attitudes which were either of direct service in their schoolwork (linguistic competence, the capacity for quiet study and independent learning), or that were rewarded indirectly by the school (such as 'good taste', 'proper' diction, linguistic fluency and confidence, or simply a respectful disposition towards the school and teachers) (*H*, 30-33). The parents of these children were also more likely to take them to theatres, museums, concerts, etc. (a frequentation provided only

---

[3] 'the pre-eminent value that the French system accords to literary aptitude, and, more precisely, to the aptitude to transform all experience into literary discourse, beginning with the literary experience, in short what defines the French manner of living literary – and sometimes scientific – life like a Parisian life' (trans. J.S.).

6. Literature and Cultural Policy 155

sporadically by the school, or not at all), providing the background of cultural knowledge and experience demanded tacitly by literary studies. According to *Les Héritiers*, nowhere was the influence of social origin more manifest than in literature departments, making literary studies 'le terrain par excellence pour étudier l'action des facteurs culturels de l'inégalité devant l'Ecole' (*H*, 19).[4]

If the mechanisms by which the French school and university system contributed to social reproduction so often went unnoticed, it was because the social differences it ratified were transformed into academic categories, grades, and percentages, which disguised social differences behind apparently objective categories based on merit. A good example of this is a document Bourdieu discovered during his research into the *Grandes écoles*, in which a professor had written down the marks of his students and his appreciation of them, and their social origin. By a simple graph, Bourdieu was able to establish a correlation between scholastic success and social class. 'Autremement dit', Bourdieu explains, 'le système de classement euphémistique a pour fonction d'établir la connexion entre la classe et la note, mais en la niant ou, mieux, en la déniant – comme dit la psychanalyse' (*I*, 94).[5]

Bourdieu considered the resulting 'verdict effect' (*l'effet de verdict*) to be one of the most important and, for many, damaging actions performed by the school. To give this point more force, Bourdieu draws an analogy with Kafka's *The Trial*, which he reads as a metaphor for the education system.[6] Like Josef K, who is condemned by a tribunal he is forced to recognise, but whose judgment he is unable to appeal nor even to understand, children 'internalise' the verdicts of their teachers (often re-enforced by their families, in different ways according to their social origin), which become part of how the children in turn see themselves. 'C'est un univers dans lequel on entre pour savoir qui on est,' Bourdieu explains, in an interview first published in 1985, 'et avec une attente d'autant plus anxieuse qu'on y est moins attendu. Il vous dira, de façon insidieuse ou brutale: "tu n'est qu'un..." – suivi généralement d'une insulte qui, dans ce cas là, est sanctionnée par

---
4 'the ideal place to study the action of cultural factors on inequality in the school' (trans. J.S.).
5 'In other words, the system of euphemistic classification has the function of establishing a connection between class and marks, but precisely by denying such a connection – by denegating it, in the psychoanalytic sense' (*Political Interventions*, 67).
6 In *Méditations pascaliennes*, Bourdieu extends this metaphor to the social world as a whole (*MP*, 279-83).

une institution indiscutable, reconnue de tous' (*I*, 205).⁷ Bourdieu describes the 'traumatismes de l'identité' that can result from this verdict effect as 'sans doute un des grands facteurs pathogènes de notre société' (*I*, 205).⁸ It leaves some children scarred with anxiety, insecurity, and poor self-esteem, while others are confirmed and legitimated in their way of being. We can notice how Bourdieu turns to literature to underline and make palpable a fundamental point, while it also helps him to put it into relief through a form of defamiliarisation (*ostrenanie*).

The belief in natural talent, intelligence, or merit, was supported and upheld by the literary mythology of inspired geniuses or 'uncreated creators'. The 'charismatic ideology' of the artist-as-prophet, graced with an artistic 'gift', had its counterpart in 'the dogma of the immaculate perception',⁹ which considered cultural reception also to be a matter of natural aptitude (*D*, 381). 'La littérature "où, comme disait Gide dans son *Journal*, rien ne vaut que ce qui est personnel"', Bourdieu writes in *La Distinction*, 'et la célébration dont elle fait l'objet dans le champ littéraire et dans les systèmes d'enseignement, sont évidemment au centre de ce culte du moi où la philosophie, souvent réduite à une affirmation hautaine de la distinction du penseur, chante aussi sa partie' (*D*, 486).¹⁰ Just as literary works were supposed to be the 'unique' expression of 'unique' creators, so students were also expected to express their 'personal' opinions and tastes, with little in fact done to provide the cultural knowledge and comparisons, or the words and concepts necessary to formulate such opinions to those who had not acquired these from their family milieu.

Importantly, Bourdieu also saw the 'charismatic ideology' of art at work in official French cultural policy in the 1960s. The main targets of Bourdieu's

---

7 'It's a world that you enter in order to know what you are, and with all the more anxious expectation, the less you are expected there. It says to you, in an insidious or brutal fashion: "You are just a..." – generally followed by an insult that, in cases such as this, is sanctioned by an institution beyond discussion and recognized by all' (*Political Interventions*, 162).
8 'these traumas of identity are undoubtedly one of the main pathogenic factors in our society' (*Political Interventions*, 162).
9 Bourdieu borrows this phrase from Friedrich Nietzsche, *Thus Spake Zarathustra: A Book for Everyone and No One*, trans. R.J. Hollingdale (Harmondsworth: Penguin, 1961), Chapter 37.
10 'Literature, in which, as Gide said in his Journal, "only the personal has any value", and the celebration which surrounds it in the literary field and in the educational system, are clearly central to this cult of the self, in which philosophy, often reduced to a lofty assertion of the thinker's distinction, also has a part to play' (*Distinction*, 52).

early cultural policy critiques were 'l'idéologie du don naturel et de l'œil neuf' (*AA*, 90-91),[11] according to which responsiveness to works of high culture was supposed to be a matter of direct intuition, and the 'l'ideologie des 'besoins culturels' (*AA*, 156),[12] according to which individuals have an innate (just not always satisfied) need for high cultural stimulation. These presuppositions were behind, for instance, the ill-fated *Maisons de Culture*, brainchild of André Malraux (then Minister of Culture). As the survey results in *L'Amour de l'art* show (and as Bourdieu's mathematical model, based on statistical probability, enabled him to predict), these flagship institutions catered primarily to people who engaged already in cultural practices, and failed in their mission to take high culture to the masses merely by opening these institutions in their locality: 'comme s'ils croyaient que la seule inaccessibilité physique des œuvres empêche la grande majorité de les aborder, des les contempler et de les savourer' (*AA*, 151).[13] The downside to this purely formal accessibility, of course, was a tendency to blame the victims of cultural dispossession if they did not make use of the opportunities and facilities that were ostensibly available.

It is no coincidence, perhaps, that André Malraux was himself a literary author, of works including *La Voie royale* (1930) and *L'Espoir* (1937). Malraux, who famously likened his *Maisons de Culture* to cathedrals, had a vested interest in the celebration of culture as a substitute or successor for religion, and in the image of cultural reception as a sort of mystical 'communion', making him and other artists prophets for a godless age.

The divisive effects of literary culture continued out into wider society. In *La Distinction*, Bourdieu describes the sense of exclusion and alienation, even revolt, experienced by members of the popular class, when confronted with works of high culture. One of his examples is avant-garde theatre, which appears to do everything possible to exclude the popular public by systematically disappointing normal expectations (*D*, 34). High culture defines itself in opposition to popular tastes, posing every possible obstacle to the *participation* the popular public demands, and finds in less 'formalised' and 'euphemistic' entertainments (*D*, 36). There is also an effect of peer pressure, which forbids any kind of 'pretentiousness' in matters of culture, language, or clothing, especially

---

11 'the ideology of the natural gift and of the fresh eye' (*Love of Art*, 54).
12 'cultural needs' (*Love of Art*, 106).
13 'as if they believed that only the physical inaccessibility of the works of art prevented the great majority from approaching, contemplating and enjoying them' (*Love of Art*, 103).

among men – in whom interests, dispositions and mannerisms held to be characteristically 'bourgeois' (against whom the working class male could only oppose his strength and 'virility'), were discouraged as 'effeminate' (*D*, 443-44). In contrast, the apparently intuitive understanding that the cultivated had of literary works was seen as a sort of instinct: opposed not only to the 'bad taste' of the popular class, but also to the 'cuistrerie' of those (petit-bourgeois) individuals who had learned the grammar, and knew the literature, but, having learned their competence in the school or later in life, still lacked the virtuoso's flair or *sens littéraire* (*D*, 73) – a fact they gave away by their tense hypercorrection and lingering taste for less legitimate genres, comic books or fantasy and science fiction (like the ape in E.T.A. Hoffmann's *Kreislerbuch*, evoked by Bourdieu in *La Distinction*, again using literature to make a point more palpable (*D*, 105 n. 109)).

Reading habits were also part of what differentiated the dominant class, according to Bourdieu: from teachers who read the most overall, especially novels, but also books on philosophy, politics and economics, but who read relatively few detective novels or adventure stories, to business bosses who read the least, and when they did read the lowest proportion of novels (the most popular genre overall) and a comparatively higher number of adventure stories and detective novels (*D*, 132). In *La Distinction*, reading habits, like sporting practices, dress-sense, table manners, or tastes in food and drink, are seen as so many markers of social position defined by volume and ratio of economic and cultural capitals.

Unsurprisingly, Bourdieu's critique of the cultural game led some to question whether he saw anything beyond its 'segregative' effects, and if the values attributed to cultural works were really reducible to their social uses and distinctiveness, as they appeared to be in Bourdieu's analysis. 'Il est donc vain', Danièle Sallenave writes, after citing a passage from *La Distinction*, 'd'opérer une distinction entre les grands livres et les autres, entre les bons films et les nanars, entre un Cremonini et les *Poulbots* de la Butte'.[14] Although Bourdieu feigned indignation at such interpretations, they are not entirely without foundation. Jeremy

---

14 Danièle Sallenave cited in Bernard Lahire, 'Présentation: Pour une sociologie à l'état vif', in *Le Travail sociologique de Pierre Bourdieu*, ed. Bernard Lahire (Paris: la Découvert, 1999), pp. 5-20 (p. 12 n. 7). 'It is therefore vain to distinguish between great books and others, between good films and junk, between a Cremonini and *Poulbots* by la Butte' (trans. J.S.).

6. Literature and Cultural Policy

Ahearne points to a tendency in Bourdieu to '"absolutize" (detach from what he also holds to be true) certain lines of argument',[15] pointing, for instance, to his critique of the historically 'arbitrary' nature of legitimate culture, which appears to offer little reason to privilege one particular culture over another:

> With the repeated insistence throughout *La Reproduction* that legitimate culture simply 'is' arbitrary, it is easy to forget the note (afterthought?) in its preface that the notion of pure arbitrariness is a logical construction without empirical referent that is necessary for the construction of the argument (somewhat like Rousseau's 'state of nature') (…) It is worthwhile, at the very least, to meditate on the extent to which the rites of culture are purely 'negative' (i.e. segregational) and its pleasures 'vain'.[16]

Pierre Salgas put this question directly to Bourdieu, in an interview published in 1985[17] on the occasion of the publication of *Propositions pour l'enseignement de l'avenir*,[18] a report commissioned by François Mitterrand from the professors of the Collège de France (where Bourdieu had held a chair since 1981). This report was not a policy critique, but policy proposal, and it is interesting that it leads Bourdieu to leave his pure critique of literature and culture and to indicate positive or 'intrinsic' uses. Salgas took this opportunity to question Bourdieu over his attitude towards literary culture. Reading his early work, in particular *La Reproduction* and *La Distinction*, Salgas observes, one could get the impression that literary values are reducible to rarity value and distinctiveness. Did the sociologist then consider literary studies to have a place in a modern education system? What about Proust, whom Bourdieu clearly admired, should he be included on the school curriculum? Bourdieu responds emphatically:

> On retombe sur l'effet de ratification. C'est un fait que les biens culturels sont soumis à des usages sociaux de distinction qui n'ont rien à voir avec leur valeur intrinsèque. Suis-je pour ou contre Proust? La question n'a pas de

---

15 Ahearne, *Between Cultural Theory and Policy*, p. 41.
16 Ibid., p. 50.
17 Jean-Pierre Salgas, 'Le Rapport du Collège de France: Pierre Bourdieu s'explique', in *La Quinzaine Littéraire*, 445 (1985), 8-10, included in *Interventions 1961-2001*, pp. 203-10.
18 *Propositions pour l'enseignement de l'avenir élaborées à la demande de Monsieur le Président de la République par les professeurs du Collège de France* (Paris: Collège de France, 1985), referred to hereafter as *PPEA*. This report will be examined more closely in the next section.

sens. Comment ne pas souhaiter que l'on puisse produire à l'infini des gens capables de faire ce qu'a fait Proust ou, du moins, de lire ce qu'il a écrit? Ceux qui m'attaquent sur ce point, ou qui prennent contre moi la 'défense' de la philosophie sont des gens dont le point d'honneur intellectuel est plus lié à l'usage social des choses intellectuelles qu'à ces choses elles-mêmes (*I*, 209).[19]

Clearly, Bourdieu saw value in literature beyond its social uses. Yet one needs to read his work quite carefully to discover just what its 'valeur intrinsèque' might be. Bourdieu, as we have seen, was not one to worship literature for its own sake.

There is a clue, however, in Bourdieu's response to Salgas that what he really wanted to see cultivated by literary education was a certain linguistic competence and 'creative' disposition – which has so long been one of the aims attributed to literary studies that it now almost goes without saying (and literary scholars, educators and policy makers can usefully be reminded of it for that reason). In the terms Bourdieu uses, literary works are 'instruments de production, donc d'invention et de liberté possible' (*RA*, 495 n. 26).[20] They are 'objectified' or externalised linguistic 'resources', like grammar books and dictionaries (or like an 'encyclopaedia', as James Joyce once described *Ulysses*, which goes through the A to Z of literary styles and content, from 'elite' literature, with allusions to Hamlet and the *Odyssey*, to glossy women's magazines[21]) (cf. *LPS*, 88). These linguistic and stylistic instruments can be accumulated and concentrated in certain works, and fresh ones generated (Proust, with his *Pastiches et Mélanges*, and stylistic experiments in *À la recherche du temps perdu*, is again a good example). And they can be 'internalised' again by readers, who are subsequently able to formulate certain ideas, and to express certain experiences, of their own.

Despite the initial strangeness of Bourdieu's terminology (and the fact that it runs counter to the general course of literary education since the late nineteenth century, which, as Lionel Gossman observes, turned

---

19 'You get back here to the effect of ratification. It is a fact that cultural goods are subject to social uses of distinction that heve nothing to do with their intrinsic value. Am I for or against Proust? How can one not want there to be countless people able to do what Proust did, or at least read what he wrote? Those who attack me on this point, or use against me the "defence" of philosophy, are people whose intellectual pride is more bound up with the social use of intellectual things than with these things themselves' (*Political Interventions*, 165).
20 'instruments of production, hence of invention and possible freedom' (*Rules*, 392).
21 James Joyce, Letter of 21 September 1920 to Carlo Linati, in *Selected Letters of James Joyce*, ed. Richard Ellmann (New York: Viking, 1975), p. 270.

away from rhetoric and became 'an activity of appreciation and not primarily a way of learning how to produce fine speeches and essays oneself'[22]), this conception of literature echoes in some ways that of the founders of literary education in the eighteenth century, whose literature programmes had as their goal the acquisition of rhetoric and the 'elevation of the mind'. The key purpose, of course, was not to produce cohorts of creative writers (although, as Bourdieu suggests, that would be no bad thing), but rather to furnish students with the linguistic and ideational resources to understand their own experiences – so freeing them from blind submission to doctrines and ideologies, and increasing their ability to express their own arguments and viewpoints. Indeed, this recalls how Proust, again, called for his own book to be read, in a famous passage near the end of *À la recherche du temps perdu*:

> Je pensais (...) à mon livre, et ce serait même inexact que de dire en pensant à ceux qui le liraient, à mes lecteurs. Car ils ne seraient pas, selon moi, mes lecteurs, mais les propres lecteurs d'eux-mêmes, mon livre n'étant qu'une sorte de ces verres grossissants comme ceux que tendait à un acheteur l'opticien de Combray; mon livre, grâce auquel je leur fournirais le moyen de lire en eux-mêmes. De sorte que je ne leur demanderais pas de me louer ou de me dénigrer, mais seulement de me dire si c'est bien cela, si les mots qu'ils lisent en eux-mêmes sont bien ceux que j'ai écrits.[23]

As the philosopher Gilles Deleuze remarked, it is not without some surprise that we find Proust, an author often thought of as a pure intellectual, expressing this instrumental vision of literature, which valorises its usefulness as a means of knowledge and self-knowledge (and so of control and self-control), and which Deleuze – using a language of symbolic struggle that could almost be that of Bourdieu – paraphrases as follows: 'traitez mon livre comme une paire de lunettes dirigée sur le dehors, eh bien, si elles ne vous vont pas, prenez-en d'autres, trouvez

---

22 Lionel Gossman, 'Literature and Education', *New Literary History*, 13 (1982), 341-71 (p. 355). Discussed and cited by Bourdieu in *RA*, 497-98.
23 Marcel Proust, *Le Temps retrouvé* (Paris: Gallimard, 1954), pp. 424-25. 'I was thinking more modestly about my book and it would not even be true to say that I was thinking of those who would read it as my readers. For, as I have already shown, they would not be my readers, but the readers of themselves, my book being only a sort of magnifying-glass like those offered by the optician of Combray to a purchaser. So that I should ask neither their praise nor their blame but only that they should tell me if it was right or not, whether the words they were reading within themselves were those I wrote'. *Time Regained* (Vol. 8 of *Remembrance of Things Past*), trans. Stephen Hudson (eBooks@Adelaide, 2010) at http://ebooks.adelaide.edu.au/p/proust/marcel/p96t/ consulted on 23/07/11.

vous-même votre appareil qui est forcément un appareil de combat'.[24]

There is clearly a tension in Bourdieu's work between literature's social uses of distinction and domination (its 'exchange value'), and its 'use-value' as an instrument of mental emancipation. As we might expect, Bourdieu did not believe that it was possible simply to separate the two. In the stark language of the first part of *La Reproduction*, there is no pedagogical action (AP) without 'symbolic violence', and Bourdieu was sceptical of 'les idéologies de l'AP comme action non violente – qu'il s'agisse des mythes socratiques ou néo-socratiques d'un enseignement non directif, des mythes rousseauistes d'une éducation naturelle ou des mythes pseudo-freudiens d'une éducation non répressive' (R, 27).[25] Every pedagogical action supposes the imposition of some historically 'arbitrary' cultural content. Indeed, discipline and didacticism are necessary in order not to disadvantage the culturally dispossessed still further. The image of the free or 'autonomous' learner, still prevalent especially in universities – and of which Bourdieu attributes the initial success, in *Les Héritiers*, to the fact that it 'venait combler les attentes les plus profondes et les plus vouées des étudiants littéraires, parisiens et bourgeois' (H, 75),[26] by assuming natural ability – presupposes that students intuitively understand what is expected of them, and already have the study skills, core knowledge, motivation, etc., required for intellectual work (cf. H, 113). Bourdieu nevertheless draws a distinction between 'abuses' of symbolic power and 'emancipatory disciplines' (we can notice the apparent oxymoron), by which, through patient repetition and exercise, 'habituses of invention, creation and liberty' can be inculcated.[27] This tension between imposition and empowerment can be felt clearly in the following passage from *Les Héritiers*, which takes as an example the case of literary studies:

---

24 Michel Foucault and Gilles Deleuze, 'Les Intellectuels et le Pouvoir', in *Dits et Écrits 1954-1988*, 306-15 (p. 309). 'treat my book as a pair of glasses directed to the outside; if they don't suit you, find another pair; I leave it to you to find your own instrument, which is necessarily an investment for combat', trans. in 'Intellectuals and Power: A Conversation between Michel Foucault and Gilles Deleuze', in *Language, Counter-Memory, Practice: Selected Essays and Interviews by Michel Foucault*, ed. Donald F. Bouchard (Ithaca, NY: Cornell University Press, 1977), pp. 205-17 (p. 208).
25 'ideologies of PA as non-violent – whether Socratic myths or neo-Socratic myths of non-directive teaching, Rousseauist myths of natural education or pseudo-Freudian myths of non-repressive education' (trans. J.S.).
26 'satisfied the deepest expectations and wishes of literary students, Parisian and bourgeois' (trans. J.S.).
27 Bourdieu cited in Ahearne, *Between Cultural Theory and Policy*, p. 61.

> Il est indiscutable que certaines aptitudes qu'exige l'École, comme l'habilité à parler ou à écrire et la multiplicité même des aptitudes, définissent et définiront toujours la culture savante. Mais le professeur de lettres n'est en droit d'attendre la virtuosité verbale et rhétorique qui lui apparaît, non sans raison, comme associée au contenu même de la culture qu'il transmet, qu'à la condition qu'il tienne cette vertu pour ce qu'elle est, c'est-à-dire une aptitude susceptible d'être acquise par l'exercice et qu'il s'impose de fournir à tous les moyens de l'acquérir (H, 110).[28]

Here we can see Bourdieu insist, not that the school should cease to make demands on students, specifically in matters of literature and language (for instance, from a well-meaning but misplaced 'respect' for cultural 'difference' and 'diversity'), but that it should develop techniques and practices (what Bourdieu refers to, in the closing pages of Les Héritiers, as a 'pédagogie rationnelle'),[29] which could transmit that culture more effectively and more universally. In the next section, we will explore Bourdieu's own proposals for a restructuring and reform of education, with a specific focus on their impact on literary culture and education, both in terms of individual classroom practice and wider cultural policy contexts.

Proposals for the future of education

By the time of the Collège de France report, published in 1985, the humanities were losing their pre-eminent place in the hierarchy of disciplines to science. On the basis of his earlier critiques of 'humanistic' culture, we might have imagined that Bourdieu would have welcomed this development, which replaced the former 'voie royale' through the série littéraire to the ENS with a route through maths and physics or sciences to one of the Grandes écoles d'ingénieurs in Paris. In fact, the Collège de France report deplores as 'un des vices les plus criants du système d'enseignement actuel (…) le fait qu'il tend de plus en plus à ne connaître et à ne reconnaître qu'une seule forme d'excellence intellectuelle, celle que représente la section C (ou S) des lycées et

---

[28] 'There is no doubt that certain aptitudes demanded by the School, such as the ability to speak and write and the multiplicity itself of aptitudes, define and will always define scholarly culture. But the teacher of literature is justified in demanding the verbal and rhetorical virtuosity which appears to him, and not without reason, to be associated with the content itself of the culture he transmits, only if he recognises this virtue for what it is, which is to say an aptitude acquired through practice, and that he is responsible to provide everyone with the means to acquire it' (trans. J.S.).
[29] 'rational pedagogy' (trans. J.S.).

son prolongement dans les grandes écoles scientifiques' (*PPEA*, 17).³⁰ Rather than verbal prowess, mathematics was now being used as an instrument of selection and elimination, making students with other competences feel and appear inferior:

> les détenteurs de ces compétences mutilées sont ainsi voués à une expérience plus ou moins malheureuse et de la culture qu'ils ont reçue et de la culture scolairement dominante (c'est là sans doute une des origines de l'irrationalisme qui fleurit actuellement). Quant aux détenteurs de la culture socialement considérée comme supérieure, ils sont de plus en plus souvent voués, sauf effort exceptionnel et conditions sociales très favorables, à la spécialisation prématurée, avec toutes les mutilations qui l'accompagnent (*PPEA*, 17).³¹

It is also useful to place this report in its broader social and political context. One year on, there were widespread student mobilisations against the 'Devaquet project' (named after Alain Devaquet, the junior minister who had drawn up the policy paper), which had proposed reforms of the university system including raising enrolment costs and increasing selection into and competition between universities. The protest was sufficiently strong to force the withdrawal of the projected reform (see *I*, 145). During the strikes, Bourdieu came out in support of the students, describing the unrest as a reaction to a broader trend of 'neo-liberal' educational policies, which were stoking competition between schools, disciplines and students, and aligning education with the needs of the economy. Bourdieu makes particular mention of the social devaluing of traditional humanities disciplines, which, because they were not directly 'vocational', were described in a dominant discourse spread by the mainstream media that also found resonances with popular anti-intellectualism as superfluous (there was an 'overproduction' of graduates, etc.). Indeed, in an interview with Antoine de Gaudemar, published during the strikes in *Libération*,³² Bourdieu describes the situation

---

30 'one of the most serious vices of the current education system (…) the fact that it tends more and more to recognise and understand only one form of intellectual excellence, represented by the section C (or S) of the colleges and its extension in the scientific *Grandes Écoles*' (trans. J.S.).

31 'the holders of these mutilated competences are thus doomed to a more or less unhappy experience both of the culture they have received and of the dominant intellectual culture (this is no doubt one of the origins of the irrationalism that is currently flourishing). As for the holds of the culture considered socially as superior, they are increasingly doomed, unless there is an exceptional effort and very favourable social conditions, to premature specialisation, with all the mutilations which accompany it' (trans. J.S.).

32 Antoine Gaudemar, 'À quand un lycée Bernard Tapie?', *Libération*, 4 December 1986.

in terms strikingly similar to those that he later would employ in *Les Règles* to characterise the cultural climate under the Second Empire, when bourgeois fathers would warn their sons not to waste their time studying philosophy, history, or literature (*RA*, 87):[33]

> Quand une mère bourgeoise ou même petite-bourgeoise parle de son fils qui veut faire de l'histoire, on croirait qu'elle annonce une catastrophe. Et ne parlons pas de la philo ou des lettres classiques. Les étudiants en lettres sont devenus des bouches inutiles. Et pas seulement pour les 'milieux gouvernementaux', de droite et de gauche: pour leur famille aussi, et souvent pour eux-mêmes (*I*, 214).[34]

The result has been what John Guillory has described in the case of America as 'a large-scale 'capital flight'' away from traditionally literature-based humanities disciplines.[35]

Finally, it is necessary to mention that the Collège de France report was not a one-off, that he went on to participate in another process of policy prescription (also with implications for literature). In 1988, Lionel Jospin as Minister for National Education set up a commission Bourdieu co-presided with François Gros to study the contents of education. The resulting report, *Principes pour une réflexion sur les contenus d'enseignement*,[36] published in 1989, restates many of the ideas expressed in the earlier *Collège de France* report, but provides useful elaborations on the application its general principles, including to the teaching

---

33 Bourdieu cites André Motte, a nineteenth-century industrialist: 'Je repète chaque jour à mes enfants que le titre de bachelier ne leur donnera jamais un morceau de pain à croquer; que je les ai mis au collège pour leur permettre de goûter les plaisirs de l'intelligence; pour les mettre en garde contre toutes les fausses doctrines, soit en littérature, soit en philosophie, soit en histoire. Mais j'ajoute qu'il y aurait pour eux grand danger à trop s'adonner aux plaisirs de l'esprit' (*RA*, 87). 'I repeat each day to my children that the title of bachelier [high school graduate] will never put a piece of bread into their mouths; that I sent them to school to allow them to taste the pleasures of intelligence, and to put them on their guard against all false doctrines, whether in literature, philosophy or history. But I add that it would be very dangerous for them to give themselves over to the pleasures of the mind' (*Rules*, 48).
34 'When a bourgeois or even petty-bourgeois mother talks of her son deciding to read history, you'd think she was announcing a catastrophe. Not to mention philosophy or literature. Students in the humanities have become useless mouths. And not only for "government circles" of both right and left, but for their families as well, and often even for themselves' (*Political Interventions*, 170).
35 Guillory, *Cultural Capital*, p. 45.
36 *Principes pour une réflexion sur les contenus d'enseignement* (Paris: Ministère de l'Education Nationale, de la Jeunesse et des Sports, March 1989). The text of the report can be found in Bourdieu, *Political Interventions*, pp. 217-26.

of literature and languages. Nor was the Collège de France report Bourdieu's first foray into the field of cultural/educational policy. In the wake of the *événements* of May 1968, Bourdieu contributed to the production of a series of collectively written thematically based documents issued by the *Centre de sociologie européenne*, including 'Quelques indications pour une politique de démocratisation'.[37] In what follows, we will focus on how these explicitly 'normative' policy proposals addressed contemporary issues and problems related to literary education in France.

The Collège de France report does not propose the simple abolition of academic hierarchies or the suppression of competition, which would seem from Bourdieu's sociology to be constants in any social configuration. Indeed, as Bourdieu notes in his interview with Salgas, 'les *Propositions* du Collège de France ne parlent de hiérarchies (et c'est une mystification que d'en nier l'existence) que pour dire qu'il faut les multiplier, ce qui est la seule manière d'affaiblir les effets liés au monopole' (*I*, 209).[38] This is one of the words, along with 'reproduction' and 'démocratisation', which one would have expected in a document produced by Bourdieu, but which (as he also noted elsewhere) do not appear in the Collège de France report.[39] Bourdieu did not want to make any unrealistic promises or proposals. The report does, however, recommend 'la diversification des formes d'excellence' (*PPEA*, 17), so that competition between disciplines would be very much attenuated.[40] Although the school does not entirely control the social value of the qualifications it distributes (which depends to a large degree on the value of the positions to which they provide access), it does wield a significant power of consecration, which can to a large extent guarantee the social value of the competences it teaches. It follows from what the report says that tackling hierarchies between subject areas within the school could contribute greatly to reducing their differential valorisation beyond it:

---

37 'Quelques indications pour une politique de démocratisation', Dossier no 1 du Centre de sociologie européenne, 6 rue de Tournon, Paris, included in *Political Interventions*, pp. 69-72.
38 'The Collège de France "Proposals" do not talk in terms of hierarchies (though it is a mystification to deny their existence) except to say that there should be a large number of these, which is the only way of wakening the effects bound up with the existing monopoly' (*Political Interventions*, 165).
39 See the quotation from an interview carried out in Tokyo in 1989 in *I*, 186.
40 On the question of how to minimise the effect of stigmatisation, the report suggests the institution of new forms of competition, such as between 'teams' bringing together students and teachers in joint projects, which would reduce 'l'atomisation du groupe et l'humiliation ou le découragement de quelques-uns' (*PPEA*, 23-24), 'the atomisation of the group and the humiliation and discouragement of certain individuals' (trans. J.S.).

travailler à affaiblir ou à abolir les hiérarchies entre les différentes formes d'aptitude, cela tant dans le fonctionnement institutionnel (les coefficients par exemple) que dans l'esprit des maîtres et des élèves, serait un des moyens les plus efficaces (dans les limites du système d'enseignement) de contribuer à l'affaiblissement des hiérarchies purement sociales (*PPEA*, 17).[41]

The Collège de France report suggests several ways in which the principle opposition and antagonism between literary and scientific disciplines, which split the French education system into different 'sections' and faculties, could be resolved. Firstly, it calls for an abolition of the division between 'practical' or 'applied' and 'pure' or 'theoretical' disciplines: not only in name, but by reintroducing 'practical' or 'theoretical' components into disciplines from which they had been excluded. This means that students in every discipline should be placed, as far as possible, in the position of 'creator' or 'discoverer', where they could learn the 'formes générales de pensée' (what are commonly called 'transferable skills') of logic, experimentation, and invention, and where equal weight would be given both to practice and to the theory that informs it (*PPEA*, 18-19). Interestingly, the Collège de France report gives the humanities disciplines, re-cast as practical and creative arts, a prominent role in the inculcation of this 'creative' or 'inventive' disposition, and suggests this as one of the ways in which their educational role could be revalorised:

> Tout en faisant sa juste place à la théorie qui, dans sa définition exacte, n'est identifiée ni au formalisme ni au verbalisme, et aux méthode logiques de raisonnement qui, dans leur rigueur même, enferment une extraordinaire efficacité heuristique, l'enseignement doit se donner pour fin, dans tous les domaines, de faire faire des produits et de mettre l'apprenti en position de découvrir par lui-même. On peut produire une 'manipulation' de chimie ou de physique au lieu de la recevoir toute montée et d'enregistrer les résultats; on peut produire une pièce de théâtre, un film, un opéra, mais aussi un discours, une critique de film, un compte-rendu d'ouvrage (de préférence à l'intention d'un vrai journal d'élèves ou d'étudiants) ou encore une lettre à la Sécurité sociale, un mode d'emploi ou un constat d'accident, au lieu de seulement disserter (…). Dans cet esprit, l'enseignement artistique conçu comme enseignement approfondi de l'une des pratiques artistiques (musique ou peinture ou cinéma, etc.), librement choisie (au lieu d'être, comme aujourd'hui, indirectement imposée), retrouverait une place éminente (*PPEA*, 19).[42]

---

[41] 'to work to weaken or abolish hierarchies between different forms of aptitude, as much at the institutional level (ratios for example) as in the minds of teachers and students, would be one of the most effective measures (within the limits of the education system) to contribute to the weakening of purely social hierarchies' (trans. J.S.).

[42] 'While giving its proper place to theory which, in its exact definition, is neither

The idea that both literary and scientific disciplines can draw on and inculcate the same general 'modes of thought' is repeated and elaborated in *Principes pour une réflexion sur les contenus d'enseignement*. The Bourdieu-Gros report identifies the aim of all teaching as to 'offrir des *modes de pensée dotés d'une validité et d'une applicabilité générales*', three of which it lists as 'le mode de pensée déductif, le mode de pensée expérimental ou le mode de pensée historique' – adding 'le mode de pensée réflexif et critique, qui devrait leur être toujours associé' (*I*, 219).[43] Again, the Bourdieu-Gros report suggests that certain broad subject areas (or the 'disciplines' into which they have been more or less adequately divided) may be better suited to transmitting particular 'modes of thought'. It also however indicates a broad underlying unity with regard to the types of general skills they each require. Thus, for instance, the report reads:

> l'enseignement des langages peut et doit, tout autant que celui de la physique ou de la biologie, être l'occasion d'une initiation à la logique: l'enseignement des mathématiques ou de la physique, tout autant que celui de la philosophie ou de l'histoire, peut et doit permettre de préparer à l'histoire des idées, des sciences ou des techniques (*I*, 225).[44]

Learning a language, students are learning how to manipulate complex logical structures, no less than they are in mathematics; while, for reasons that, as we will see, are inseparably social and scientific, each discipline

---

identified with formalism or verbalism, and to the logical methods of reasoning which, through their very rigour, hold extraordinary heuristic power, the aim of education, in every domain, should be to enable the apprentice to produce things and put him in a position to discover for himself. One can perform an "experiment" in physics or chemistry instead of encountering it all set up and registering the results; one can produce a theatrical play, a film, an opera, but also a discourse, a film review, a synthesis of a work (preferably for a real student journal) or else a letter to Social Security, an instruction manual or an accident report, instead of only writing essays (…). In this spirit, artistic education conceived of as in-depth training in one of the artistic crafts (music, painting, cinema, etc.), freely chosen (instead of being, as it is today, imposed indirectly), would rediscover its eminent place' (trans. J.S.).

43 'Education should privilege all teaching capable of offering modes of thought endowed with a general validity and applicability (…). Decisive privilege must be given to teaching charged with ensuring the considered and critical assimilation of fundamental ways of thinking (such as deduction, experiment, and the historical approach, as well as reflective and critical thinking, which should always be combined with the foregoing' (*Political Interventions*, 175).

44 'The teaching of languages can and must be, just as much as physics of biology, an opportunity for initiation into logic: the teaching of mathematics or physics, just as much as that of philosophy or history, can and must prepare students for the history of ideas, science and technology' (*Political Interventions*, 180).

should study its own history, as part of a broader social and cultural process, which also opens out onto broader historical enquiry. This last point is made prominently in the Collège de France report, under both the first principle, 'L'unité de la science et la pluralité des cultures' (*PPEA*, 13-14),[45] and the sixth, 'L'unification des savoirs transmis' (*PPEA*, 33-34).[46] 'Un des principes unificateurs de la culture et de l'enseignement', the report suggests, could be 'l'histoire sociale des œuvres culturelles (des sciences, de la philosophie, du droit, des arts, de la littérature, etc.), liant de manière à la fois logique et historique l'ensemble des acquis culturels et scientifiques' (*PPEA*, 33).[47] An awareness of the common genesis and historical process of differentiation and autonomisation (such as that outlined in Chapter 3 of the present study with a particular focus on literature) would integrate the different subject areas – most notably literary and scientific cultures – within a shared social and intellectual history, reducing their opposition and antagonism.

The purpose of instilling the historical mode of thought across the faculties would not only be the social integration of the academic and student bodies. There were also scientific reasons to study scientific and cultural history. An awareness of the social conditions and historical process and of scientific progress would give scientists both a more realistic understanding of their own enterprise, and serve as an antidote 'contre les formes anciennes ou nouvelles d'irrationalisme ou de fanatisme de la raison', by fostering 'un respect sans fétichisme de la science comme forme accomplie de l'activité rationnelle' (*PPEA*, 13-14).[48] By showing the social and historical rootedness of scientific knowledge as one field among many, science would cease to hold the status of the final or unique source of truth, and students would gain an improved appreciation and understanding of the different forms of research and knowledge (including literary and artistic). The report thus indicates a subtle path, which would seek to 'réunir l'universalisme de la raison qui est inhérent à l'intention scientifique et le relativisme qu'enseignent les sciences historiques, attentives à la pluralité des sagesses et des

---

45 'Unity of science and plurality of cultures' (trans. J.S.).
46 'Unification of transmitted knowledge' (trans. J.S.).
47 'One of the unifying principles of culture and education [could be] the social history of cultural works (science, philosophy, law, the arts, literature, etc.), relating at once in a logical and historical manner the ensemble of cultural and scientific achievements' (trans. J.S.).
48 'against both the old and new forms of irrationalism and rationalist fanaticism' by fostering 'a respect without fetishism for science as the most accomplished form of rational activity' (trans. J.S.).

sensibilités culturelles' (*PPEA*, 15).[49]

The Collège de France report recommends therefore teaching, 'tout au long de l'enseignement secondaire, une culture intégrant la culture scientifique et la culture historique, c'est-à-dire non seulement l'histoire de la littérature ou même des arts et de la philosophie, mais aussi l'histoire des sciences et des techniques' (*PPEA*, 33).[50] This history should be taught also in its international, notably European, dimension (*PPEA*, 34), in order to take account of 'les innombrables emprunts de techniques et d'instruments à travers les différentes civilisations' (*PPEA*, 15).[51] Again, this educational practice would have both scientific and social benefits: 'notamment les progrès assurés par la méthode comparative',[52] which is a potent method of learning; and 'la découverte de la différence, mais aussi de la solidarité entre les civilisations',[53] which is particularly important in today's world, in which people from different cultural backgrounds are more likely than ever to live alongside each other, develop trade, etc. (*PPEA*, 14). To this end, the report also calls for the production of histories and anthologies of European culture and civilisation, to foster greater collaboration between literature and languages teachers (who appear to be the obvious choices for this sort of work) in different specialisms and nations (*PPEA*, 34).

The call for greater collaboration and coordination between subjects and specialisms is again echoed and amplified in the Bourdieu-Gros report. 'Tout devrait être fait pour encourager les professeurs à coordiner leurs actions' (*I*, 223),[54] the report urges, including by organising regular staff meetings, encouraging teachers to explore beyond their subject specialism, and by programming joint classes (which should be given equal value to single teacher lessons, in terms of pay and the number of hours for which they count). To give a clearer picture of what this last proposal might look like in practice, the Bourdieu-Gros report suggests that we imagine a class taught jointly by a professor of languages

---

49 'to unite the universalism of reason which is inherent to the scientific project and the relativism taught by the historical sciences, attentive to the plurality of wisdoms and cultural sensibilities' (trans. J.S.).
50 'throughout secondary education a culture integrating scientific culture and historical culture, that is, not only literary history or even the history of the arts or philosophy, but also the history of sciences and technology' (trans. J.S.).
51 'the innumerable exchanges of techniques and instruments between the different civilisations' (trans. J.S.).
52 'notably the progress assured by the comparative method' (trans. J.S.).
53 'the discovery of difference, but also of the solidarity between civilisations' (trans. J.S.).
54 'Everything should be done to encourage teachers to coordinate their actions' (*Political Interventions*, 179).

(or philosophy) and a professor of mathematics (or physics), in which it would be demonstrated, for example, 'que les mêmes compétences générales sont exigées par la lecture de textes scientifiques, de notices techniques, de discours argumentatifs' (I, 225).[55] The skills of interpretation and close reading (which literature and language studies currently provide) are no less useful in deciphering complex scientific texts than they are for analysing literary works. Again, this is presented as one of the ways in which the harmful social schism could be healed between scientific and literary cultures:

> L'opposition entre les 'lettres' et les 'sciences', qui domine encore aujourd'hui l'organisation de l'enseignement et les 'mentalités' des maîtres et des parents d'élèves, peut et doit être surmonté par un enseignement capable de professer à la fois la science et l'histoire des sciences ou l'épistémologie, d'initier aussi bien à l'art ou à la littérature qu'à la réflexion esthétique ou logique sur ces objets, d'enseigner non seulement la maîtrise de la langue et des discours littéraire, philosophique, scientifique, mais aussi la maîtrise des procédures logiques ou rhétoriques qui y sont engagés (I, 225).[56]

Bourdieu's thought had moved on from his earlier reflections in 'Quelques indications pour une politique de démocratisation'. There, he had put his name to a proposal for the establishment of a common basic curriculum up to sixth-form level, to delay as far as possible the choice between 'humanities' and 'sciences' and enable everyone to acquire both cultures (I, 71). Both of the later reports counsel against the temptation towards 'encyclopaedism' this appears to suggest (i.e., trying to pack as much as possible onto the curriculum), concentrating instead on the transmission of the 'general forms of thought', and of what the reports refer to as a 'minimum culturel commun' (*PPEA*, 27) or 'minimum commun de connaissances' (I, 222),[57] by analogy with the national minimum wage (the difference being, as Bourdieu explains, that 'ceux qui sont dépourvus de ce minimum ne savent pas qu'ils peuvent et doivent le revendiquer comme

---

[55] 'the same general skills are required for the reading of scientific texts, technical notices and arguments' (*Political Interventions*, 180).
[56] 'The opposition between "science" and "humanities" that still dominates the organization of teaching today, as well as the mentalities of teachers and parents, can and must be overcome by a teaching able to profess both science and the history of sciences or epistemology, to induct students into art and literature as well as asthetic or logical consideration of these subjects, to teach not only mastery of language and litearture, philosophical and scientific discourse, but also active mastery of the logical and rhetorical procedures that these involve' (*Political Interventions*, 180).
[57] 'common minimum of knowledge' (*Political Interventions*, 178).

ils le savent lorsqu'il s'agit du salaire minimum' (I, 208).⁵⁸ Unlike economic poverty, cultural dispossession tends to exclude awareness of one's own state of deprivation. As Ahearne observes, Bourdieu's early critique of 'l'ideologie des "besoins culturels"' did not lead him, therefore, to turn his back on the project of providing universal access to 'high' culture, but rather to insist that this state of unconscious deprivation was an important factor that any cultural policy aimed at democratising culture should take into account.⁵⁹

As part of this core competence, the Collège de France report specifies 'une maîtrise réelle de la langue commune, écrite et parlée' (PPEA, 30)⁶⁰ as one of the main conditions that make learning possible. The cultural minimum also includes the background knowledge and experience that, as we have seen, is necessary to appropriate cultural (including literary) works. In order more effectively to transmit this cultural minimum, the Collège de France report encourages 'l'usage des techniques modernes de diffusion', especially video and television (PPEA, 37).⁶¹ The 'Démocratisation' dossier had mentioned previously the need to provide students with experiences which pupils from favoured classes receive from their families (museum trips, trips to historical and geographical locations, theatre outings, listening to records, etc.), or with substitutes for these (I, 69).

This proposed use of modern media to teach traditional 'literary' disciplines is a response to the rise of new media, which have displaced written communication, and which threaten the school itself as the main authoritative source of information. One of the most serious challenges to the school, the report observes, has come from 'le développement des moyens de communication modernes (en particulier la télévision), capables de concurrencer ou de contrecarrer l'action scolaire' (PPEA, 9).⁶² Now, no doubt, the internet has become the greater threat. The report proposes therefore putting these modern instruments to pedagogical use – recommending for instance the creation of a dedicated State 'cultural channel', which indeed soon after came into existence (PPEA, 27; 46).⁶³

---

58 'those who are deprived of this minimum are unaware that they can and should claim it, in the same way that they might claim the minimum wage' (*Political Interventions*, 164).
59 Ahearne, *Between Cultural Theory and Policy*, p. 58.
60 'a mastery of the common language in written and spoken form' (trans. J.S.).
61 'the us of modern technologies of diffusion' (trans. J.S.).
62 'the development of modern means of communication (in particular television), capable of competing with or counteract the action of the school' (trans. J.S.).
63 The Franco-German cultural channel *LA SEPT*, later to become *ARTE*. See also

Cultural programmes, created with the participation of teachers and specialists, and recorded onto video-tape for use in the classroom, offer, the report argues, powerful 'instruments de transmission des savoirs et des savoir-faire élémentaires, c'est-à-dire fondamentaux' (PPEA, 37)[64], including in the case of literary studies:

> Il n'est pas douteux, par exemple, qu'en matière d'art et de littérature, et tout spécialement de théâtre, et aussi de géographie ou de langues vivantes, l'image pourrait contribuer à ôter à l'enseignement le caractère assez irréel qu'il revêt pour les enfants ou les adolescents dépourvus de l'expérience directe du spectacle ou du voyage à l'étranger (PPEA, 37-38).[65]

A related proposal is the notion that cultural 'creators' (researchers, artists, writers) and intermediaries (publishers, journalists, curators) should be brought into schools; and that schools should also co-ordinate their actions with those of other cultural institutions, such as libraries, museums, orchestras, etc. This proposal is again designed to combat the school's tendency towards insularity and 'irreality'. In a comment that (if we know Bourdieu's work) can be assumed to have been directed at the humanities, the *Collège de France* report specifies that 'il faut éviter que le système scolaire ne se constitue en univers séparé, sacré, proposant une culture elle-même sacrée et coupée de l'existence ordinaire' (PPEA, 41).[66] It was important therefore to reintroduce the social contexts to the school's activity as one of several instances of transmission, in order to raise students' awareness of its (and their own) role and contribution in cultural life, and to 'rappeler la distinction, sans doute partiellement irréductible, entre la culture et la culture scolaire' (PPEA, 42).[67]

In this way, the report aimed to strengthen the relations between the different agents and institutions of cultural production and diffusion, with the school at their centre (PPEA, 44). The report does not ignore the 'résistances psychologiques' to active cooperation between cultural agents and institutions

---

Ahearne, *Between Cultural Theory and Policy*, p. 64.
64 'instruments for the transmission of basic, which is to say fundamental, knowledge and know-how' (trans. J.S.).
65 'It is not to be doubted, for example, that in the case of art and literature, and especially of theatre, and also of geography or modern languages, the image could contribute to release education from its rather unrealistic character which it has for children or adolescents who lack direct experience of spectacles or trips abroad' (trans. J.S.).
66 'the school system must be prevented from becoming a separate and sacred universe, proposing a culture which is itself sacred and cut off from ordinary existence' (trans. J.S.).
67 'to remember the distinction, which is no doubt partially irreducible, between culture and scholastic culture' (trans. J.S.).

who more often compete against each other, and which rank alongside other bureaucratic, legal, and financial obstacles to the participation of figures from the artistic, literary, and professional worlds in education (*PPEA*, 42). On the one hand, their presence is likely to be viewed as an invasion and threat by teaching professionals. On the other hand, cultural producers may resent what could appear to be pedagogical demands being placed upon their artistic projects. The report specifies however that such exchanges could be organised 'non dans la logique d'un contrôle qui ne peut que susciter des réactions de fermeture et de défense corporatiste, mais dans la logique de la participation aux responsabilités, même financières, à l'inspiration et à l'incitation' (*PPEA*, 41).[68] Building mutually beneficial relations between the school and other cultural institutions, through which each would reinforce and prolong the actions of the other, could contribute not only to the success of the educational enterprise, but also to that of the cultural environment around it.

Admittedly, the reports met with mixed success. Of the nine principles set out in the Collège de France report, President Mitterrand retained only three: 'l'unité dans le pluralisme, l'ouverture dans et par l'autonomie, la révision périodique des savoirs enseignés' (*I*, 199),[69] and the last of these was only acted on after it was repeated in the Bourdieu-Gros report, when Jospin set up, as a direct response to it, the 'Conseil national des programmes d'enseignement' to oversee the ongoing revision of national subject curricula.[70] Yet as Bourdieu admitted during an appearance on *Apostrophes*, many of the propositions had been made and even tried before, here and there; what was new was that they had never been brought together and implemented as a whole, across the education system – especially as some of its proposals appeared contradictory.[71] The impact of the report was therefore no doubt reduced by its partial implementtion. Twenty years later, the proposals have hardly dated, and continue to be read as valuable and suggestive resources in their

---

68 'not in the logic of an inspection which could only provoke reactions of corporatist defense and closure, but in the logic of participation in the responsibilities, including even financial, of inspiration and incitement' (trans. J.S.). On this point, see also Ahearne, *Between Cultural Theory and Policy*, pp. 63-64.
69 'unity within pluralism, openness in and through autonomy, and periodic revision of the subjects taught' (*Political Interventions*, 156).
70 For further detail, see Jeremy Ahearne, *Intellectuals, Culture and Public Policy in France: Approaches from the Left* (Liverpool: Liverpool University Press, 2010).
71 *Apostrophes* (Paris: Antenne 2), 10 May 1985. At http://www.ina.fr/video/I00002866/p-bourdieufait-une-proposition-pour-l-enseignement-du-futur.fr.html consulted on 12/12/09.

own right, for individual classroom practice as much as for wider policy contexts.

Finally, although they were co-authored and co-signed, the reports discussed in this section do express Bourdieu's own views. Bourdieu placed great store on the fact that the Collège de France report, especially, was a collective work, and expressed the consensus of some forty specialists across a range of fields, as this gave force to the proposals, as the expression of a collective body. It was also important to him that this consensus had been achieved not simply over the minimum (for instance, that students should be taught to read, write, and count), or at the expense of detail (*PPEA*, 9). Nevertheless, Bourdieu does seem to have been the main, if not sole, author of both reports which are written in his characteristic style, and are included in his compilation of political writings, *Interventions*. It seems reasonable therefore to use these two reports to support our central thesis that, far from an enemy of literary culture who sought to reduce literature to an instrument of cultural distinction, Bourdieu saw its positive value and uses, as is shown as evidence in the proposals made in these reports regarding literary education.

Between the state and the free market

Bourdieu also provides cultural policy indications targeted at the cultural field around the school, although these generally take the form of asides, given informally in interviews or more directly political speeches, or are implied by his research findings. The main context for these interventions was what Bourdieu saw as the increasing commercialisation and concentration of the cultural field, which was in his view cutting off more challenging writers, artists, and filmmakers from the public space, where they would need to create their own markets, in favour of more conventional works, for which there was pre-existing demand. Bourdieu studied this context in his last major piece of empirical research, 'Une Révolution conservatrice dans l'édition',[72] in which Bourdieu and his co-workers had shown that editorial policies vary as publishers go up and down in size, and as a factor of competition. It followed that, as publishers and booksellers were bought out or merged, their editorial

---

72 Pierre Bourdieu, 'Une Révolution conservatrice dans l'édition', *Actes de la recherche en sciences sociales*, 126 (1999), 3-28.

policies would become more conservative and oriented towards profit.

This was a case Bourdieu put before a meeting of the *Conseil international du musée de la télévision et de la radio* (MTR) on Monday 11 October 1999, in a paper entitled, forthrightly, 'Maîtres du monde, savez-vous ce que vous faites?'[73] Among those present were Peter Chenin, the president of Fox, Greg Dyke, the director-general of the BBC, Rémy Satter, president of CLT-UFA, Patrick Le Lay, CEO of TF1, as well as business leaders from Hollinger, Bertelsmann, Mediaset, etc., representatives from American pension funds, and the European Commissioner for culture, Viviane Reding. Citing Plato's (dubious) dictum, 'nul n'est méchant volontairement',[74] Bourdieu began by trying to dispel certain 'false ideas' or 'myths', which were obscuring the real effects of concentration and the quest for short-term profit maximisation. Against the idea that commercial competition leads to a diversification of supply, for instance, Bourdieu points to the fact of increasing homogenisation of cultural products. His examples are television programmes – 'le fait que les multiples réseaux de communication tendent de plus en plus à diffuser, souvent à la même heure le même type de produits, jeux, *soap operas*, musique commerciale, romans sentimentaux du type *telenovela*', etc. – but he could equally have mentioned bestsellers and paperbacks that could have been published by indifferent imprints: 'autant de produits issus de la recherche des profits maximaux pour des coûts minimaux' (*I*, 419).[75]

Referring directly to the publishing industry, Bourdieu cites the example of Thomas Midlehoff, then chief executive of the transnational media corporation Bertelsmann which had in 1998 acquired Random House (already the largest general trade book publisher in the Anglophone world), as an example of the sort of commercial pressures editors were under from their managers and parent companies: 'Selon

---

73 Pierre Bourdieu, 'Maîtres du monde, savez-vous ce que vous faites?', published in *L'Humanité*, 13 October 1999, *Le Monde*, 14 October 1999, and *Libération* 13 October 1999. Included in *Political Interventions* under the title 'Questions aux vrais maîtres du monde', pp. 417-24. 'Masters of the world, do you know what you are doing?' (trans. J.S.).
74 'No one is bad by choice' (*Political Interventions*, 340).
75 'to the idea of the extraordinary diversification of supply, we could oppose the extraordinary uniformity of television programmes, the fact that the various communications networks increasingly tend to broadcast the same type of product at the same time – games, soaps, commercial music, sentimental "*telenovelas*", police series that are no better for being French, like *Navarro*, or German, like *Derrick*. So many products issuing from the quest for maximum profit for minimum cost' (*Political Interventions*, 341).

le journal *La Tribune*, "il a donné deux ans aux 350 centres de profit pour remplir les exigences. (...) D'ici à la fin 2000, tous les secteurs doivent assurer plus de 10% de rentabilité sur le capital investi"' (*I*, 419-20).⁷⁶ The result was that editors were forced to compete for commercial bestsellers, especially when publishers were integrated with big multimedia groups, re-orienting the entire field towards commercial production, meaning that writers that did not fit the business model would have more difficulty making it into print. We can imagine that his audience did not welcome such criticism. Conscious, perhaps, that appealing to the better nature of the 'Maîtres du monde' might not be the most successful strategy, Bourdieu tried next to excite their interest in profit:

> Si l'on sait que, au moins dans tous les pays développés, la durée de la scolarisation ne cesse de croître, ainsi que le niveau d'instruction moyen, comme croissent du même coup toutes les pratiques fortement corrélées avec le niveau d'instruction (fréquentation des musées ou des théâtres, lecture, etc.), on peut penser qu'une politique d'investissement économique dans des producteurs et des produits dits 'de qualité' peut, au moins à terme moyen, être rentable, même économiquement (à condition toutefois de pouvoir compter sur les services d'un système éducatif efficace) (*I*, 422).⁷⁷

As Ahearne writes, 'this may well be casuistry' (subtle but unsound reasoning, with a view to promoting a given point of view): 'such harmony between the interests of media entrepreneurs and autonomous cultural producers seems improbable'.⁷⁸ Bourdieu's argument was coherent, however, with his ruse (discussed above) of using economic arguments against economic arguments – 'retourner contre l'économie dominante ses propres armes, et rappeler, que, dans la logique de l'intérêt bien compris, la politique strictement économique n'est pas nécessairement économique' (*CF1*, 45).⁷⁹

---

76 'I could cite the example of Thomas Middlehoff, president of Bertelsmann, as reported in *La Tribune*: "He gave the 350 profit centres two years to meet their targets. (...) Between now and the end of 2000, each sector must ensure a profit of more than 10 per cent on the capital invested"' (*Political Interventions*, 342).
77 'Since we know that, in all the developed countries at least, the length of school attendance is still steadily growing, as well as the average educational level, and all those practices strongly correlated with it such as museum or theatre attendance, reading, etc., we can imagine that a policy of economic investment in producers and products described as "quality" could even be economically profitable at least in the medium term, on condition however that this could count on the services of an effective educational system' (*Political Interventions*, 344).
78 Ahearne, *Between Cultural Theory and Policy*, p. 72.
79 'to turn back against the dominant economy its own weapons, and point out that,

In the final instance, it was to the State that Bourdieu looked to protect the interests of cultural producers. Of course, the French literary field already receives an enviable package of State support, from the famous 'Loi Lang', to the 'Fonds d'intervention pour les services, l'artisanat et le commerce' (FISAC), and a reduced rate of value added tax on books. In the conclusion to 'Une Révolution conservatrice dans l'édition', entitled (and signalling another 'normative' shift) 'La morale de l'histoire',[80] Bourdieu suggests, however, that the contemporary distribution of State subsidies, which went primarily to the oldest and most prestigious publishers (such as Gallimard and Seuil), should have been be re-directed toward small and often fledgling publishers, which are the main conduits for the newest and most innovative writers (cf. *RC*, 45). Yet, even if these measures have not been as effective or efficient as they might have been, they have still helped undeniably to maintain a diverse book market in France, which has few equivalents in other countries.

We can understand Bourdieu's concern, then, when the ability of independent States to protect the cultural and public sectors of their economies seemed threatened by neo-liberal reforms in the 1990s, aiming to 'open' national markets even further to global capital. In an open letter the director-general of UNESCO published in 2000, Bourdieu cites a memo from within the World Trade Organisation (WTO), which states its intention to extend free market rules to education, health, and culture.[81] This last category includes 'des services comme l'audiovisuel dans sa totalité, les bibliothèques, archives et musées, les jardins botaniques et zoologiques, tous les services liés aux divertissements (arts, théâtre, services radiophoniques et télévisuels, parcs d'attractions, parcs

---

according to the logic of well-understood interest, strictly economic policies are not necessarily economical' (trans. J.S.).

80 'The moral of the story' (trans. J.S.).

81 'Le mandat de la négotiation est ambitieux: supprimer les restrictions sur le commerce des services et procurer un accès réel à un marché soumis à des limitations spécifiques. Notre défi est d'accomplir une suppression significative de ces restrictions à travers tous les secteurs de services, abordant les dispsitions nationales déjà soumises aux règles de l'AGCS et ensuite les dispositions qui ne sont pas actuellement soumises aux règles de l'AGCS et couvrant toutes les possibilités de fournir des services' (*I*, 451). 'The mandate of this negotiation is ambitious: to suppress restrictions on trade in services and obtain real access to a market subject to specific limitations. Our challenge is to accomplish a significant suppression of these restrictions across all sectors of services, tackling the national mechanisms already subject to GATT rules and covering all possibilities of providing services' (*Political Interventions*, 370).

récréatifs, services sportifs' (*I*, 453).⁸² The result, Bourdieu warns, would be disastrous – and totally counter to UNESCO's mission to 'assurer à tous le plein et égal accès à l'éducation, la libre poursuite de la vérité objective et le libre échange des idées et des connaissances' (*I*, 454).⁸³ States would give up their powers (treated as so many 'obstacles to commerce') to protect their national identities, and citizens exercising a right to free education, libraries, museums, etc., would be turned into simple consumers. Bourdieu and his co-signatories called therefore on the director-general to join their opposition to the GATT agreement (a call which went unheeded).

Bourdieu made a similar case in an address to anti-globalisation protestors in Québec in 2001. The policy of globalisation, he argued, was leading to the destruction of 'tous les *systèmes de défense* qui protègent les plus précieuses conquêtes sociales et culturelles des sociétés avancées' (*I*, 461),⁸⁴ such as domestic regulations, subsidies, licences, etc. The Canadians were well placed, as it were, to observe the effects of 'free trade' between unequal partners, including to their publishing industry: 'L'union douanière n'a-t-elle pas eu pour effet de déposséder la société dominée de toute indépendance économique et culturelle à l'égard de la puissance dominante, avec la fuite des cerveaux, la concentration de la presse, de l'édition, etc. au profit des États-Unis?' (*I*, 463).⁸⁵ Bourdieu's well-publicised support for the anti-globalisation movement was therefore closely allied with his defence of cultural and so also literary autonomy.

Yet State protection was not without its own dangers. State support did not necessarily go to the most autonomous and competent but, as it had under the Second Empire, to the most conventional and compliant producers. It could also influence the direction taken by research, whether

---

82 'the negotiations under way (...) cover services such as the entire range of audio-visual material, libraries, archives and museums, botanical and zoological gardens, all services associated with entertainment (arts, theatre, radio and television services, fun fairs, recreational and sports facilities)' (*Political Interventions*, 372).
83 'to promote (...) full and equal opportunities for education for all, in the unrestricted pursuit of objective truth, and in the free exchange of ideas and knowledge' (*Political Interventions*, 372).
84 'the destruction of all the *defence systems* that protect the most precious social and cultural conquests of the advanced societies' (*Political Interventions*, 377).
85 'The customs union has had the effect of dispossessing the dominated society of all economic and cultural independence from the dominant power, with the brain drain, the concentration of press and publishing, etc. to the benefit of the United States' (*Political Interventions*, 378).

by inspiring a cynical search for symbolic profits or by more insidious co-optation (giving recognition for recognition, as it were). In this context, Bourdieu even criticises the apparently pro-intellectual socialist government in France in the 1980s and 1990s, for having 'appuyé sur les faiblesses et les failles des champs littéraires et artistiques, c'est-à-dire sur les moins autonomes (et les moins compétents) des créateurs, pour imposer ses sollicitations et ses séductions' (*LE*, 23).[86] This is a reference, no doubt, to the Mitterrand government's attempts to woo famous authors, artists, film stars, and intellectuals, and through them the electorate, with invitations to well-publicised working lunches and ministerial receptions, discussion groups and committees, etc.[87] Bourdieu also writes of the constraints imposed by

> le mécénat d'Etat, bien qu'il permette d'échapper en apparence aux pressions directes du marché, (...) soit à travers la reconnaissance qu'il accorde spontanément à ceux qui le reconnaissent parce qu'ils ont besoin de lui pour obtenir une forme de reconnaissance qu'ils ne peuvent s'assurer par leur œuvre même, soit, plus subtilement, à travers le mécanisme des commissions et comités, lieux d'une cooptatation négative qui aboutit le plus souvent à une véritable normalisation de la recherche, qu'elle soit scientifique ou artistique (*RA*, 554).[88]

Bourdieu's solution to this antinomy (autonomous producers need State protection, which puts them in a position of dependence on the State) was, as we might expect, to assert it as such. Cultural producers at once can claim the resources they need from the State, and control over how such resources are used. Bourdieu put this point strongly to Hans Haacke, as he explained the apparent contradiction between his defence of the possibility of State intervention in culture, and his vigorous critiques of its cultural policy:

> Il faut qu'ils travaillent simultanément, sans scrupule ni mauvaise conscience, à accroître l'engagement de l'Etat et la vigilance à l'égard de l'Etat.

---

86 'exploited the weaknesses and flaws of the literary and artistic fields, that is, the least autonomous (and least competent) creators – to impose its solicitations and enticements' (*Free Exchange*, 13; trans. modified J.S).
87 See Ahearne, *Between Cultural Theory and Policy*, p. 124.
88 'state sponsorship – even though it seems to escape the direct pressures of the market – whether through the recognition it grants spontaneously to those who recognize it because they need it in order to obtain a form of recognition which they cannot get by their work alone, or whether, more subtly, through the mechanism of commissions and committees – places of negative co-optation which often result in a thorough standardization of the avant-garde' (*Rules*, 345).

Par exemple, s'agissant de l'aide de l'Etat à la création culturelle, il faut lutter à la fois pour l'accroissement de cette aide aux entreprises culturelles non commerciales et pour l'accroissement du contrôle sur l'usage de cette aide. (...) C'est à la condition de renforcer à la fois l'aide de l'Etat et les contrôles sur les usages de cette aide (...), que l'on pourra échapper pratiquement à l'alternative de l'étatisme et du libéralisme dans laquelle les idéologues du libéralisme veulent nous enfermer (LE, 77-78).[89]

Only the State, Bourdieu argued, is capable of guaranteeing the existence of a culture without a market, just as it alone is able to provide public services, hospitals, transport, schools, etc. which are not run simply for profit. Without such state assistance, writers and researchers would have to rely on the good will of rich patrons, as they did in the seventeenth century, with the result that it is unlikely that some types of work would ever be written. Bourdieu offers himself as an example: if he had to find sponsors for his work, he admits, he would have a lot of difficulty. For this reason, he writes, 'le libéralisme radical, c'est évidemment la mort de la production culturelle libre parce que la censure s'exerce à travers l'argent' (LE, 75).[90]

For a corporatism of the universal

Yet Bourdieu's solution to the problem of how to maintain an autonomous cultural sector left important questions unanswered. Why should the State relinquish control over the use of public funds? And why should public money be used to support minority – and elite – interests, such as avant-garde literature? Convincing the State that it should do these things (or justifying their continuation) may sound as impossible as managing to convince the commercial pole of literary production to hand back market share to independent bookshops and publishers. What it has in its favour, however, particularly in France, is the State's historical commitment to

---

[89] 'They must work simultaneously, without scruples or a guilty conscience, to increase the state's involvement as well as their vigilance in relation to the state's influence. For example, with regard to state support of cultural production, it is necessary to struggle both for the increase of support for non-commercial cultural enterprises as well as for greater controls on he use of that assistance (...). It is only by reinforcing both state assistance and controls on the uses of that assistance (...) that we can practically escape the alternative of statism and liberalism in which the ideologues of liberalism want to enclose us' (Free Exchange, 73).
[90] 'Radical liberalism is evidently the death of free cultural production because censorship is exerted through money' (Free Exchange, 70).

'universal' values (freedom, truth, beauty, justice, and so on). According to Bourdieu, the claim to 'universality' could be used as a way to win support for cultural practices that were now in a process of decline:

> C'est au nom de cet idéal, ou de ce mythe que l'on peut encore, aujourd'hui, tenter de mobiliser contre les entreprises de restauration qui sont apparues, un peu partout dans le monde, au sein même des champs de production culturelle; c'est au nom de la force symbolique qu'il peut donner, malgré tout, aux 'idées vraies' que l'on peut tenter de s'opposer avec quelques chances de succès aux forces de régression intellectuelle, morale, et politique (*I*, 288).[91]

The reason for Bourdieu's cautious wording is, of course, that (as he had spent the first part of his career demonstrating) the dispositions informed by values which we sometimes think of as 'universal' (they are, for many, the sign of our 'humanity') are far from being universally distributed. We are not spontaneously moral, rational, or disinterested beings. These may be universal anthropological possibilities, but they can be realised fully only under particular social and economic conditions, which, Bourdieu points out, are by no means universally satisfied. It follows that works of great art and literature, which are held for a time to be universal, and even eternal, are no such things. They are the preserve of a privileged few, who have the desire and competence (both acquired through socialisation and education) required to appropriate them.

Yet if universal values are no more than a 'myth' or a strategic ploy, Bourdieu's position of defending 'legitimate' culture is exposed to the most elementary anti-intellectualist attack. Why should State money be used to subsidise the '*happy few*', who, in Bourdieu's own words, enjoy 'le *privilège de lutter pour le monopole de l'universel*' (*RP*, 224)?[92] From facing charges of barbarism in the early days of his career, Bourdieu now found himself, in its later phase, accused of elitism. 'On objectera que je suis en train de tenir des propos élitistes', Bourdieu anticipated in *Sur la télévision*, 'de défendre la citadelle assiégée de la grande science et de la grande culture, ou même

---

91 'It is in the name of this ideal or myth that we can still seek to mobilize today against the enterprises of restoration that have sprung up almost everywhere in the world, even within the fields of cultural production themselves; it is in the name of the symbolic force that it can give, despite everything, to "true ideas", that we can seek to oppose with some chance of success the forces of intellectual regression' (*Political Interventions*, 236).
92 'the privilege of fighting for the monopoly of the universal' (*Practical Reason*, 135).

de l'interdire au peuple' (T, 76).[93] Yet, Bourdieu argued, there was not necessarily a contradiction between defending the conditions necessary for the production of specific, specialised works, and a concern to democratic culture. The way past this problem (and the way for the 'mandataires de l'universel' (I, 287)[94] to earn their privilege and status), was for the creators and custodians of culture to work simultaneously both to protect the social and economic conditions necessary to sustain such culture (including the 'droit d'entrée'[95] which excludes non-specialists from participation), and to promote the conditions under which more people could acquire the competences and resources necessary to engage in the cultural game (implying a 'devoir de sortie', to leave the ivory tower and participate actively in society). Bourdieu writes

> En fait, je défends les conditions nécessaires à la production et à la diffusion des créations les plus hautes de l'humanité. (...) Il faut défendre à la fois l'ésotérisme inhérent (par définition) à toute recherche d'avant-garde et la nécessité d'exotériser l'ésotérique et de lutter pour obtenir les moyens de le faire dans de bonnes conditions. En d'autres termes, il faut défendre les conditions de production qui sont nécessaires pour faire progresser l'universel et en même temps, il faut travailler à généraliser les conditions d'accès à l'universel, de sorte que de plus en plus de gens remplissent les conditions nécessaires pour s'approprier l'universel (T, 77).[96]

In reality, the two sides of this coin turn into each other. By working to universalise the conditions of access to works which are of potentially 'universal' value (whether in science, literature, or art), the custodians of culture can win greater recognition and support for what they do, and more symbolic and material resources to continue doing it. Meanwhile, by helping to make the 'universal' progress by making works of potentially universal value, and by working simultaneously on their particularly skilled and creative habitus, producers can also make themselves more useful to society.

---

93 'People may object to this as elitism, a simple defence of he besieged citadel of big science and high culture, or even, an attempt to close out ordinary people' (On Television, 65).
94 'mandatories of universality' (Political Interventions, 236).
95 'right of entry' (On Television, 65).
96 'In fact, I am defending the conditions necessary for the production and diffusion of the highest human creations. (...) It is essential to defend both the inherent esotericism of all cutting-edge research and the necessity of de-esotericizing the esoteric. We must struggle to achieve both these goals under good conditions. In other words, we have to defend the conditions of production necessary for the progress of the universal, while working to generalize the conditions of access to that universality' (On Television, 65-66).

This is how Bourdieu concludes *Les Règles*, with a call 'pour un corporatisme de l'universel': a sort of politico-ethical project or *Realpolitik de la raison*, in which intellectuals would put their symbolic capital and specific skills at the service of 'universal' causes. Despite his repeated insistence on the 'modesty' of this programme, its scope is clearly massive: almost too huge to be meaningful. Unlike the limited aims of the 'intellectuel spécifique' embodied by Foucault, it is not restricted to a specific area of expertise, but expands to take account of social and economic factors. Yet it is also clearly more targeted than the scatter-gun approach of Sartre's 'intellectuel total', who would try to solve the totality of the world's problems. It provides, perhaps, as the French expect from public intellectuals, a *framework* within which to inscribe and make sense of more localised actions (such as, for example, the publishing or teaching of non-commercial forms of literature).

This project would not be entirely altruistic. 'Il y a une reconnaissance universelle de la reconnaissance de l'universel'(*RP*, 165), [97] Bourdieu writes: a symbolic profit that goes to those who work for the benefit of the group, and which, he hypothesises, is a sort of anthropological constant, observable in every culture and society. If cultural producers could generate more demand for their products, they would also be better paid. We can notice how Bourdieu's *Realpolitik* feeds back into his cultural policy proposals (discussed above) to foster stronger relations between the school and cultural institutions, including with the literary and publishing fields, and intersects with his support for the anti-globalisation movement and defence of the State. For these reasons, Bourdieu admits in *Les Règles*'s final lines, 'cette *Realpolitik de la raison* sera sans nul doute exposée au soupçon de corporatisme', the meshing of particular interests. 'Mais il lui appartiendra de montrer, par les fins au service desquelles elle mettra les moyens, durement conquis, de son autonomie, qu'il s'agit d'un corporatisme de l'universel' (*RA*, 558).[98]

---

[97] 'The universal is the object of universal recognition and the sacrifice of selfish (especially economic) interest is universally recognized as legitimate' (*Practical Reason*, 59).

[98] 'This *Realpolitik of reason* will undoubtedly be suspected of corporatism. But it will be part of its task to prove, by the ends to which it puts the sorely won means of its autonomy, that it is a corporatism of the universal' (*Rules*, 348).

Conclusion

Bourdieu's work on literature provides a wide-ranging and theoretically sophisticated framework for understanding the processes and patterns of literary production and reception. Bourdieu's work on cultural tastes, education and his cultural policy proposals intertwine with his substantive work on literature to provide a view of literature's place and function in French society. This is a model that can and has been used as the basis for comparison of literary production in other countries, facilitated by the re-application of Bourdieu's concepts and theories. Bourdieu's theory has, moreover, been extended to the transnational level of 'world literary space', to take account of the relations of domination and subordination between different literary traditions. Bourdieu's work on literature in turn has implications for cultural policy and politics. His account of how Flaubert and others broke free from subordination to the market, and of how Zola used this position of autonomy and authority to intervene in the political sphere, is a model that can be followed and extended. The broad historical panorama Bourdieu supplies of how literature became differentiated from other discourses, and of how the writer gained his prestigious place in French culture, can also help educators, researchers, writers, publishers and others with a vested interest in literature to understand the reverse process, which we appear now to be witnessing.

Literary critics can learn from Bourdieu new concepts and methods for analysing literary texts and their social contexts. Several of Bourdieu's notions have antecedents in established approaches. The concept of field, for instance, has similarities with the notion of a republic of letters, while the theory of habitus relates to questions more usually dealt with in biographies. The notion of cultural capital was anticipated by Paul Valéry, and Bourdieu's starting point for his project to reconstruct the author's point of view was a challenge bequeathed by Flaubert. Yet the originality of Bourdieu's theory is not the individual components, but the way they are connected – and for this reason

DOI: 10.11647/OBP.0027.08

this study has also argued that a systematic appropriation of Bourdieu's method is preferable to a pick-and-choose approach. The three key concepts of capital, habitus and field, for instance, only have their full explicative force in relation to each other: capital is a product of a field of individual habitus, of which the positions are defined by the distribution of capital, and so on.

Teachers of literature can take away from their reading of Bourdieu a keener sense of purpose, and a clearer understanding of their role as guardians and guarantors of literary culture. Certainly, in his early work Bourdieu was a harsh critic of literary education, which was then dominant, and which he describes as a prime example of how the school ratifies social and economic differences. Rather than leading pious celebrations in the classroom, however, Bourdieu encourages teachers to treat literature as a store of expressive and ideational resources, and textual analysis as a way of training students' critical faculties. Unequal distributions of cultural capital could find their remedy in the proposal for a core cultural minimum, which would provide to all students, regardless of social background, the foundation of skills and knowledge necessary to engage in literary and cultural life. And students from across the disciplines could be given a sharper sense of the diversity of forms of excellence, and of the analogies between different forms of knowledge, to counter-balance the now rising supremacy of science.

Literary writers, publishers and booksellers can gain insight from Bourdieu's work into their own activities, to position themselves and others in the field, identify and understand possible conflicts, and recognise shared interests. Reminding these crucial players in the field of the 'heroic' times when the French literary field freed itself from domination by the Church, State and market could also give these actors courage to keep to those principles of autonomy which can now seem precarious, or even anachronistic. At a time when the value of literary culture is questioned routinely, and the differences between great works and mediocrities blurred, Bourdieu offers realistic arguments for the conservation of the fragile eco-system of specialists and enthusiasts, and a simple framework for action. Bourdieu argues for the State to help protect publishers and booksellers from direct commercial pressures, such as the rise of publishing giants and media megastores. And he led by example, founding the self-consciously autonomous sociology journal *Actes de la recherche en sciences sociales*, and the ill-fated literary journal *Liber*, to counter the disappearance of independent instances of consecration and transmission.

Bourdieu's work on literature can also inspire literary writers directly. Annie Ernaux, in particular, has found inspiration in Bourdieu's writing on social inequality and reflexivity. More generally, aspiring writers may find in Bourdieu's deflated image of the literary 'genius' a more attainable, and arguably no less impressive, ideal.

Yet Bourdieu's work is not complete. He himself saw his sociology in general as only a 'work in progress' (*E*, 90), and encouraged his readers to view the analyses in *Les Règles* as so many 'sketches', which could be completed and revised by further research (*RA*, 303). His theory itself, Bourdieu insisted, benefits less from critical exegesis than from being put to use in new analyses, which could confirm its hypotheses, or prompt further modifications and refinements. The relation Bourdieu draws between works and their social contexts, in particular, needs to be tested on works less amenable to Bourdieusian analysis than *L'Éducation sentimentale*. And the differences between the notions of literary field, microcosm, institution and grouping should be defined to describe more or less loose or transient relationships.

Bourdieu himself took inspiration from literary texts and writers as he developed his theory. He found solutions to problems in the reporting of interviews in Flaubert's *style indirect libre*. He was inspired by writers who broke with traditional linear narratives, such as Faulkner and Robbe-Grillet, to look beyond conventional interpretations and accounts of life histories. And he found in the multi-layered prose of Proust, and in the polyonomasie of Flaubert, Joyce or Faulkner, techniques to help him describe the complexity of reality. Bourdieu's key concept of 'field' was, moreover, developed during his research into literature and culture. All this proves that literature and sociology, although opposed and at times conflicting, have much to learn from each other.

Returning to the central allegations with which we began this study, it should by now be clear that Bourdieu by no means sought to 'reduce' literary works to their social conditions of production. Indeed, his theory was developed partly in opposition to Marxist sociological approaches, which explained works directly in terms of their political or economic contexts – a sort of 'short-circuit'. Bourdieu keeps the notions of a 'space of works' and the 'space of positions' separate, and introduces the concept of a 'literary field', to chart the complex mediations that relate a work to its social conditions of production. Then again, Bourdieu was equally critical of the post-structuralist tendency to discredit any and all attempts to analyse and interpret works as ultimately impossible, and even unethical. Instead, he developed an epistemological position that can be understood as realist (despite certain confusing and contradictory statements), in which theoretical models are taken to approximate reality, and tested on their heuristic and predictive power. While no model might ever match the complexity of the phenomenon it describes, there are degrees of accuracy.

Secondly, although Bourdieu's sociology can seem, at first, pessimistic and despairing, he was in fact highly optimistic about the ability of both literature and sociology to make a positive social impact. This is obvious in his efforts to found an international literary journal, Liber, which was initially distributed freely in national newspapers. It can also be seen in his efforts to reach a wider general readership by adopting a more literary style in La Misère du monde. Bourdieu believed that literature and sociology could help people to understand their own experience and that of others, and could help to counter-act a dominant ideology that was not in the interest of the common good. Literature, in particular, could be a space in which to imagine and act out alternative futures, which may even galvanise real political struggles. Indeed, Bourdieu's optimism sometimes out-steps the bounds of the possible. This was the case with Liber, which soon lost its commercial backers and retreated between the pages of his sociological journal Actes de la recherche en sciences sociales; and also with his ambitious plans for the International Parliament of Writers, which were ignored. With these projects, Bourdieu was trying to institute a new position in the cultural field, that of a 'collective intellectual', which could intervene from a position of autonomy, as Zola did during the Dreyfus Affair, but with the combined symbolic capital of a collective grouping.

Finally, far from an 'attack' on literary culture, Bourdieu's theoretical work on literature was the basis of his apparently incongruous defence of literature as a 'universal' culture. Bourdieu may have been a caustic critic of high culture's universalist pretentions, and actual segregational effects. But this does not contradict his normative Realpolitik to universalize the conditions of access to works which could be, potentially, of universal value. Once the myths of 'immaculate perception' and 'uncreated creators' are shattered, then educators, policy makers, cultural producers and society at large could work together to sustain the social conditions in which intellectual (including specifically literary) culture can survive. This is what Bourdieu referred to in Les Règles' final lines as a 'corporatisme de l'universel', a recognition of the solidarity and shared interests behind apparent divisions and antagonisms, which could be the basis for collective and individual acts of support and co-operation.

We can conclude by summarising these points as a sort of programme for applying Bourdieu to literary studies. On a theoretical level, Bourdieu's works demand not only retrospective comprehension, but a productive or generative use, which would apply its empirical findings and the conceptual system behind them in new research, including in different national contexts. At an institutional level, Bourdieu's work on literature also provides a strong rationale for developing closer interdisciplinary links between literature and sociology. From a cultural policy perspective, Bourdieu's texts provide suggestive resources for individual classroom practice as much as for wider policy contexts. And in terms of cultural politics, Bourdieu reminds writers, researchers and the larger intellectual community of how they can reconcile the demands of autonomy and activism, and suggests new collaborative strategies in the pursuit of universal values. This programme cuts across not only Bourdieu's individual oeuvre, but also across disciplinary and national boundaries, taking us necessarily 'beyond' Bourdieu. And many of the concerns and problems it addresses, in theory, cultural policy, and politics, are no less pressing today. Two decades after the publication of *Les Règles*, and ten years since his death, Bourdieu's work on literature remains a 'work in progress'.

References

A. Works by Pierre Bourdieu

and Jean-Claude Passeron, *Les Héritiers: les étudiants et la culture* (Paris: Éditions de Minuit, 1964).

and Alain Darbel, *L'Amour de l'art: les musées d'art européens et leur public* (Paris: Éditions de Minuit, 1966).

'Champ intellectuel et projet créateur', *Les Temps Modernes*, 246 (1966), 865-906.

'Structuralism and Theory of Sociological Knowledge', *Social Research*, 35 (1968), 681-706.

and Jean-Claude Passeron, *La Reproduction: éléments pour une théorie du système d'enseignement* (Paris: Éditions de Minuit, 1970).

'Systems of Education and Systems of Thought' in *Knowledge and Control*, ed. Michael F.D. Young (London: Collier-Macmillan 1970), 189-207.

'Le Marché des biens symboliques', *L'Année Sociologique*, 22 (1971), 49-126.

'L'Invention de la vie d'artiste', *Actes de la recherche en sciences sociales*, 1 (1975), 67-93.

'La Spécificité du champ scientifique et les conditions sociales du progrès de la raison', *Sociologie et Sociétés*, 7 (1975), 91-118.

and Monique de Saint Martin, 'Anatomie du goût', *Actes de la recherche en sciences sociales*, 5 (1976), 5-81.

'Le Champ scientifique', *Actes de la recherche en sciences socialess*, 2/3 (1976), 88-104.

and Luc Boltanski, 'La Production de l'idéologie dominante', *Actes de la recherche en sciences sociales*, 2/3 (1976), pp. 3-73.

'Champ du pouvoir, champ intellectuel et habitus de classe', *Scolies*, 1 (1977), 7-26.

'La Production de la croyance', *Actes de la recherche en sciences sociales*, 13 (1977), 3-43.

and Monique de Saint-Martin, 'Le Patronat', *Actes de la recherche en sciences sociales*, 20/21 (1978), 3-83.

La Distinction: critique sociale du jugement (Paris: Éditions de Minuit, 1979).

Questions de sociologie (Paris: Éditions de Minuit, 1980).

'Sartre', *London Review of Books*, 22 (1980), 11-12.

Le Sens pratique (Paris: Éditions de Minuit, 1980).

and Yvette Delsaut, 'Pour une sociologie de la perception', *Actes de la recherche en sciences sociales*, 40 (1981), 3-9.

Leçon sur la Leçon (Paris: Éditions de Minuit, 1982).

'The Field of Cultural Production, or: The Economic World Reversed', *Poetics*, 12 (1983), 311-356.

Jean-Claude Chamboredon and Jean-Claude Passeron, *Le Métier de sociologue: préalables épistémologiques*, 4th edn (Paris: EHESS, 1983).

'La Dernière Instance', in *Le Siècle de Kafka*, eds. Yasha David and Jean-Pierre Morel (Paris: Centre Georges Pompidou, 1984), 268-270.

Homo academicus (Paris: Éditions de Minuit, 1984).

'Existe-t-il une littérature belge? Limites d'un champ et frontières politiques', *Études de lettres*, 4 (1985), 3-6.

'The Genesis of the Concepts of Habitus and Field', *Sociocriticism*, 2 (1985), 11-24.

'The (Three) Forms of Capital', trans. Richard Nice, *Handbook of Theory and Research for the Sociology of Education*, ed. John G. Richardson (New York: Greenwood, 1986), 241-255.

Choses Dites (Paris: Éditions de Minuit, 1987).

'The Historical Genesis of a Pure Aesthetic', *The Journal of Aesthetics and Art Criticism*, 46 (1987), 201-210.

'L'Institutionnalisation de l'anomie', *Les Cahiers du Musée national d'art moderne*, 19-20 (1987), 6-19.

'Flaubert's Point of View', *Critical Inquiry*, 14 (1988), 539-562.

Homo Academicus, trans. Peter Collier (Stanford, CA: Stanford University Press, 1988).

'Les Conditions sociales de la circulation internationale des idées', *Romanistische Zeitschrift für Literaturgeschichte/Cahiers d'Histoire des Littératures Romanes* 14 (1989), 1-10; also published in *Actes de la recherche en sciences sociales*, 145 (2002), 3-8.

'The Corporatism of the Universal. The Role of Intellectuals in the Modern World', *Telos*, 81 (1989), 99-110.

Distinction: a Social Critique of the Judgment of Taste, trans. Richard Nice (London: Routledge, 1989).

La Noblesse d'État: grandes écoles et esprit de corps ([Paris]: Éditions de Minuit, 1989).

'Le Champ littéraire', *Actes de la recherche en sciences sociales*, 89 (1991), 3-46.

Pour une Internationale des intellectuels', *Politis*, 1 (1992), 9-15.

The Logic of Practice, trans. Richard Nice (Standford, CA: Stanford University Press, 1990) .

In Other Words: Essays Towards a Reflexive Sociology, trans. Matthew Adamson (Stanford, CA: Stanford University Press, 1990).

The Craft of Sociology, ed. Beate Krais, trans. Richard Nice (Berlin and New York: Walter de Gruyter, 1991).

'Der Korporatismus des Universellen: Zur Rolle des Intellektuellen in der modernen Welt', trans. Jürgen Bolder et al., *Die Intellektuellen und die Macht* (Hamburg: VSA-Verlag, 1991), 41-65.

An Invitation to Reflexive Sociology (Cambridge: Polity, 1992).

'Pour une Internationale des Intellectuels', *Politis*, 1 (1992), 9-15.

Les Règles de l'art: genèse et structure du champ littéraire (Paris: Éditions du Seuil, 1992).

The Field of Cultural Production, ed. Randall Johnson (Cambridge: Polity, 1993).

'My Feelings about Sartre', *French Cultural Studies*, 4 (1993), 209-211.

'A Propos de la famille comme catégorie réalisée', *Actes de la recherche en sciences sociales*, 100 (1993), 32-36.

ed. *La Misère du monde* (Paris: Éditions du Seuil, 1993).

'Un parlement des écrivains pour quoi faire?' *Libération*, 3 November 1994.

Raisons pratiques: sur la théorie de l'action (Paris: Éditions du Seuil, 1994).

and Hans Haacke, *Libre échange* ([Paris]: Seuil/Les Presses du Réel, 1994).

—, *Free Exchange*, trans. Randal Johnson (Stanford, CA: Stanford University Press, 1995).

The Rules of Art: Genesis and Structure of the Literary Field, trans. Susan Emanuel (Stanford, CA: Stanford University Press, 1996 [1992]).

Sur la télévision: suivi de L'emprise du journalisme ([Paris]: Liber Éditions, 1996).

Méditations pascaliennes ([Paris]: Éditions du Seuil, 1997).

Pascalian Meditations, trans. Richard Nice (Stanford, CA: Stanford University Press, 1997).

and Dubios, Jacques, 'Champs littéraire et rapports de domination', *Textyles*, 15 (1998), 12-16.

Contre-feux: propos pour servir à la résistance contre l'Invasion néo-libérale (Paris: Liber, 1998).

La Domination masculine (Paris: Éditions du Seuil, 1998).

On Television, trans. Priscilla Parkhurst Ferguson (New York: The New Press, 1998).

Practical Reason: On the Theory of Action, trans. Randall Johnson (Stanford, CA: Stanford University Press, 1998)

'Maîtres du monde, savez-vous vraiment ce que vous faites?' in *L'Humanité*, 13 October 1999, *Le Monde*, 14 October 1999, and *Libération*, 13 October 1999.

'Une Révolution conservatrice dans l'édition', *Actes de la recherche en sciences sociales*, 126 (1999), 3-28.

and Günter Grass, 'La tradition "d'ouvrir sa gueule"', *Le Monde*, 3 December 1999.

ed. *The Weight of the World, Social Suffering in Contemporary Society* (Cambridge: Polity, 1999).

Esquisse d'une théorie de la pratique: précédé de trois études d'éthnologie kabyle (Paris: Éditions du Seuil, 2000).

Interventions, 1961-2001: science sociale et action politique, ed. Franck Poupeau and Thierry Discepolo (Marseille: Agone, 2000).

Propos sur le champ politique (Lyon: Presses Universitaires de Lyon, 2000).

Contre-feux 2: pour un mouvement social européen (Paris: Raisons d'Agir, 2001).

Langage et pouvoir symbolique (Paris: Fayard, 2001).

Masculine Domination, trans. Richard Nice (Stanford, CA: Stanford University Press, 2001).

and Loïc Wacquant, 'Neoliberal Newspeak. Notes on the New Planetary Vulgate', *Radical Philosophy*, 105 (2001), 2-5.

Science de la science et réflexivité: cours du Collège de France 2000-2001 (Paris: Raisons d'Agir, 2001).

and Pierre Carles, *La Sociologie est un sport de combat* ([France]: C-P Productions, 2001).

and Günter Grass, 'The "Progressive" Restoration', *New Left Review*, 14 (2002), 63-77.

Science of Science and Reflexivity, trans. Richard Nice (Chicago, IL: Polity, 2004).

Esquisse pour une auto-analyse (Paris: Raisons d'Agir, 2004).

Sketch for a Self-analysis, trans. Richard Nice (Cambridge: Polity, 2007).

Political Interventions: Social Science and Political Action, ed. Franck Poupeau and Thierry Discepolo, trans. David Fernbach (London: Verso, 2008)

and Luc Boltanski *La Production de l'idéologie dominante* (Paris: Raisons d'Agir, 2008).

B. Secondary sources

Ahearne, Jeremy, *Intellectuals, Culture and Public Policy in France: Approaches from the Left* (Liverpool: Liverpool University Press, 2010).

—, *Between Cultural Theory and Policy: The Cultural Policy Thinking of Pierre Bourdieu, Michel de Certeau, and Régis Debray* (University of Warwick: Centre for Cultural Policy Studies, 2004).

Albright, James and Allan Luke, eds. *Pierre Bourdieu and Literacy Education* (New York: Routledge, 2008).

Anderson, Benedict, *Imagined Communities: Reflections on the Origin and Spread of Nationalism* (London: Verso, 1983).

Bachelard, Gaston, *La Valeur inductive de la relativité* (Paris: Vrin, 1929).

—, *Le Nouvel esprit scientifique* (Paris: Librairie Félix Alcan, 1937).

—, *La Poétique de l'espace* (Paris: Presses Universitaires de France, 1957).

—, *La Formation de l'esprit scientifique: contribution à une psychanalyse de la connaissance objective*, 4th edn (Paris: Vrin, 1965).

Barthes, Roland, *Mythologies* (Paris: Éditions du Seuil, 1957).

—, 'Éléments de sémiologie', *Communications*, 4 (1964), 91-135.

—, 'L'Effet de réel', *Communications*, 11 (1968), 84-89.

—, *Le Degré zéro de l'écriture: suivi de Noveaux essais critiques* (Paris: Éditions du Seuil, 1972).

—, *Le Bruissement de la langue* (Paris: Éditions du Seuil, 1984).

Becker, Howard, 'Art as Collective Action', *American Sociological Review*, vol. XXXIX (1974), 767-776.

Beckett, Samuel, *Watt* (New York: Grove, 1959).

Benson, Rodney D. and Erik Neveu, eds. *Bourdieu and the Journalistic Field* (Cambridge: Polity, 2005).

Bergson, Henri, *Œuvres*, 2nd edn (Paris: Presses Universitaires de France, 1963).

Bhaskar, Roy, *A Realist Theory of Science* (Hemel Hempstead: Harvester Wheatsheaf, 1975).

Bhaskar, Roy, *The Possibility of Naturalism* (Hemel Hempstead: Harvester Wheatsheaf, 1989).

Boschetti, Anna, *Sartre et 'Les Temps Modernes': une entreprise intellectuelle* (Paris: Éditions de Minuit, 1985).

—, 'Bourdieu's Work on Literature: Contexts, Stakes and Perspectives', *Theory, Culture & Society*, 23 (2006), 135-155.

—, 'How Field Theory Can Contribute to the Knowledge of the World Literary Space', unpublished paper given on 16 May 2009 at the *Bourdieu and Literature* conference, University of Warwick.

—, ed. *L'Espace culturel transnational* (Paris: Nouveau Mondes Éditions, 2010).

Bouvaist, Jean-Marie, *Crise et mutations dans l'édition française* (Paris: Éditions du Cercle de la librairie, 1993).

Brown, Nicholas and Imre Szeman, eds. *Bourdieu: Fieldwork in Culture* (Lanham, MD: Rowman & Littlefield Publishers, 1999).

Caillé, Alain, 'Esquisse d'une Critique de l'Économie Générale de la Pratique', *Cahiers du LASA*, 12-13 (1992), 109-220.

Calhoun, Craig, Edward LiPuma and Moishe Postone, eds. *Bourdieu: Critical Perspectives* (Cambridge: Polity, 1993).

Carpet, Oliver, ed. *Le Prix du livre 1981-2006: la loi Long* (Paris: IMEC, 2006).

Casanova, Pascale, *The World Republic of Letters*, trans. M. B. Debevoise (Cambridge, MA: Harvard University Press, 2005).

—, *La République mondiale des lettres* (Paris: Éditions du Seuil, 2008).

Cassirer, Ernst, *Substance et fonction* (Paris: Éditions de Minuit, 1977).

—, *Individu et cosmos* (Paris: Éditions de Minuit, 1983).

Champagne, Patrick, *Faire l'opinion: le nouveau jeu politique* (Paris: Éditions de Minuit, 1993).

Charle, Christophe, *Naissance des 'intellectuels' 1880-1900* (Paris: Éditions de Minuit, 1990).

Charpentier, Isabelle, 'Quelque part entre la littérature, la sociologie et l'histoire...', *Contextes*, 1 (2006), at http://contextes.revues.org/index74.html consulted on 26/08/2011.

Ferguson, Priscilla Parkhurst, *Literary France: The Making of a Culture* (Berkeley, CA: University of California Press, 1987).

Cleary, Joe, 'Review: The World Literary System: Atlas and Epitaph', *Field Day Review*, 2 (2006), 196-219.

Collier, Peter, 'Liber: Liberty and Literature', *French Cultural Studies*, 4 (1993), 291-304.

Critchley, Simon, *Very Little... Almost Nothing* (London: Routledge, 1997).

—, *On Humour* (London: Routledge, 2002).

Delattre, Lucas, 'Le président de la Bundesbank parie sur l'euro en 1999', *Le Monde*, 17 October 1996.

Dixon, Keith, 'Les Évangélistes du Marché', *Liber*, 32 (1997), 5-6.

Dubois, Jacques, 'Bourdieu and Literature', *Substance*, 93 (2000), 84-102.

Dunn, Allen, 'Who Needs a Sociology of the Aesthetic? Freedom and Value in Pierre Bourdieu's *Rules of Art*', *Boundary* 2:25 (1998), 87-110.

During, Simon, *Foucault and Literature: Towards a Geneology of Writing* (London: Routledge, 1992).

Durkheim, Émile, *Le Suicide* (Paris: Presses Universitaires de France, 1981).

DuVerlie, Claude and Pierre Bourdieu, 'Esquisse d'un projet intellectuel: un entretien avec Pierre Bourdieu', *The French Review*, 61 (1987), 194-205.

Ernaux, Annie, 'Bourdieu: le chagrin', *Le Monde*, 5 Febuary 2002.

—, *La Place* (Paris: Gallimard, 1983).

Firth, Raymond, *Elements of Social Organization* (Boston, MA: Beacon Press, 1963).

Flaubert, Gustave, 'Lettre à Louise Colet, 1852', *Correspondance*, Series 3, 1852-1854 (Paris: Conard, 1927), 67.

—, *L'Éducation sentimentale* (Paris: Librairie Générale Française, 2002).

Foucault, Michel, 'Réponse au cercle d'épistémologie', *Dits et Écrits 1954-1988*, 4 vols., ed. Daniel Derfert and François Ewald (Paris: Gallimard, 1994), I (1968), 696-731.

—, and Gilles Deleuze, 'Les Intellectuels et le Pouvoir', in *Dits et Écrits 1954-1988*, 4 vols., ed. Daniel Defert and François Ewald (Paris: Gallimard, 1994), II (1972), 306-315.

Fowler, Bridget, *Pierre Bourdieu and Cultural Theory: Critical Investigation* (London: Sage, 1997).

Freeland, Cynthia, *But is it Art? An Introduction to Art Theory* (Oxford: Oxford University Press, 2001).

Frodon, Jean-Michel, 'La réaction de Jacques Derrida', *Le Monde*, 24 January 2002.

Glaser, Barney and Anselm Strauss, *Awareness of Dying* (Chicago: Aldine, 1965).

—, *Time for Dying* (Chicago: Aldine, 1968).

Goodman, Jane E. and Paul A. Silverstein, eds. *Bourdieu in Algeria: Colonial Politics, Ethnographic Practices, Theoretical Developments* (Lincoln, NE and London: University of Nebraska Press, 2009).

Gossman, Lionel, 'Literature and Education', *New Literary History*, 13 (1982), 341-371.

Grass, Günter, *From the Diary of a Snail*, trans. Ralph Manheim (London: Secker & Warburg, 1974).

Graw, Isabelle 'Que suis-je? Une entrevue avec Pierre Bourdieu' (first publ. as 'Ein interview mit Pierre Bourdieu von Isabelle Graw', *The Thing*, 1996), trans. Véronique Gola, at www.homme-moderne.org/societe/socio/bourdieu/entrevue/quesui.html consulted on 30/05/09.

Greenway, John, *Literature among the Primitives* (Hatbors, PA: Folklore Associate, 1964).

Geldof, Koenraad and Alex Martin, 'Authority, Reading, Reflexivity: Pierre Bourdieu and the Aesthetic Judgment of Kant', *Diacritics*, 27 (1997), 20-43.

Gerhards, Jürgen and Helmut K. Anheier, 'The Literary Field: An Empirical Investigation of Bourdieu's Sociology of Art', *International Sociology*, 4 (1989), 131-146.

Grémion, Pierre, *Preuves: une revue européenne à Paris* (Paris: Julliard, 1989).

—, *Intelligence de l'anti-communisme: le congrès pour la liberté de la culture à Paris 1950-1975* (Paris: Fayard, 1995).

Grenfell, Michael, *Pierre Bourdieu: Agent Provocateur* (London: Continuum Press, 2004).

—, and Cheryl Hardy, *Art Rules: Pierre Bourdieu and the Visual Arts* (London: Berg, 2007).

—, and David James, with Philip Hodkinson, Diane Reay and Derek Robbins, *Bourdieu and Education: Acts of Practical Theory* (London: Falmer Press, 1998).

Griswold, Wendy, 'Review of The Rules of Art, Genesis and Structure of the Literary Field', *The American Journal of Sociology*, 104 (1998), 972-975.

Guillory, John, *Cultural Capital: The Problem of Literary Canon Formation* (Chicago, IL: University of Chicago Press, 1993).

Haacke, Hans, 'A Public Servant', *October*, 101 (2002), 4-6.

Habermas, Jürgen, 'Modernity Versus Postmodernity', *New German Critique*, 22 (1981), 3-14.

Jakobson, Raymond and Claude Lévi-Strauss, '"Les Chats" de Charles Baudelaire', *L'Homme*, 2 (1962), 5-21.

Jameson, Frederic, 'How Not To Historicize Theory', *Critical Inquiry*, 34 (2008), 564-582.

Jouhaud, Christian, *Les Pouvoirs de la littérature: histoire d'un paradoxe* (Paris: Gallimard, 2000).

Joyce, James, 'Letter to Carlo Linati, 21 Sept. 1920', *Selected Letters of James Joyce*, ed. Richard Ellmann (New York: Viking, 1975), 270.

Jurt, Joseph, 'Gattungshierarchie und Karrierestrategien im XIX. Jahrhundert', *Lendemains*, 36 (1984), 33-41.

—, 'Autonomy and Commitment in the French Literary Field: Applying Pierre Bourdieu's Approach', *International Journal of Contemporary Sociology*, 38 (2001), 87-102.

Lahire, Bernard, ed. *Le Travail sociologique de Pierre Bourdieu: dettes et critiques* (Paris: La Découverte, 1999).

—, 'Répéter ou inventer', *Le Monde*, 25 January 2002.

—, *La Condition littéraire: la double vie des écrivains* (Paris: La Découverte, 2006)

Lane, Jeremy, *Pierre Bourdieu: A Critical Introduction* (London: Pluto, 2000).

—, *Bourdieu's Politics: Problems and Possibilities* (London: Routledge, 2006).

Latour, Bruno and Steve Woolgar, *Laboratory Life: The Construction of Scientific Facts* (Princeton, NJ: Princeton University Press, 1979).

Lecourt, Dominique, *L'Épistémologie historique de Gaston Bachelard* (Paris: Vrin, 1969).

Leenhardt, Jacques, 'Les Règles de l'Art de P. Bourdieu', *French Cultural Studies*, 4 (1993), 263-270.

Lemire, Maurice 'L'Autonomisation de la "Littérature Nationale" au XIXe siècle', *Études Littéraires*, 20 (1987), 75-98.

Lévi-Strauss, Claude, *Tristes Tropiques* (Paris: Plon, 1955).

Loesberg, Jonathan, 'Bourdieu and the Sociology of Aesthetics', *English Literary History*, 60 (1993), 1033-1056.

Lord, Alfred B., *The Singer of the Tales* (Cambridge, MA: Harvard University Press, 1960).

Mallarmé, Stéphane, *La Musique et les lettres* (Paris: Librairie Académique Didier, 1895).

Martin, Jean-Pierre, ed. *Bourdieu et la littérature* (Nantes: Cécile Defaut, 2010).

Mauger, Gérard, 'Lire Pierre Bourdieu', *Politis*, 686 (2002), 26-27.

—, and Claude F. Poliak, 'Les Usages sociaux de la lecture', *Actes de la recherche en sciences sociales*, 123 (1998), 3-24.

McLemee, Scott, '"Not a Fish in Water": Close Colleague of Bourdieu Reflects on His Influence', *The Chronicle of Higher Education*, 25 January 2002, 18.

Moi, Toril, 'The Challenge of the Particular Case', *Modern Language Quarterly*, 58 (1997), 497-508.

Nietzsche, Friedrich, *Thus Spake Zarathustra: A Book for Everyone and No One*, trans. R.J. Hollingdale (Harmondsworth: Penguin, 1961).

Orwell, George, *Nineteen Eighty-Four* (London: Secker & Warburgh, 1997).

Phillips, Dianne, 'Correspondance Analysis', *Social Research Update*, 7 (1995), at http://sru.soc.surrey.ac.uk/SRU7.html consulted on 14/07/09.

Plato, *Theaetetus* (Newburyport, MA: Focus Philosophical Library, Pullins Press, 2004).

Poyet, Thierry and Fabrice, eds., *Lettres en première autobiographie: 'Ernaux'*, in *L' École des Lettres*, 9 (2002-2003).

Proust, Marcel, *Le Temps retrouvé* (Paris: Gallimard, 1954).

—, *Time Regained* (Vol. 8 of *Remembrance of Things Past*), trans. Stephen Hudson (eBooks@Adelaide, 2010) at http://ebooks.adelaide.edu.au/p/proust/marcel/p96t/ consulted on 23/07/11.

Reed-Danahay, Deborah, *Locating Bourdieu* (Bloomington, IN: Indiana University Press, 2005).

Robbins, Derek, *Bourdieu and Culture* (London: Sage, 2000).

Rouet, François, *Le Livre: mutations d'une industrie culturelle* (Paris: Documentation française, 1992).

Rouanet, Henry, Werner Ackermann and Brigitte Le Roux, 'The Geometric Analysis of Questionnaires: The Lesson of Bourdieu's La Distinction', *Bulletin de Méthodologie Sociologique*, 65 (2000), 5-15.

Sachs, Joe, 'Introduction', in Aristotle, *Nicomachean Ethics*, trans. Joe Sachs (Newburyport, MA: Focus Philosophical Library, Pullins Press, 2002).

Salaün, Jean-Michel, Review of Jean-Marie Bouvaist, 'Crise et Mutations dans l'Édition Française', BBF, 1 (1995), 100-101, at http://bbf.enssib.fr/ consulted on 23/07/2011.

Salgas, Jean-Pierre 'Le Rapport du Collège de France: Pierre Bourdieu s'explique', *La Quinzaine Littéraire*, 445 (1985), 8-10.

Sapiro, Gisèle, 'La Raison Littéraire: le champ littéraire français sous l'occupation', *Actes de la recherche en sciences sociales*, 111 (1996), 3-35.

—, ed. *L'Espace intellectuel en Europe: de la formation des États-nations à la mondialisation. XIXè-XXè siècle* (Paris: Éditions du Nouveau Monde, 2009).

Sartre, Jean Paul, *Critique de la raison dialectique*, 2 vols (Paris: Gallimard, 1960).

—, *Qu'est-ce que la Littérature?* (Paris: Gallimard, 1964).

—, *L'Idiot de la famille: Gustave Flaubert de 1821-1857*, 3 vols. (Paris: Gallimard, 1971-1972).

Steiner, Peter, *Russian Formalism: A Metapoetics* (Ithaca, NY: Cornell University Press, 1984).

Swartz, David, *Culture and Power: The Sociology of Pierre Bourdieu* (Chicago, IL and London: University of Chicago Press, 1997).

Thomson, Stephen, 'The Instance of the Veil: Bourdieu's Flaubert and the Textuality of Social Science' in *Comparative Literature*, 55: 4 (2003), 275-292.

Valéry, Paul, *Cahiers*, 2 vols (Paris: Gallimard, 1974).

—, 'La Liberté de l'Esprit', in *Regards sur le monde actuel*, *Œuvres*, 2 vols., ed. Jean Hytier (Paris: Gallimard, 1960), vol. 2, pp. 1077-1106.

—, 'Fonction et mystère de l'Académie', *Regards sur le monde Actuel*, *Œuvres*, 2 vols., ed. Jean Hytier (Paris: Gallimard, 1960), vol. 2, pp. 1119-1127.

Vandenberghe, Frédéric '"The Real is Relational": An Epistemological Analysis of Pierre Bourdieu's Generative Structuralism', *Sociological Theory*, 17 (1999), 32-67.

Verdès-Leroux, Jeannine, *Le Savant et la politique: essai sur le terrorisme sociologique de Pierre Bourdieu* (Paris: Grasset, 1998).

Viala, Alain, *Naissance de l'écrivain: sociologie de la littérature à l'âge classique* (Paris, Éditions de Minuit, 1985).

Wacquant, Loïc 'Towards a Reflexive Sociology: A Workshop with Pierre Bourdieu', *Sociological Theory*, 7 (1989), 26-63.

Wacquant, Loïc, 'From Ruling Class to Field of Power: An Interview with Pierre Bourdieu on *La Noblesse d'État*', *Theory Culture Society*, 10 (1993), 19-44.

Weber, Alfred, *History of Philosophy*, trans. Frank Thilly (New York: Charles Scribner's Sons, 1904).

Young, Robert J.C., ed. *Untying the Text: A Post-Structuralist Reader* (Boston: Routledge, 1981).

—, *White Mythologies: Writing History and the West* (London and New York: Routledge, 1990).

Žižek, Slavoj, *Organs Without Bodies* (London: Routledge, 2004).

Zola, Émile, *Le Roman expérimental* (Paris: Garnier-Flammarion, 1971).

C. Collectively or anonymously authored works

'A Declaration of Independence', *Liber*, 17 (1994), 29.

Propositions pour l'enseignement de l'avenir élaborées à la demande de Monsieur le Président de la République par les professeurs du Collège de France (Paris: Collège de France, 1985).

Principes pour une réflexion sur les contenus d'enseignement (Paris: Ministère de l'Éducation Nationale, de la Jeunesse et des Sports, March 1989).

Index

amor intellectualis 113-14, 120
L'Amour de l'art (Pierre Bourdieu) 30, 151, 157
anamnesis 75, 84
anti-intellectualism 29-30, 151, 164-65

Bachelard, Gaston 21, 40-45, 110, 126
banalisation 66 See also defamiliarisation (*ostrenanie*)
Barthes, Roland 83, 85, 106, 124-25
Baudelaire, Charles 30, 35, 67, 92, 108, 117, 140-41, 150-51
Belgian literary field 71
belief 20, 73, 77, 108, 110-12, 118, 141, 156 See also illusio
belief effect 106, 111
Bhaskar, Roy 58-59
biography 39, 59, 104
Blanchot, Maurice 31, 111
boundaries 57-58, 71, 95-96
Boschetti, Anna 26, 58-59

Casanova, Pascale 46, 49, 71-73, 82
canonisation 51, 72
censorship 15, 30, 92, 107, 115, 151, 181
change 21-22, 44, 58, 62, 63, 64, 66-68, 77, 127, 140, 141
charismatic ideology 26, 156
collective intellectual 30, 92, 142, 146-51 See also International Parliament of Writers
Coluche (Michel Colucci) 142
creative project 63
cultural capital 47-50, 53, 72, 158, 185 See also symbolic capital
cynicism 89, 112, 123, 139, 179

defamiliarisation (*ostrenanie*) 156
denegation 104-08

Derrida, Jacques 24, 31, 111, 124, 125, 148
La Distinction 118, 157-60
Le Dictionnaire des idées reçues (Gustave Flaubert) 133
La Domination masculine (Pierre Bourdieu)
Duchamp, Marcel 98-99, 115

L'Éducation sentimentale (Gustave Flaubert) 15, 34, 35, 46, 47, 70, 103-09
Ernaux, Annie 122-24, 187
existentialism 25, 28, 29 See also Sartre, Jean-Paul
external analysis 64 See also biography, Marxism

Faulkner, William 37, 99, 116, 187
feel for the game 61-62
fetishism 98, 112-13, 169
The Field of Cultural Production (Pierre Bourdieu) 38
field 18, 28, 44, 185
field of power 38, 46-50, 51, 53, 105
literary field 50-59, 70, 80-85, 93
first beginnings (illusion of) 84, 91
Flaubert, Gustave 45, 47, 70, 75, 87, 88-89, 97-98, 100, 103-09, 115, 116, 133, 151, 185 See also *L'Éducation sentimentale*, *Le Dictionnaire des idées reçues*
formula (generative) 69, 105, 114
Foucault, Michel 31, 33-34, 65-66, 68, 92, 124, 125, 149, 184

generation 62, 66-67, 93, 99
Grass, Günter 120-22, 143, 146

Haacke, Hans 101, 143-46, 181
Habermas, Jürgen 32-34, 43
habitus 28, 59-63, 66, 105, 134-35, 186
hermeneutic analysis 64, 135-37
Les Héritiers (Pierre Bourdieu) 154-55
hierarchy 51, 80, 95
historicisation (double) 19
homology 51, 56, 64-65, 104
humour 120-22, 132-33

illusio 111-12
interest 34, 55, 85, 88, 111, 182 *See also illusio*
internal reading 46, 54-70, 77
International Parliament of Writers 142, 148-50, 188
involution (of the literary field) 92-96, 185

Le Jour et la Nuit (Didier Bezace) 122
Joyce, James 116, 187

Kafka, Franz 155
knowledge (opposition between literary and scientific) 128-29
Krauss, Karl 143-44
Kuhn, Thomas 44, 85

Laboratory Life: The Construction of Scientific Facts (Bruno Latour and Steve Woolgar) 125-27
lector 27
Leenhardt, Jacques 108-09
Lévi-Strauss, Claude 21, 26-29, 58, 121
Liber 144-45, 147-50, 188
liberty (margin of) 75
Libre-échange (Pierre Bourdieu and Hans Haacke) 143-46
linguistic turn 124-25
Literary France, The Making of a Culture (Priscilla Parkhurst Ferguson) 23, 48

Mallarmé, Stéphane 31, 74, 110-13
Malraux, André 157
Manet, Édouard 38, 90, 150
Marxism 43, 46, 58, 67-69, 87, 187
Mauss, Marcel 21, 108

Le Métier de sociologue (Pierre Bourdieu, Jean-Claude Passeron and Jean-Claude Chamboredon) 40, 42, 126
La Misère du monde (Pierre Bourdieu et al) 119-22, 139, 188
multiple correspondence analysis (MCA) 53-56
My Century (Günter Grass) 143

naivety 115
nihilism 31
Nineteen Eighty-Four (George Orwell) 140
nomos 80, 85, 151

origin (social) 24-25, 68, 70, 154-55

patronage 93, 101, 180
La Place (Annie Ernaux) 123
point of view 45-46, 70, 116
Ponge, Francis 138
position-taking 20, 55, 64, 67, 80
positivism 42, 127
postmodernism 32, 125
problematic 45, 57
La Production de l'idéologie dominante (Pierre Bourdieu and Luc Boltanski) 131-35,
Proust, Marcel 75, 115-16, 159-61, 187

Quebecois literary field 51-52

reading 77-8, 158, 171 *See also* belief effect
realism (scientific) 58-9, 124-29 (literary) 106-07 *See also* belief effect
relationalism 27-28, 40-42, 46, 54, 57, 128
reflexivity 36, 60, 70, 75-78, 89, 118, 121, 122, 125, 187
Les Règles de l'art (Pierre Bourdieu) 21, 34-38
La Reproduction (Pierre Bourdieu and Jean-Claude Passeron) 154-55
resistance 20, 61, 71, 114, 120, 133, 137-38, 174 (to analysis)
Robbe-Grillet, Alain 63, 116, 187
Rushdie, Salman 148
Russian Formalism 65-66

Sartre, Jean-Paul, 21, 24, 25-26, 27, 28
  63, 75, 85, 92, 131, 140, 149, 184
scholastic bias, 77
Science de la science et réflexivité (Pierre
  Bourdieu) 33, 75, 125
scientific field 33-34, 115
seriousness 104, 121-22, 128, 136
short-circuit error 187 *See also* Marxism
Simon, Claude 116, 118
social capital 62
space of positions 64, 187
space of possibilities 45, 64-70 *See also*
  problematic
space of works 46, 64-70, 187 *See also*
  internal reading
Spinoza, Baruch 64, 109, 113, 118
structuralism 26-29, 40, 41, 58, 124 *See
  also* Lévi-Strauss, Claude
style 20, 107, 115-22, 160, 187
symbolic capital 51, 52, 62, 79, 86-88,
  121
symbolic revolution 140-41

Tietmeyer, Hans 135-38
To the Lighthouse (Virginia Woolf) 117
trajectory 59-63

universality 30, 44, 47, 52, 72, 74, 101,
  145, 169, 181-84, 188

Valéry, Paul 45, 49-50, 185

writing 20, 107-08, 115-24
Woolf, Virginia 87, 116, 117 *See also To
  the Lighthouse*
world literary space 46, 71-74, 185

Zola, Émile 63, 75, 79, 84, 89-92, 123,
  131, 140, 149, 151, 185, 188

This book does not end here...

At Open Book Publishers, we are changing the nature of the traditional academic book. The title you have just read will not be left on a library shelf, but will be accessed online by hundreds of readers each month across the globe. We make all our books free to read online so that students, researchers and members of the public who can't afford a printed edition can still have access to the same ideas as you.

Our digital publishing model also allows us to produce online supplementary material, including extra chapters, reviews, links and other digital resources. Find *Bordieu and Literature* on our website to access its online extras. Please check this page regularly for ongoing updates, and join the conversation by leaving your own comments:

http://www.openbookpublishers.com/product.php/80

If you enjoyed the book you have just read, and feel that research like this should be available to all readers, regardless of their income, please think about donating to us. Our company is run entirely by academics, and our publishing decisions are based on intellectual merit and public value rather than on commercial viability. We do not operate for profit and all donations, as with all other revenue we generate, will be used to finance new Open Access publications.

For further information about what we do, how to donate to OBP, additional digital material related to our titles or to order our books, please visit our website.

Knowledge is for sharing

www.ingramcontent.com/pod-product-compliance
Lightning Source LLC
Chambersburg PA
CBHW070547170426
43201CB00012B/1747